MARION COUNTY VIEW OF PEO

MW01230653

MEMORIES, ETC., --2023—By Donnie Powell Includes articles (with permission) by Dennis Parker and Jack Christopher.

+++++++++++++++

This is disorganized and has some repetition. These are not in any particular order. They are taken from my earlier books so I can put the Marion County entries together into one book and donate one or more to the library in my original home county there in Buena Vista, GA. (If they will take it.) I noticed I put some items in more than one book (or in one book twice)—and some are "fuzzy", when you get my age, you will understand—please pardon.

I plan to self-publish on Amazon. Please ignore the mistakes.

I HOPE YOU WILL WRITE SOME OF YOUR MEMORIES, STORIES, ETC.

Hope you enjoy.

Donnie

++++ (Positive thoughts being sent to you.)++++++++

Excerpts from:
Boy in Georgia
Powell's Miscellaneous Thoughts and Stories (2018)
Powell's #2 Miscellaneous Thoughts and Stories. (2020)
Powell's #3 Miscellaneous Thoughts and Stories (2020)
Powell's #4 Miscellaneous Thoughts and Stories (2021)

Powell's #5 Miscellaneous Thoughts and Stories (2022)
Powell's #6 Miscellaneous Thoughts and Stories (2022)
Powell's #7 Miscellaneous Thoughts and Stories (2023)

TABLE OF CONTENTS

It is longer than expected. So it may have to be Part I and Part II.

(Sorry I was unable to give page numbers so am guessing at how many pages.)

Powell's #4 Miscellaneous Thoughts and
Stories (2021)
Coke Bottle (in "the Journal" Oct 2020)
Graduation Speech (Fiction) Wish I had
said
Powell Home Place
Bull Fight

((END OF PART 1))

HOPE TO INCLUDE THESE AND MORE IN
PART II
Rural Stores in Marion County—Some Pictures
    --Brantley
    --Carter
    --Eddie Wells
    --Tazewell With good write up by Jack
Christopher

    Boarding House memories by Joyce

About   Powell's #5 Miscellaneous Thoughts and
Stories (2022)
Page 390   Marion County High School Picture
    --Class of 1962
    Teachers
    My "historic Hallways" memories

    Chicken House Memories—
    --Jack Christopher, Doug Jones, Dennis
Parker, Donny Finkle

About   Powell's #6 Miscellaneous Thoughts and
Stories (2022)
            Buena Vista Square Pictures
            Wight Motor Memories
            First Baptist Church Memories
            Pasaquan Pictures
            Veterans Stat Park
            --Boy Scout Memories
            --Camp Safety Patrol memories
            Powell Home place Pictures

            Powell's #7 Miscellaneous Thoughts and
            Stories (2023)
            Massee Lane Camellia Gardens—Marvin
            Jernigan (cousin)
            Quilt—Mom's Family tree
            Powder rocks
            Davis Picture –about 1895
            Davis Picture
            Powell Pictures
            My Books—List of (so far)

#.I. FROM   BOY IN GEORGIA

WHEN I WAS A BOY IN GEORGIA   BY DONNIE
POWE

(9473) (Illustration by Richard Powell)

+++++   +++++++

(9685) My parents. Roy Alton ("Tom") and Mina Davis Powell. Married in 1926. (This picture taken about 1970?)

++++++++++++++++++++++++++++++++++

SECTION I INTRODUCTION

Although we lived within the city limits of a small town, I grew up in a rural environment. Therefore, many of the things I remember may seem somewhat brutal (e.g. hog killing time), they were often just a part of normal farm life. Others will reflect a streak of mean. The happenings and stories written here are a lot like my memory, unorganized and faded with years. I want to thank my wonderful family, relatives, and friends who helped me have a wonderful life as a boy in Georgia. I also want to thank my son Richard for the illustrations. I apologize if anyone is offended because none was meant. These stories are "non-serious", based on factual events with some exaggeration-for humor and effect thrown in for good measure.

FAMILY MEMBER CAST

Dad and Mom (R. A. "Tom" and Mina) (Dad born 1904, Mom in 1912)
Joyce (14 years older--wouldn't let me tell her age)
Clements (10 years older)
Stout (6 years older)
Brenda (21 months older)
Me (Donnie, born in 1944)

Ricky (born in 1953)

(The drawings by Richard not shown in computer).

++++++++++++++++++

SECTION II --STORIES/MEMORIES 1-177

INDEX (Partial 1-129)

28. Foot in bicycle spokes
29. Baptist Ping Pong
30. Movies
31. The Loop
32. Kirven's Store
33. Neices at Kirven's
34. Flour shirts
35. Train wreck
36. Dry lake
37. Oil well
38. Church sermons
39. Santa
40. Haskell and the heater pipe
41. Dancing with a tall girl
42. T-T-Talking to a girl
43. Hamburgers on Saturday
44. Five gallons of lard on the floor
45. Water fights
46. Snake under the board
47. July 4th BBQ and near drowning
48. Fight in the potato pit
49. Water on the hill
50. Pinching
51. Mom's "baby"
52. Ricky hits the screen door
53. Women talking all at one time
54. Dinner on the ground
55. Indians in the jungle
56. KKK on the square
57. Ringing the big bell
58. One traffic light
59. "Psycho" movie

60. Letters to Bim
61. Clem seasick in the Army
62. Jim drove fast
63. Churning milk
64. Hand churned ice cream
65. Wood burning stove
66. Milking a cow
67. Picking cotton
68. Cotton at the gin
69. Animals in cages
70. Rooster fight
71. Mother hen on my back
72. Moving at night
73. Dad shot his finger off
74. Tempers
75. Sawmill motivated education
76. Whipping in school meant one at home
77. Dressed in a storm
78. Afraid of Halley's Comet
79. Big whirlwind
80. Blacksmith shop
81. Dad snatched fish
82. Dad drove gas truck
83. Dad's only lie
84. Wringing chicken's neck
85. To the dentist
86. Tonsils out
87. Ricky hid under the seat
88. Clem pinched off tail
89. RA camp at Clayton
90. Scouts to Lake Blackshear
91. Stepped on rusty nails

92. Dad hit in the eye by nail
93. Ricky, pie safe door, and boomerang
94. BB in my ear
95. My "red rover" concussion
96. Playground games
97. Hugh hit by a brick
98. Overnight at Ernest's house
99. Shep outran me too
100. Ain't no boogers out tonight
101. Gator game
102. Slap hands
103. Jumped off ladder
104. Cafe tip
105. To cow sales
106. War stories gave me stomach ache
107. Ricky got into my stuff
108. Savings bond stamps at school
109. Finkle outran me in Scouts
110. Planting pine trees
111. Tommy in the woods all night
112. Dad and I to the pond
113. Scout barometer
114. Yankees in BV
115. Manger set
116. Prom at our house
117. Boxes inside boxes
118. Frog gigging (spell check suggested giggling)
119. Trips to the fair
120.   Panama City, Atlanta Zoo, Cyclorama, Stone Mountain
121. FSU circus at Callaway Gardens (water skied on my face)

122. Water hose in the ground.
123. Line sounds like lion
124. Nicknames
125. I ate a persimmon
126. Stores closed on Wednesday afternoon
127. Collecting pine cones
128. Trim mule's hooves
129. Cornsheller and Croker sack

+++++++++++++++++++++++++++++++++++

1. Walking through our front yard as a child taught me the love of shoes. When barefooted, I really hated, I mean really hated, to feel that warm, squishy feeling between my toes. Fresh chicken droppings feel awful, trust me on this one. A more painful barefoot happening was when I stubbed my toe on a pine tree root. If you have ever stubbed your toe, have you noticed that you never do it lightly? I guess we all subconsciously think that as long as we are going to stub it, we might as well do a good job. Going barefoot after a rain felt great, but would--so we were told--result in getting ground itch, which is a worm that gets under the skin and wiggles its way all over your foot until you kill it by soaking your foot in kerosene, or by following some other exotic home remedy.

2. Dogs were a big part of our lives. We had all kinds but they were he-man type dogs. They never, never saw the inside of our house. They would have thought we were calling them sissies if we had brought them inside. They were tough, they were hunting dogs, they were always hungry--we could have put a rock in the middle of a plate of biscuits and thrown it to them and they

would have swallowed the biscuits and rock whole without batting an eye. If they took time to chew a mouthful the other dogs would get what was left so they just swallowed things whole as much as they could as fast as they could. The way my brother mentioned the rock on the plate of biscuits, it is possible he was not dealing in just theory. They were great watchdogs because nobody, and I mean nobody, jumped out of the car at our house unless some of us were there to call them off, or if need be, sic them on. They were death on cats. I guess I was half grown before I realized cats weren't extinct like dinosaurs. Our dogs were smart too, but they were also dumb. For example, my older brothers showed me a sure fire way of making two dogs fight. I had to show that to my friend. We would take dogs that were the best of friends and make them fight each other. Now if they had been smart, they would have jumped on me and chewed my legs off instead of fighting each other. Like I said, they were also dumb. Now that I am grown, I consider making dogs fight cruel and mean, but back then it was something kids did, well something mean kids did.

3. My parents had many home remedies--but the most hated was Castor Oil. They had the biggest spoon ever manufactured. It held one, maybe two, gallons or more. Mom would heat it up (I still do not know why) and tell us to take it all in one swallow. There is no way we could swallow that huge spoonful in one swallow. Then my Mom would say, "If you throw it up, I will give you another dose." Once down, the last thing we wanted, was to throw it up--but for me, few powers on earth could keep it down. (Even after all these years, when I

think about it, like right now, a lump comes into my throat, and I have trouble swallowing.) I called the spoon "the ten gallon spoon" , just like a ten gallon hat. One of my brothers (I think) helped that spoon miraculously disappear. To this day, no one will admit it--still afraid of Mom I guess. One day I felt a little sick and stayed home from school. Later when I was feeling better, I went outside to play. Mom called me inside and guess what she gave me. I never played hooky again, ever, even in college at Georgia Southwestern and Georgia Southern. Not long ago, I picked up a bottle of Castor Oil (hadn't touched a bottle in years) and was surprised to see that we had been taking normal doses-- normal for King Kong. One thing for sure, when we took those big doses, we stayed close to home--real close to the throne room. Many family traditions are passed from parents to their children. To this day, I don't think any of us children have ever purchased even one bottle of Castor Oil, let alone given doses to our children. They will never know how lucky they are.

4. As a teenager I got to drive--a mule. We had a garden area and my Dad let me have the privilege of plowing. He told me Gee meant go to the right and Haw meant go to the left, but he never told me what to say to get the dumb mule to go straight. Those furrows may have been an artistic statement, but they surely didn't please Dad. I don't know who was the dumbest, me, the mule, or the plow. But plowing was a good lesson in life--it helped teach me the value of education. If I had tried to be a sixth generation Georgia farmer, I would have starved to death. Maybe our education system should have a Basic Plowing with a mule course for

about seventh or eighth grade students. Then they would be very, very interested in school and I think dropout rates would drop.

5. I rode a calf. My older brothers were always doing things for me and yes, to me. One of them and some of his friends were trying to break a fairly large calf so they could ride him. They were a little afraid to get on him so my brother gave me the honor of being the first one to ride. Like I said earlier, I wasn't always bright, so I got on--after all, my big brother wanted me to do it. I got on and immediately began my first attempt at flying. I learned several things that day. That a calf doesn't want people on his back, that they are a pretty good launching pad, that flying can be fun but the landing can be rough, that I need to think before I sit and jump, and that my brother really needed me sometimes. What a brother.

6. My other brother was always teaching me things too. Like the time he took two long stems of smut grass with lots of yucky seeds and showed me a trick. He crossed the weeds and told me to bite down. I bit. Then he yanked the grass and left all those yucky seeds in my mouth. Yuck. However, it was also a learning experience worth trying on my little brother and any others I could con into it. I even told by children to be careful if their uncle said he wanted to show them a trick and that they should not bite any grass he offered them. I need to ask him if he ever pulled that trick on his own kids. Knowing him, I would bet that he did, with glee.

7. Have you ever had someone try to stuff a basketball in your ear? It happened to me in the eighth grade.

After lunch the older boys would play basketball on one end of the gym and us younger boys on the other end shooting about a dozen balls. Because we interfered with their game, the older boys would throw our loose balls as hard as they could back to the other end when our balls got in their way. So as I was dribbling along one day minding my own business, the lights almost went out in Georgia. I staggered outside and sat down to try to get back to normal. My good friend Ernest came out and stayed with me. He knew I was hurt but I don't think he believed me when I mumbled that the basketball went in one ear and out the other.

8. Learning to drive was a trip--short, bumpy, and jerky. Our yard was large enough so we could practice driving around and around in it. But did everyone have to yell and run and hide behind trees or into the house? When I first learned to drive, I was very unsure of my driving ability, and there everyone was, yelling and hiding. Operating the clutch was a hard to learn trick requiring considerable coordination. I usually managed to grind off a little of the gear shift each time I changed gears. Why, they even teased me about that. They said something about the people in town saying, "I hear the Powell boy coming, get out of his way." Really now. Changing gears a minute-- Stout had a car that he could make backfire when he wanted it to. I heard one man say, every time they saw his car, his kids and dogs would run screaming and barking into the house. Why don't we hear cars backfire anymore? As a kid I liked it. I am just glad it was my brother's car that backfired and not mine, I didn't need any more teasing.

9. On a camping trip, one Scout set a new Georgia record for tripping over a tent rope. He seemed to have some strange magnetic force drawing him to that rope, time after time. He never did a complete flip but he did everything else, including a half gainer. We were always supportive and thought about rushing to his aid, but instead just gave him scores just like it was an Olympic event. His best score on a ten point scale was a 9.5. It was a beauty. Speaking of Olympic events, I wonder if the committee would like a suggestion for a new event--the tent rope trip and flip.

10. On another Scout camping trip--We should all thank all the people who freely give of their time and energy supporting Scouting activities and who let us camp on their property--I remember we paddled around the lake and the fog was lifting and things were so peaceful. Maybe that is one reason I sometimes like to get outdoors early in the morning. One boy was in a boat by himself--except for a metal drum (open on one end and just large enough for a nice dry one-boy house boat) he sat on--what a picture--a boy on a metal drum, in a boat, on a lake with fog lifting all around--and a couple of other dingbats splashing water on me--that drum looked mighty inviting.

11. I also had two older sisters. Brenda, the one about 21 months older than me, always liked to boss me around, and being the runt, beat me up if I didn't do what she said. I remember one time I finally got the best of her and got her down and made her give up. She started crying and was so pitiful and I felt sorry for her, so I let her up. Then feeling real proud, I turned and started

walking to the house. My brother yelled but before I could turn around, my sister clobbered me from behind and knocked me down and commenced to pound on me. So much for pitiful stories--they really hurt--especially if you are looking the other way.

12. Brenda and I played Monopoly a lot, and I mean a lot. We played so much that we knew things without having to look them up or to count spaces. For example, with hotels the rent on Oriental was $550 and $950 for Tennessee. The distance between railroads is ten spaces. Landing on Free Parking by our rules was worth $500. Also, since we didn't like to pay taxes on houses and hotels, we threw those Chance and Community Chest cards away. At least once we had a marathon game that we continued for days and days. I guess we were evenly matched because it lasted so long. We broke the bank by passing Go and hitting Free Parking so many times. Then we wrote out bank I-owe-you's (an early model for the Federal budget) and continued playing. That may have been the longest Monopoly game in history. In another game, luck was with me because I finally cleaned her plow. She didn't have any monopolies and I had a bunch. She owed me money and couldn't pay. Then she kind of shed a tear or two and asked if we could make a trade so she could have a monopoly. Tenderhearted me agreed to a really dumb swap of property and I forgave her all her debts. Then she pulled out all this money she had hidden and started building houses and hotels and, and,--to make a long story short--she beat the tar out of me. But those were valuable lessons in life. Trust people, even your sister, but keep an eye on them. Be nice, but don't be stupid.

13. My dog's name was Rusty. He was a great little dog. He helped me hunt rats and birds with my BB gun. A Daisy Red Rider 500 shot BB gun that didn't shoot my eye out, thank goodness. My uncle gave Rusty to me when we visited them because the dog usually wasn't friendly to strangers but just seemed to like me. (Felt sorry for the runt I guess.) We spent many hours together. Only a boy who has had his own dog and lived in a small town or in the country really knows how wonderful having a dog can be. I talked to him and played with him and he was my best friend. But best friend or not, he had to stay outside and take his chances with all the other dogs. I remember one day when several of us boys were moving some lumber and killing rats as they came out. Our neighbor Boyce grabbed one rat by the tail as he tried to escape and hollered for his younger brother Barney to hit it with a stick. (As mean as Boyce was to Barney, it is a wonder that he didn't use it as an opportunity to hit Boyce in the head with that stick.) Before Barney could act, Rusty jumped up and grabbed the rat and killed him pronto. We worked on the rat population that day, but that just gave the remaining ones a little more elbow room. We would go out to the barn at night, shine our light under the barn and shoot the rats we saw. The rats fought us to a standstill until we cheated. We started using rat poison and that turned the tide of battle in our favor. You know, of all the animals on the endangered list, it is a shame that we can't get rats to sign up--they probably think the same thing about us.

14. I never professed to be the smartest boy around. But maybe part of that was a hearing problem that the

doctors haven't been able to detect. Maybe that basketball is still in there or maybe I fell off one too many calves. Anyway, I had trouble knowing the difference between 15 cents and 50 cents. In Mr. Brady's hardware store there was a knife that I liked. He said it cost 50 cents and since I had two dimes, I told him I would take it. When he saw my dimes, he explained the difference. Now wouldn't this story have had a happy ending if I said he gave me the knife for 20 cents? But he didn't, so I learned the difference between 50 cents and 15 cents. Isn't it amazing how many things you learn early in life that you never forget--like eating and walking and sleeping. (I can almost hear Gomer Pyle saying that.)

15. They probably don't have hog killings now days like they did when I was a boy. It was a happening. Back then it didn't take much to get us excited. Anyway, everyone loved it, except the hogs, of course. We would boil water in a black iron kettle shaped like a ball with the top cut off. It held about 30 gallons. We would build a fire under the pot and keep it going to have plenty of hot water. After killing the hog, we'd dunk him in a drum full of hot boiling water to help loosen the hog hair so we could scrape the hair off. Then they would hang him upside down by his hind legs and gut him. One of my jobs was to play in the fire and maybe add some wood. I was multi--what is the opposite of talented? I could do many things with equal ability. I remember Mom would tell me to help Dad, and Dad would tell me to help my brother, etc.--obviously I was multi-talented. I could help turn the sausage grinder. I even pinched my finger badly once in that grinder and it

really hurt; almost had ground up finger (ouch and yuck). I was amazed when they blew the intestines like a balloon and stuffed them with sausage. I remember once getting nauseated around the greasy boiling of the fat to get lard. Surprisingly, the family reminded me of my squeamishness every hog killing after that. Another benefit of hog killings was the great fresh food afterward. Some people have never had crackling bread—cornbread made with cracklings. Now that is real good eating. Take a glass of buttermilk, crumble up some crackling bread, add some salt and pepper, maybe a spoonful of baked sweet potato dipped in the milk and cornbread. Ummm, that was good food. And if it was hot cornbread it was even better. Some people like sweet milk but I preferred buttermilk. Wonder what would happen if I walked into a swanky restaurant and asked for some cornbread in milk. They would probably give me a swanky trip to the door.

16. One day we had a near tragedy when a horse used for plowing went wild and ran wide open through a yard full of children. I never did find out what caused the horse to turn crazy and run crazy. But I do remember other occasions when my older brother sort of lost his temper (actually, we Powell's have never been known to have a temper long enough to lose it, so I don't see how he could have lost one.) when dealing with a dumb brute. Whenever that happened, he usually tried to get their attention by cleaning out their ears with a two by four. So if I had been that horse and was due for an ear cleaning, I might have stampeded too.

17. My eldest brother Clem never used a two by four to clean my other brother's (Stout's) ears out. He preferred to clean them out with his fists. Clem really believed in keeping Stout's ears clean. They would have terrific wresting fights inside the house and outside. I remember one time they were fighting and fell on Mom and Dad's bed and broke it. That didn't slow them down, they just kept it up outside. I thought the fights were kind of neat, so I was surprised to see Mom crying. I don't know whether it was because they broke her bed, because they were hurting each other, or because it would be several years before they left home.

18. Stout had an adventure--sort of stumbled into it. He and a friend went into the woods behind the house and got lost. I remember how all the neighbors and our friends came over to help look for him. One cousin even went into an old shack half sunk into the mud looking for them. (I still have a yearning for the closeness and support of the small town and the multitude of relatives that were always instantly there to help.) They followed a creek downstream and eventually reached a road and started walking home when a friend gave them a ride home. He said they weren't lost and he knew where he was. Maybe he just took so long to get home so everyone would have time to visit. We always took advantage of every situation to visit--weddings, funerals, etc. Maybe Mom just told him to get lost so she could have some visiting. It finally dawned on me the other day, if Stout wasn't lost, why did he follow the creek downstream when he could have got home quicker by following it upstream. I guess the most surprising thing about the adventure was

that Dad did not beat the tar out of him. Dad had a long history of taking the belt to my older brothers, Scared me so bad that I was always the perfect angel and never got into trouble. I remember a lot of Stout's friends and cousins were there when he came home. They were teasing him about his forthcoming punishment and Dad walked into the room. You could have heard a pin drop. He got something out of the room and left and Stout started breathing again. I don't think he ever did get that belting. If Dad reads this he may go find Stout and collect on that overdue whooping. (We called them "whooping" which means it is a lot tougher than a whipping. Dad always gave whooping.)

19. Living in rural America had many advantages. One was we could have--and did have--just about any kind of pet we wanted. We had the usual dogs, cats (but only as long as they could stay away from the dogs), rabbits, a few squirrels-gray and flying, chickens (one pair dyed green and pink or blue for Easter) and you guessed it--a pair of pet pigs. My sister and I really loved those biddies and pigs. Unfortunately, one of the chicks discovered the bath room, the commode, and that he/she couldn't swim--all in the same day. We played with those chicks and pigs and really had fun with them (we were desperate for any diversion). I was really excited when we sold those pigs. We had great plans for the money. I guess I was much older when I realized that those pigs were sold to the market and were not being the pets of some other kids but instead were someone's pet bacon. Those pigs were great friends--but I never let friendship get in the way of money.

20, Dad tells of his logging days, that one day as he was walking around looking up at the trees to be cut, he felt something flopping around on his foot and leg. He looked down and saw that he was standing on the head of a rattlesnake. I asked him how he got off. He said, "Oh, that wasn't hard to do." He also tells that once a mule got tangled up in the lines after getting into a yellow jacket nest. The "hand" driving the mule had run for cover and the poor mule was really getting stung by the yellow-jackets. (Let me digress. If you have never had a run in with a bunch of yellow-jackets, count yourself lucky. With most wasps, if you get away from their nests, they will leave you alone. But the yellow jackets follow you home and he is like a kamikaze. They also hit you going full steam. It is like a bullet hitting you. The sting will continue to irritate you about a week or so after the sting. So needless to say stay away from yellow jackets.) My Dad was always one of my heroes, so he did the heroic thing, he ran in, untangled the mule, and drove him out of the yellow jacket line of fire. Of course with yellow jackets, if it had been me, first of all I wouldn't have gone in there to help the mule, and if I had I would kept driving the mule all the way home and would have run into the house and hid under the bed. Dad also tells of the time I was with him in the woods and after he stepped over a log I stopped and said, "Look at that big snake." And sure enough Dad had stepped over a really large snake. To me there are only two kinds of snakes poisonous or dead. So Dad made him nonpoisonous.

21. We had cousins on my Mom's side and cousins on my Dad's side and cousins on all sides. One group of

the men decided to go fishing in a large lake in Florida. In retrospect, it would be sort of like Spanky and Our Gang going out in a boat. None of the men had a life preserver, only Bernie, the only boy, had one. There were about seven or eight in what was probably a five person boat. The motor worked well enough to get them about a mile from shore. The boat then proceeded to transform itself into a submarine and they could not bail fast enough to keep it afloat or perhaps they turned too fast and just sunk it. Anyway, here we have a lake full of cousins with only one life preserver. Fortunately, the good Lord looks after fools and cousins and they all survived. One said later, after he swam ashore and got his breath, he kissed the ground and went to get help for the others. I guess that was one reason Dad always kept us away from boats--just too dangerous--especially in the hands of a cousin.

22. To paraphrase a portion of a poem about Paul Revere's ride, "hardly a man in now alive who remembers...", hardly a person is now alive who remembers their first television set. Well, I do. One of our cousins got one and we would come home from school and walk (or run) to their house every day to watch our favorite (favorite because it was the only thing on TV) program which was "Howdy Doody". We really loved that program. Of course we began a campaign to convince Dad and Mom that we needed a TV. Their reply was an honest one of "we cannot afford one". But somehow they did it and we were able to watch all those wonderful programs. I just thought, do you suppose our uncle whose house we visited every day before we got the TV, do you suppose he might

have bought the TV for us just to keep us at home? Naahh. Those were vintage TV programs, black and white, live, no re-runs, and we became a TV generation. Without TV the Mickey Mouse club and Davy, Davy Crockett would not have been so successful. I still remember how to sing all the verses of the Davy Crockett songs. I also learned how to spell e-n-c-y-c-l-o-p-e-d-i-a thanks to Jiminy Cricket. So early on, I learned that TV can be educational and enlightening-- what could be more enlightening and artistic than Davy Crockett and Annette Funicello.

23. One of the truly great inventions of all time is indoor plumbing. We had indoor plumbing but it would sometimes stop up and then we would all go to our back up system--the old outhouse. If you have never experienced the joys of the outhouse you can't really truly appreciate how great things are with indoor bathrooms. When the weather was nice, it is not too bad. When it is cold outside, it is even colder in the outhouse, so you wait as long as you can and then get the job done as quickly as possible. Soft toilet tissue is also a major invention, which you can really appreciate if you ever used newspaper or Sears catalog. Ouch, Ouch! One side benefit of that type paper is no one ever complained of hemorrhoids, One other thing about outhouses is the aroma. You can hold your breath only so long and then you wish you could have held it longer. One other disadvantage is the insects in warm weather. Sometimes there would be wasps but there would always be flies--lots of flies. (Thank you Lord that I was born in America!) I can also remember taking a bath in a tub-not a modern bath tub, but a wash tub. It

was cold and we learned to take a fast bath. We also took mini-baths that we referred to a spit baths. Just a little water on a bath cloth, then hit the hot spots. So next time I am feeling down about not being able to buy a bigger house, I will try to remind myself that things could be a lot worse--I could be owner of a house with an outhouse. There were six of us kids but with only one bath. How we managed that, I really don't know. We have three kids, two baths and we still have more bathroom conflicts than we did back then.

24. I guess I was the scaredest (like in easiest to scare the worst and most often) kid around. I remember on one Scout campout the leaders were "setting the stage" by telling us about some unknown monsters that made a strange noise and might even be in our part of Georgia. One of the Scouts was in on it and had brought his clarinet mouth piece and was on the other side of the lake. Naturally it was dark. When Mark blew that mouthpiece it really sounded wild. I was so scared I was ready to go home. I think my hair stood on end. Someone asked what that knocking sound was. Some of the boys in the boat paddled over to the sound. I never would have done that. Of course they had frog gigs and paddles as weapons. By then, I was busy guarding the inside of the truck because all I had was a machete knife, a long stick of fire wood, and a glowing fire. So with so little protection, it was only right that I should have been more afraid than they were. They finally convinced me it was a gag and coaxed me out of the truck. My hair returned to normal about 2 days later. (The other day my 11 year old son wanted to take his sister's clarinet mouthpiece on his Scout camping trip

and try to scare all his friends. I told him not to that they might not scare and might attack him. Kids don't scare these days like I did--maybe nobody ever scared as easily as I did. Maybe I was in the top 10 of all time. Maybe we could start a Hall of Fame for those who scare easily--I'd be famous--right up there with Don Knots--one of my boy hood heroes.)

25.   Another "scary adventure" occurred at Future Farmers of America summer camp. (I would have starved to death if I had tried to be a farmer, but I liked their summer camp a lot--maybe because it was also a camp for Future Homemakers of America (girls))   Our leader "set the stage" by waiting till night and saying there were some mountain lions or panthers along the river and the boys should not sneak off into the woods with the girls. Some older boys were in on it and were outside and one or two who were in on it were inside to help spread the panic. They did their job very well. One shouted that he had seen something near the window. One looked out and said something is out there.   I had overheard another cabin leader telling our leader how he had scared his cabin about a monster outside and one of the boys had led the others in the Lord's Prayer. But fear doesn't always let you think clearly. I should have realized it was a gag but all 1 could think about was that I was about ready to start the Lord's Prayer. I suggested to all the other frightened guys that we should get the mops and brooms and set them on fire if the panther got inside. About that time someone outside scratched on a window screen and Frank jumped about 3 double bunks and said "Th-th-there's something at the window." I was glad to have

some company on the upper bunk, so I handed him a mop. Finally Shep the brave one (I thought he was crazy and told him not to) said he would go outside and prove nothing was out there.   (Shep would never be allowed in our hall of fame but Frank would have been a definite possibility). It would have been terrible if I told you the panther ate him up. So I will tell the truth--they told Shep they saw something go under the cabin right under this window and when he came over to the window and beat around under the cabin with his stick, they poured a bucket of cold water on him.   Then everyone laughed and laughed, even Shep the brave was a good sport about it and had a good laugh while he put on a dry shirt.   About 30 minutes later, Frank and I finally realized it was a gag and came down off the upper bunks and had nervous laughs. I don't remember about Frank, but I slept with my trusty mop--just in case.

26.   Firecrackers were legal in Georgia when I was a boy. I know a lot of people got hurt by being careless or stupid but is that any reason to outlaw something as much fun as firecrackers. If people getting hurt was a criteria Georgia would have outlawed cars, trucks and guns by now. Anyway, I can remember especially at Christmas always getting sparklers and firecrackers. We would light the sparklers at night and throw them and pretend they were shooting stars. We always thought it was neat when the grass caught on fire and we would stomp it out.   I would hold one of the smallest firecrackers in the tip of my fingernails and if I did it right it didn't hurt. I would also put some in the mouth of a coke bottle and pretend it was a cannon. I put some under an old can or hub cap and watch them kick the can

into the air. We would set fire to a whole pack and listen to them go off like machine gun fire. We would set off Roman candles and cherry bombs and anything else we could afford. Some idiots would even set off a whistler among a crowded street and watch it chase people as it spewed along the ground. That was not my idea of fun--besides it would probably hit some big guy who would have shown me how funny he thought it was. I remember once we were on a field trip to some part of town and three classmates got in trouble over one firecracker. One brought it, one lit it and one threw it. Shep was one of them I think--braver (or dumber) than me again. I never heard of anyone ever sticking one in a gasoline tank--I guess we weren't totally dumb with the firecrackers. They are still legal in Alabama and South Carolina. Are they smarter and more enlightened than Georgia or vice versa. Of course if they were legal today, as many Georgians as there are today, we would probably burn more of the state down than Sherman did.

27. One of my happiest memories is the summer day my Dad brought home a beautiful little red bicycle with training wheels. It wasn't even my birthday or anything. He didn't go into a lot of emotional stuff, he just set it down on the ground and told me it was mine. I surely hope I told him thank you and hugged him but I don't remember. I rode that bike all day. With training wheels, I even took rest breaks while sitting on it. I might have even eaten supper on it or even brought it into my bedroom. I really loved that red bike and rode it for years. Unfortunately, I was also very selfish and when Mom loaned it to a boy down the street, I rushed outside and checked the tires to see if he had worn them

out. Our front yard was not a lawn, but was bare ground just right for playing. We would go up the road about 100 yards and come riding into the yard as fast as we could and stomp on the brake and leave a long skid mark--the longer the better. We would see who could make the longest mark. Fortunately, none of us were ever seriously injured. One thing we did that kids don't do today is we would use a clothespin to attach about a 2 inch by 5 inch piece of cardboard so the cardboard would flap against the spokes and make a sound sort of like a motorbike. The more we attached, the more noise we make and the more we liked it. Is it an international truism that kids love noise? We did. I told my 11 year old about the clothespins and cardboard and he wanted to try it on his bike. We may just try it--I may even put them on my bike too. I may not be able to be a kid again, but I can act childish--I have been accused of that before--and worse.

28. When I was in the fourth grade, Frank offered me a ride on the back of his bike. I was going to his house to play. So I hopped on and he took off. I guess he was going so fast it sort of scared me and I clamped down tight--hands, arms, legs, feet. Somehow my foot got caught in the spokes of the bike and next thing I know I am having awful pains in my heel. I guess he thought I was screaming because of the fast ride so he sped up, and I screamed louder, and he sped up and so on. Finally he stopped and I checked my foot. The shoe was torn through, and my foot was bleeding. Those spokes had skinned my heel and it hurt. I guess I limped on home, and I am sure Mom was sympathetic but I am also sure she didn't like me grinding up a shoe. She

didn't say it but she may have thought it, "next time take your shoes off before you hitch a ride." You see, skin will grow back but shoe leather doesn't. I was always one to try to evoke sympathy from others, so the next day with my foot all bandaged up, I limped into my class and asked the teacher if I could borrow her stool so I could prop my foot up. She was nice and let me use her stool several days. Just think, if I had had my shoes off, we could have ground my heel down to the bone and I could have milked the hurt heel for several weeks at school, instead of a few days. On the other hand, for those who have not stuck a foot into bicycle spokes, I recommend you don't, the sympathy is real but so is the pain.

29. I was a member of the First Baptist Church in Buena Vista. (A town that small calling their church First is a little ironic. They could have named it "The" Baptist or "The One and Only" Baptist Church of BV.) In a small town the church is often a major source of social life--very nearly the only social life in BV. The church built a Sunday School Building with a social hall on the first floor. During one Vacation Bible School, they built a folding ping pong table. Several of us guys played a lot and the table became part of our social life and meeting place. We would play after church and some afternoons. Fortunately, the preacher had kids our age so we could play just about any time. In reality, I guess we used ping pong as an excuse to be together and talk about things, like girls, and movies, and school, and our basketball teams, and girls, and cars, and girls, and jokes, and girls, and part time jobs, and girls, and guy things. Anyway, through the years I played a lot of ping

pong and I thought I was pretty good. I was not the best in BV but pretty good. It is amazing how cocky I was. I didn't brag, but I thought I could beat anyone until they proved me wrong and I figured I would win next time. (Years later, when I was working at Robins Air Force Base, I had a chance to play ping pong at lunch with some men who were the Robins champs. When I met the champ, I was surprised, He was sort of stooped over and didn't look too mobile or quick. I remember thinking, if he is the best then maybe I will be the new champ. Why, he can't even stand up straight. I think I got 2 points against him in the game--a couple of his slams missed my end of the table. I couldn't believe it. He put some kind of super spin on the ball and if I got my paddle on it, the ball just shot off in a crazy direction that I had no control over. That man was mean to me. I soon found excuses not to go down there to be humiliated. I have told my kids this story and encouraged them to never judge someone by appearance. Also, I am glad I didn't brag that I was good. Getting beat--skunked--is bad enough, but having to eat crow would have made it worse.) Of course there was a price to pay to use the Church's ping pong table. That price was attending church. But you know, some of the sermons were good. After all these years, I even remember a few things the preacher said. But after evening church we would rush over to play ping pong--and talk. I remember Arthur would get a little upset when he lost and would throw his paddle. So, if you won, you better be prepared to duck, which I did. I bet I could still beat him--he stands up straight so I would have a chance. Wonder if he still throws his paddle.

30. Saturday afternoon movies were a big part of my growing up. Up to age 12, we paid $0.15, and at age 12 the cost was $0.40, a mere pittance, compared to today's $5 and up prices. What was so neat about the old days, you paid one price and could stay all day--you could see the movie over and over, and I did. No wonder I remember some scenes from old movies. I saw the previews several times, and the movies several times. In those days, we would have a movie or two--usually westerns--a cartoon, a serial, previews and news. Kids now days don't know what a serial is or how exciting they could be. Time after time, the hero--Batman, Flash Gordon, etc.--would end the weekly serial obviously about to die a horrible death, but the next Saturday he would be saved or save himself at the last minute. The cartoons were great too. I see a lot of them on TV that I remember from when I was a kid. The movies were magic. I could ride the range or be with Tarzan in the jungles or Ulysses (Kirk Douglas), or Moses, or Drums Along the Mohawk when Henry Fonda outran those three Indians, or with Satch in the Bowery Boys, or pirates, or knights, ad infinitum. The movies were great and I learned a lot there. Sometimes, on TV they aren't as good as I remember, but sometimes they are just as good or better. Saturday afternoon movies, Roy Rogers, Gene Autry, Rex Allen, and many monster movies, even some classics, some about a boy and his dog (Old Yeller, Good-bye My Lady), movies about Bible characters, and many, many more. A silver screened magic carpet for a young boy to ride time and again and thankfully the good guy always won. Audie Murphy, the most decorated soldier of World War II, was one of

my heroes. He may not have been a great actor but I never missed one of his movies. I also liked Charles Bronson. Did you know he played the role of Captain Jack an Indian chief in one movie?--that was many years ago. I imagine I even played cowboys and Indians and was Captain Donnie Jack. I do remember saying lets play Black Indians in the jungle because they have better wild animals--elephants, lions, zebras, hippos, etc. In fact I would often "play like" I was a Black Indian. As the Statler Brothers song goes, "Thank you Mr. Edison for giving us the best years of our life".

31. One night my sister Brenda (about 21 months older than me) and I were at the same movie but she was quite a bit later getting home. So when Mom asked where she and her date had been, I cheerfully chimed in with my little brother two cents worth. I said they had gone to Lovers Loop and parked. Brenda never said a word. So I proceeded to tell Mom where the Loop was--out near the Gypsy Camp store and that people would go out there and park. Brenda had sort of drifted out of the room. Later when Mom wasn't around, she came up to me and said, "You keep your mouth shut about me and what I do, especially when I am on a date! Do you understand me?" After such a clear explanation, I understood perfectly--especially since she had her fist under my nose at the time.

32. Kirven's was a big department store in downtown Columbus. Shopping in Columbus was always a treat. My sister Joyce and her husband, Gene, took us many places and really helped expand my horizons and were especially generous in taking us shopping in Columbus.

35

When we were old enough to go off on our own, we would have to meet back at a certain time and place. The back of Kirven's was where we always met, partly because they had a couple of benches inside that we could wait on. Now my sister Joyce could tell time, but when shopping she just didn't tell time, she just shopped until the stores closed--even though we had been told to meet an hour or two before the stores closed. It is a standing joke in the family even today, that we spent countless hours waiting and that eventually we would take possession of the bench because those there when we arrived would always leave before we did. If they had had a parking meter on that bench, they would have made a lot of money off us because we did "park" there a lot.

33. Another time two of my nieces were waiting behind Kirven's and the older (Connie) scared the younger (Peggy Joyce) by telling her they would be locked up in jail by the police if their parents (yep, Joyce and Gene late as usual) didn't come soon. Poor little Peggy was in tears and very upset. When she finally saw her parents round the corner half a block away, she yelled and waived her arm, "Come On! Hurry! Come On!" Connie still relishes retelling that story--but, Peggy isn't too crazy about it.

34. Mom always did whatever she could to hold costs down. Flour used to come in cloth sacks that were often white but sometimes in floral designs. She would keep the sacks and make dresses or shirts from them. She was a good seamstress and they always looked good but I really preferred store bought shirts because then I

would have one that didn't look like the shirts all the other kids wore to school. I preferred to have her make sheets out of the 25 pound flour sacks--I was always "unselfish" like that.

35. There was a freight train wreck at a crossroads we called Putnam, about 7 miles east of Buena Vista. We all had to go down and take a first hand look. I remember it was awesome--all those train cars scattered all over the place. Someone said one Putnam resident got there first and some of the wrecked merchandise--like in whiskey--was so badly wrecked that it was almost like it disintegrated--or more appropriately, disappeared. Some said he finally sobered up about six months later. The wreck at least gave us something to talk about. In a small town, life was always sort of dull and routine, so anything out of the ordinary was almost always welcome--and to one Putnam resident, the train wreck was remembered often and fondly for years (after he sobered up).

36. Putnam had another boyhood memory. One of the more well-to-do families decided to make a lake there. The construction began and to help fill it up, they had water pumped into the lake bed. As the months went by, the level of the lake water did not rise. We heard later that the soil was sandy in that area and the water just kept soaking down into the ground. We never did get to sneak in there and catch some fish. We boys didn't appreciate the lack of planning--after all we had some big plans for that lake--but none that included a dry lake bed.

37. Putnam was also the site of the first (and I guess last) oil drilling in Marion County. We were all hopeful they would hit oil. It would have meant more money, more jobs, maybe more girls moving into the area (there was definitely a shortage of girls--the shortage should have been listed in Ripley's Believe It or Not). So we were all excited about this possible new undertaking. But alas, there was no oil and finally, our dreams had to be laid to rest. I could have been a star or at least an extra in the movie about oil being discovered in Georgia. I could just see it, my name in lights, the money, the travel, the girls, etc. Oil would have been only one thing "discovered" in Marion County. The world would just have to wait--what a shame, what a loss to the world. Oh well, the world took their loss well.

38.   Our Baptist church was a place for social gatherings, but was also a place for spiritual renewal. I think some of it took because I turned out pretty--well, sort of pretty--well. But I guess I remember some of the stories and jokes. For example, one pastor said a chip on the shoulder came from a block head. Now, as they say, I resemble that remark--well half way, you see I strive to ensure I do not have a chip on my shoulder. He also told about the time his commanding officer called him in and said I understand you don't like cursing--I will try to keep that in mind. I whispered to his son, and then he cussed him out. We were always afraid of being called on to say a prayer out loud in front of everyone. Talking to God is easy. But talking out loud in front of a lot of people is really tough. Sometimes I would look around and if I was the oldest

one around, I would seriously consider ducking out the side door. You know, even today, I sit near the side door, just in case.

39. Christmas was always--and still is--a very special time. I can remember all the things we wanted and how fortunate we were in all the things we got. I always wanted a "gun and holster" set, a B-B gun, toys, toys and more toys. Clothes were nice but, well kids want toys. Christmas traditions are nice but there are some that we didn't continue with our kids. My sister and I would "wake up" after Santa came and we would stay up all night. Now as an adult, I cannot believe we actually stayed awake all night, but we did--how excited we were--how dumb we were. How patient our parents were--I am not that patient. I have to have my sleep-- some of it. Santa did not wrap presents back then, at least not at our house. I remember we would just stand a few seconds and just look at all the stuff. Then we would just dive in. I would sometimes try to claim Stout's stuff, but he was bigger and it didn't work. But when he went on to bed, I would "check" it out--one other advantage of staying up all night. We got fruit, candy, nuts, etc. and we tried to eat a lot of it during the night. It is a wonder we didn't have upset stomachs but I guess we were tough. We ate as much as we could so our brothers and cousins wouldn't get "our share". Our share was all we could eat--we were selfish too, even at Christmas. But Santa wraps our children's gifts--maybe he found it was easier to wrap than to assemble. Anyway, our kids emphatically state they want them wrapped--the name tags reduce disputes over who gets

what. You see, our kids are also selfish and greedy, just like us. Boy, do we love Christmas.

40. When I went to college I left a boy and returned, well a boy. But Haskell lived down the hall and he was a strong former football player. He loved to sip a few beers and one night he returned feeling rather uninhibited. He grabbed the one inch steam pipe running down the wall to the heater and pulled with all his might. The pipe bent about a foot from the wall. As luck would have it, the floor monitor came out about that time and asked who bent the pipe. Naturally a crowd gathered--we would quit studying at the slightest--or no--excuse. The floor monitor continued to play Sherlock Holmes and finally accused Haskell, and said I saw you bend the pipe. But Haskell continued to deny it. After about 20 minutes, the monitor said, off the record and man to man, Haskell did you bend that pipe? Haskell said, something like, off the record and man to man, you darn right I bent that pipe. The monitor shouted, Haskell why did you bend the pipe? (Since they were back on the record), Haskell said, I didn't bend that pipe. That cracked us all up.

41. Do you remember the first time you danced with a girl? I do. It was a romantic and exciting time. Unfortunately, I was still very short, totally scared, and devoid of rhythm. She was very gracious and understood a very insecure, younger student who could not dance a step. She got me through it and to this day have sweet memories of holding her close (within 12 inches of each other), smoothly gliding across the floor, and sweeping her off her feet. Her version may be

slightly different. At later dances, I would start over to her but somehow when I got to where she was, she wasn't there--guess she had to go powder her nose--doesn't know what she missed.

42. Most girls don't know the following deep, dark secret but here it is--The female magnet waves have a befuddling effect on the male tongue, especially if hormones have kicked in. The normal male conversation would roughly translate hello and how are you doing. It is good to see you and I think you are a very special person. However, when the female is physically present and her magnetic waves are waving, the poor teenager actual comments would come out something like, uh, go up no wow see no what school back around ugh uh. Now all the guys understood exactly what he said--one is even thinking, gosh I wish I had said that and I why can't I say things like that around girls. All the other guys think he has won her heart with such eloquence. The girl thinks he is a complete nut, but says something like I thank you for your comments and she smiles and glides away with every boys heart in her hand and every boys eve on her ----. God gave girls that special magnetic power, but He also endowed them with a sixth sense to be compassionate and understanding that it is just a phase that all boys go through and that it will end--in about 50 years. Women think men don't express their feelings to the women in their lives, but we do, using the same words we used as teenagers--with similar results. We know what we mean and we say it beautifully in spite of the magnetic impact. We can't help it if the women can't hear what we meant and think we are nuts. If a woman

wants a clearer explanation, I will be glad to explain it in words any man could understand. Maybe if I learned sign language they would understand--I'd probably get my fingers tangled up and never get them unstuck.

43. Mom cooked hamburgers on Saturday night. My two older brothers were teenagers, had usually worked hard all day, needed lots of energy for their fights, and were hoping for a long Saturday night. As a result, they didn't just eat, they consumed as if they were about to hibernate for the winter. I staggered to eat just one or two, but they each ate 6 or 8 or 10--I lost count. Boy could they eat, and eat and eat. To this day I still don't believe what I saw. How did Dad afford to feed them? I know he must have been secretly thrilled when they finally got married and left home. I think he finally actually gained a little weight after that--up to then he was skin and bones. Come to think of it, they ate sort of like our dogs--gobbling up everything before the others could get it. I wonder if Mom ever played a trick on them for fighting so much and slipped something into their hamburgers--like maybe a laxative or something. It might not have made them better, but they had to spend some time apart--our outhouse was not a two seater, just one.

44. I was lucky to get a job in a grocery store--there were not very many jobs available. I made a whopping $ 5 a day. Later I got a promotion up to $ 6 and was really thrilled. (In Buena Vista, we had a low threshold for thrills.) Even at this pay, I was able to save some money for the one and only time of my life. Anyway we did all sorts of work in the store. One day Fred was

going to take a five gallon bucket of lard out to the customer's pickup truck. It was hotter than you can imagine. Macho Fred grabbed that lard can with one hand and easily lifted if off the floor. In the heat, the lard was liquid and the top was not taped on. You guessed it. The lid flew off and the liquid spilled all over the wooden floor. Few people would believe it but I was there. That lard spread out and like the oil in the Bible it didn't diminish. It was like a tidal wave, it went on and on. We helped Fred by seeing the humor in the situation, but we were sensitive--we didn't roll on the floor--after all there was lard all over it. We did rush out and warn passing motorists and pedestrians to clear the area--that there had been a major oil spill. Poor old Fred mopped up lard for hours. Of course one good thing for the wooden floors, with all that grease in them, they never rotted--preserved for eternity. Once I was lifting a big sack of groceries up to set into the back of a pickup truck and the eggs on the top fell out when I tilted the bag. Did you know those cartons don't protect the eggs in a fall of about six feet onto asphalt? We had poor quality cartons even back then. My biggest goof was much bigger than Fred's lard episode. As we closed up we cleaned up and finally turned out the lights. One night I volunteered to turn the lights and accidentally turned off an extra switch--it was to the ice cream cooler. They told me about it the next Saturday-- fortunately I didn't have to pay for it but since I had flunked "turning off electric switches 101" I never was allowed near them again. With help like Fred and me, I guess I shouldn't have been surprised when the store closed a few years later. You know, if that ice cream hadn't been contained in the cooler, it would have probably covered the lard and then some--might have renamed the town to Ice Vista or Buena Cream.

45. Kids today complain about being bored but back then we had to make up games out of nothing. For example, I remember one time a relative came visiting and we entertained ourselves most of the day with water fights. We would fill up pans and buckets and whatever and just chase each other and when caught, literally pour it on. We had a lot of fun. I have noticed when my kids get away from the TV and go outside to play, they often invent games and have just as much fun and get along better. Water fights, one of the simplest and most fun. I recommend it.

46. When getting some wood for our wood stove, I picked up one board and there was a snake. I was too little to do anything except run screaming into the house. My Mom and brother Stout accompanied me back to the wood shed and I proceeded to tell them where the snake was. I would point to the board and they would say this one and I would say no that one. Stout was moving around and stepping on different boards and asking if it was that one. Finally, he got the right board and I said it is the one you are standing on. That is the fastest I have ever seen him move.

47. For years my uncle would have a big bar-be-cue each July 4th. There was an old mill pond there and the older kids swam and we younger kids just waded. I was wading and Stout said look out there is a deep hole there. Being a know-it-all even then, I said I won't step in it. That statement was promptly followed by glub,

glub, glub. I remember sinking like a rock and seeing all these bubbles floating up and I just looked around. The Good Lord was looking after me because my other brother swam over grabbed me and took me to the surface. My first reaction was to scream and cry and holler. In retrospect, it is really scary how close it could have been. Had my brothers not seen me go under,.....After that I played below the mill pond, down where the creek was shallow and I could see the bottom and stand up and breathe at the same time. That is the right depth for non-swimmers. After all these years I can still see those bubbles--whew. Another time at the swimming pool I was running down toward the deep end and--is there a magnetism of an open pool that draws little kids into the pool?--with extreme coordination and attention to where I was going, I fell into the pool. Couldn't swim a lick. Did my rock imitation again. Fortunately, again my older brother Clem saw me and rescued me again. Just think, if he had never been born, I would have drowned twice (Can you drown more than once?). As Jimmy Stewart said in my favorite movie of all time "It's A Wonderful Life". I think I will ask Clem if he had it to do over again, would he still have rescued me. Then again, if you can't stand the answer, don't ask the question.

48. Stout told me about the potato (or potatoe) pit. He said Clem and cousin Clyde were mean to him and another cousin Wayne. Since C and C were bigger and stronger, they made life pretty miserable for them. There was this sweet potato pit, or hole about five feet deep that was used to store sweet potatoes during the winter. When properly stored the potatoes would not

rot.   When empty, the pit was just another hole in the ground.   But to boys, a hole in the ground is always more than just a hole in the ground.   It can become a fox hole for playing Army or it can be a tiger pit to capture tigers, or whatever.   For Clem and Clyde it was a fighting pit or wrestling pit--for Stout and Wayne.   C and C threw them in and wouldn't let them out until one beat up the other.   I am glad Clem never threw me and my sister into the pit and made us fight, she would have beaten the tar out of me.

49.   Another story I only heard about was the watered down hill.   This was before paved driveways--and before my cousins developed any IQ.   One of our Aunt's lived on a hill with a driveway that was red Georgia clay.   In dry weather they could drive to her house without any problem, but when it was wet--forget it. During one of the get-togethers at the house on the hill, one of the boys had the bright idea to pour water on the hill so the others that were coming could not get up the hill. Everyone seemed to think that was a great idea and started drawing water from the well and hauling it to the hill and pouring it down the ruts.   If their parents had made them haul that much water the boys would have protested vigorously and probably founded a child abuse organization.   But since it was their idea and helped them with a practical joke--why are they called "practical jokes", they are definitely not practical and they are not jokes, they are usually a form of meanness-- that they could probably get away with.   So they kept hauling the water.   Just as they hoped, the hill got so slick no one could get up the hill in a car.   They all had to walk up--and down.   Probably even had to get some

cars out of the ditch--an added bonus. One uncle was heard to say, there could be a drought all over the county but that hill was always wet when they came. I am glad the hill was not on the edge of a cliff--they probably would have thought it great fun to watch cars plunge over the edge and bounce all the way down. I take that back, they were just mean, not criminal. But 40 years later, they still talk about it and laugh at how much fun it was.

50. Clem loved to pinch. Not just a little love pinch but a real honest to goodness--or badness--hurting, mark-leaving, pinch. I would be sitting at the breakfast table and every time he would come by my chair, reach over and pinch my neck. I don't remember, but I don't believe I was singled out for this special attention but rather anyone he could reach. I developed a defensive maneuver of raising my shoulder and tilting my head down to cover up that side of my neck. However, he was ambidextrous and could and did pinch equally well with either hand. So I started just about every day with my morning pinch, whether I wanted it or not. From Clem's point of view, I guess he was just paying attention to his younger brother and I guess he would rather be the pincher than the pinchee.

51, I was Mom's "baby" for nine years. Mothers don't seem to call their youngest "my baby" any more. But when I was a boy, my Mom was always calling me her baby. I was too big to be called a baby. I didn't like it at all. So when my younger brother Ricky was born when I was nine, I was delighted and announced to Mom, I am not your baby any more. She thought that was funny but

I was serious and hoped she would not call me her "baby" any more. I gladly introduced my new brother as Mom's "baby" and that I was no longer her baby. So needless to say, I have always had a special feeling for my younger brother. [And yes, I think Mom still calls him her "baby" even though he is now over 40.]

52. When Clem married Weone, they lived in a small house about 100 yards from our house. Ricky was 5 or 6 and would visit them to watch TV until time for bed. He would always call us on the phone and say "Watch me home". He was afraid something would get him in the dark so we would watch him home. It is a wonder Clem didn't hide out and scare him half to death, but he would have had to be very fast because when Rick started home he really moved. One night we forgot to unhook the screen door and he hit it going wide open. I never knew boys could bounce so far back from the door but he bounced about half way back to Clem's. It is a wonder his neck wasn't broken. After that he always reminded us to unhook the door and he also slowed down when he got to the door. Ricky always was a fast learner. ["Watch me home'" has such a comforting sound. I somehow think when we die and start to heaven God will be right there to "Watch us home".]((Note: I wrote this story into Ricky's eulogy in 2012.))

53. We always did a lot of visiting with relatives. It always amazed me to sit and listen to Mom and all the Aunts talking. If you have never seen it you won't believe it. All, yes all of them were talking at once. And I could never get a word in edgewise. They talked

without periods or semicolons, or even commas. I couldn't believe they were listening to each other but I guess they did. Maybe they were just starved for female company and to be able to talk about female things--the Powell men have a long history of not listening to female talk or topics. After waiting about 30 minutes for a break, I would just finally have to interrupt--or try to--because when Mom was on automatic pilot she just kept on and on. She was trying to keep up with everyone else. I don't know who the fastest and longest-talking person in the US is supposed to be but they would only be a distant second in that room full of women. In fact, he too would have had to wait 30 minutes just to get a word in edge-wise--but then he could have just jumped in and started talking and no one would have heard him at all.

54. When I was little, I took everything literally. I remember hearing Mom saying she had asked some colored people about something. I got all excited. I wanted to see some purple or green or orange people. I had been missing out on something. You can imagine my disappointment when she cleared it up. Shoot, our town was just like early television, just black and white. Another time when we went to all day singing at a rural church the preacher said we were going to have dinner on the ground--maybe he said grounds, but I heard ground. So later when the food was outside on some tables, I asked Mom when are we going to have dinner on the ground. She said right now. I just shook my head. Obviously, she didn't understand the difference between dinner on a table and on the ground. We never did put the food on the ground.

55. I remember when we played I would sometimes suggest we play wild Indians, but sometimes I wanted to be those black Indians in the jungle where they had all kinds of exciting wild animals like lions, rhinos, zebras, etc. Their life seemed so much more exciting than ours. I envied them. They also had neat spears and set up traps for wild animals. They had jungle vines to swing on and neat boats to paddle. They had rivers to swim in and quickmud (like quicksand) to avoid. They had neat nearly nothing clothes to wear, along with wild masks or costumes. They had neat jungle huts. They did wonderful dances and could pound out quite a tune on those drums. They had tall trees to climb. They had all kinds of unusual food to gather and eat--bananas, coconuts, fish, deer. etc. They fished whenever they wanted to. They really had it made--no wonder I pretended to be a black Indian.

56. One night as we were finishing work at the grocery store, the KKK arrived on the square. All these people dressed up in white sheets. My friend and co-worker Billy and I thought it was neat. When I went home to change clothes I told my parents and said we wanted to go watch to see what happened. My Dad said not to get in the way. We were dumb enough not to see the danger so we went trooping back up to the square to see what happened. Of course, since they were in BV, the town where nothing happened, the KKK had a rousing meeting and nothing happened. I think our town just bored them to death.

57. Speaking of bored. One of the teen age thrills was to ring the big antique bell on the square and run before

the policeman arrived. When ringing a bell and running is the biggest thrill in town, you can just imagine how boring it seemed at the time. When I hear my kids say they are bored, I speak a platitude, the only bored person is one with a lazy mind. There are many things to do-- make up a story, imagine an exciting childhood, read a book, ask someone what they did when they were kids, imagine what you would do if you won a million dollars, etc. My kids usually yawn and repeat themselves. The other day when we rode by that big old bell, I was tempted to go and ring it and run--ringing it in daylight might add some degree of excitement if not intelligence.

58. Speaking of bored again. Our little town had only one traffic light. We found it exciting to go and watch it change from red to green to yellow to red. Wow what excitement. It was exciting compared to what we usually did. I guess teenagers all over the world are bored no matter where they are raised--but in retrospect, I think our little town cornered the market and was proud of their accomplishment.

59. "Psycho" was a terrible movie for a young, impressionable, scary teenage kid to see. My sister and I saw it. I was totally unprepared--probably thought it was a western and that was the cowboy's horse's name. Was I ever wrong. In that darkened theater with a larger-than-life killer on the screen, and the stereo (I think) shrieking loudly, and the shower scene....Whew. It was terrible. My sister had to explain the ending to me a couple of times on the way home from Columbus before it finally sunk in. Of course I was still in shock

and it took me that long to come around. Why, I probably had--and still have--some form of serious emotional problems as a result of that movie. Even as an adult, when I was away from home and taking a shower, guess what I thought about. I hoped I had locked the door. That movie is probably mild by today's standards. But back then it was scary stuff, maybe because it was or could be real stuff. The only time I want to see that movie again is on a small screen in the daytime with the lights all on and the VCR turned down low.

60. My cousin Clinton--we called him Bim--went into the Army. They lived near us and I was surprised to see his widowed mom cry when he left, because as a kid, going into the Army seemed like a great thing to do. Bim was always a fun loving and good-natured person. I still like talking to him today. I never was much of a letter writer but I wrote Bim occasionally and he found time to write to me too. My letters were probably terrible but were probably very welcome to a probably homesick Army soldier [that sentence was "probably" bad.]. I guess everyone likes to get mail, even a little kid who had no idea of why Bim was in the Army or where he was or what he was doing. I remember once I wrote what I called a poem. Bim was so desperate for mail that when he wrote back he said he liked the poem. At that age, any of my poems had to be dumber than dumb and worse than bad. So the moral of the story is, if you know someone in the military service, write them, they will love it. ((As a way to honor Bim, in 2012 I placed a small flag on his grave and one on his veteran father-in-law.))

61. Later my older brother Clements went into the Army--not a volunteer. He used to tell us many stories. Fortunately, they weren't war stories. He told of going overseas on a boat, getting into a big, big storm and everyone getting seasick. He said he would be sitting there trying to eat and the ship would shift and the trays would slide down the table. He would look down and there would be a tray containing not his breakfast but the former breakfast of a seasick buddy who had thrown up his breakfast onto the tray. I don't think he gained much weight on the ship. He often said everybody should have to spend a year or two in the Army, and get exposed to all kinds of people. He told of one who had a really bad drinking problem. After he shaved, the man would put on his after shave lotion and also take a drink of it. Clem told us they were always trying to get them to reenlist. He played along and had a some posters in his locker saying reenlist or make it a career.   He said they would leave him alone but harass those who spouted off about getting out right away. Clem always was pretty shrewd. He would save his money and loan it to other Army buddies--often requiring collateral. He brought home a catcher's mitt that he had gotten that way. No way was I ever, ever going to be a catcher. So I sold it to a catcher on the town baseball team for $10. (Back then, several of the small towns had baseball teams.) I think I kept the money, because I considered the mitt a gift.   He once brought a buddy home for a short visit and my sister Brenda quickly changed her clothes and fixed herself up. When Mom offered to get them some cokes, Brenda insisted on serving the refreshments. Being younger and dumber, I couldn't figure out what

was wrong with Brenda. She never volunteered for any chores before, especially after prettying herself up. Girls were sure a puzzle, especially around soldiers in uniform. Now Clem would say, you should see how the uniform impacts those running the Army--they are all nuts.

62. Cousin Jim was a wild driver. I did not like riding with him. But he was nice enough to drive Clem to the bus station in Macon so he could go back to his beloved Army. Clem's wife, Weone (pronounced we-on) would ride with Clem and I would often go the keep them company. But I was always scared to death when Jim was driving. He tried to make that car fly. I even figured on one trip to keep the windows rolled down to slow the car down. It didn't work. I guess if I had been smarter I would have figured out to just stay home. But logic at that level was above my head. In retrospect, it seems so simple--don't get in the car with Jim. After all nobody made me go. Another example of my intellectual level (if any) at that age. ((Note: Jim was wounded in WWII and had a plate in his head and walked with a limp. Wish I had talked to him about WWII. Belatedly, in 2012, to honor him, I put a small flag on his grave. Thanks for your service Jim.))

63. Churning is a lost art--thank goodness--and may it never be found. Mom believed we should have chores and be hard working. For me, it didn't take. But I did get to churn. A churn is a big wooden, ceramic, etc. container into which you pour fresh-from-the-cow milk (after straining through a clean cloth). Then you put on a lid with a hole in it with a stick with a wooden board

or blade on the end. Next you grab the stick, pull it up, push it down, pull it up, push it down, ad infinitum. By paraphrasing a tune, you get the idea--"Churning in the morning, churning in the evening, churning at supper time". Eventually, the butter will be beaten out of the cow milk and begin to float to the top. Lest you misunderstand, this is not exciting work. Jobs like these make me take my hat off to my pioneering ancestors. If the cow had to work half as hard to produce the milk, I am sure they would have stopped producing milk eons ago. Churns were probably a great invention, but if I had to churn all the butter I ate, I would have learned to eat without butter a long time ago.

64. The ice cream churn was another work-related form of torture, but with sweeter results. In the old days, Mom would put the ice cream mixture into the ice cream churn, the guys would pour ice and salt around the outside, and then turn the handle, turn the handle, turn the handle. After a long long time, the cream would freeze. I usually got to sit on top of the churn to help hold it steady, or keep me out of the way. I would also help keep the ice level up. I even got to turn the handle some. After all that work, I have to admit, the ice cream was great--it was worth all that work. Now days, I just go to the store and pick up a half gallon--but it isn't quite as good. Maybe nothing in life is as good if it is easy, if you don't work for it. To be sure, that was the best ice cream ever.

65. We had a wood burning stove in the kitchen. I remember when it was replaced by a new electric stove. For some reason it was stored outside near the smoke

house. I don't know whether Mom and Dad kept it as a back up just in case the new fangled electric stove didn't work for long or whether that was just a convenient place to put it or whether it was to serve as a warning to the electric stove. Whatever the reason, Brenda and I played with it for a long time. We cooked many a pretend meal on it. It was like an old friend who had been put out to pasture. So many things in life have been replaced, not because they didn't do what they had been created to do but because they became obsolete because of technology. This was probably one of my earliest experiences with technology. Through the years, technology has continued to bring great changes but often with some negative impacts. How many have lost their jobs due to technology and like that old wood stove, put out to pasture--remembered fondly but no longer able to do the job they want to do. But I digress. That old stove was eventually sold for scrap--maybe it was reincarnated into something useful that wouldn't become obsolete, like an American made car.

66. Milking a cow is no fun. Fortunately, my older brothers got to do that chore. I tried a few times, but as one friend said, I was an "udder" failure. I just didn't have the hand strength to get the job done--and recognized the benefit of not developing that capability. But it was interesting to watch the milking. The milk would make a neat sound as it went into the bucket and would foam up. Fresh milk was mighty good. Now whenever milking, the milker had to watch out for the cow and her tail. She would sometimes try to kick the milker and she always swished her tail and the really talented cows could hit the milker right in the eye with

that tail. One un-ingenious fellow supposedly tied a brick to the cow's tail so she wouldn't swish her tail. Unfortunately, he didn't realize how strong a cow's tail is. She swished her tail and hit him in the head with the brick and knocked him hat over milk stool into never, never land. So after testing that invention under field conditions, he decided not to file a patent on it.

67. Picking cotton helped me strive for an office job. I do believe that new employees should be required to pick cotton, work as a roofer in the summer, work as a coal miner, etc. for about a week before going onto their nice office job. I especially think it is a good idea for these prima donna ball players. If nothing else, they would at least be motivated. I only had to pick a little cotton but my parents talked about having to do it for weeks every year. (Thank you Lord that I wasn't born 50 years earlier.) For those who have never picked cotton, it is kind of fun--for about 10 minutes. It is not exciting, it is hot, the pods stick your fingers, and it is rough on the back. Lets see, if you are paid two cents for each pound you pick, and you pick 100 pounds in a day, you could make $2 a day. Now cotton is picked by machines, but in the old hand picking cotton picking days, it could build character and a strong appreciation for inside jobs.

68. Cotton was a big crop in Marion County when I was a kid. I grew up with cotton, as well as peanuts, corn, watermelons, wheat, etc. Now almost no cotton is grown. There is more money in something called soybeans. Cotton was part of the background fabric of my childhood. The trucks, and even the mule drawn

wagons, with cotton packed in them being brought to town to the cotton gins to be processed and put into bales which weighed several hundred pounds. They would line up at the gins and wait their turn. It made a picturesque setting that at the time didn't seem very interesting. Cotton may not have been king, but it was still a big crop when I was a boy in Georgia.

69. We had rabbits, pigeons, dogs in a kennel, and squirrels in cages. We even had a flying squirrel a time or two. Do zoos have flying squirrels? If not, kids may not know what I am talking about. They are neat and very fast. My brothers also had squirrels in cages. I don't know how they caught them but they did. I don't know why they caught them either. A wild squirrel is not something you pick up and pet--well technically, you could pick one up, but with those sharp teeth, he starts biting fast and keeps on until either you are all eaten up or you go away and leave him alone. Either way, you don't get in a lot of petting time. ((Note: Our older son Richard brought his roommate's flying squirrel home. It climbed on younger son Ben's back, Delores grabbed it off Ben, squirrel instantly began biting her fingers and kept biting even when they were bleeding. Had it bit me, I would have "flown" that flying squirrel into the wall.)) Once the older brothers two, had a lot of rabbits up on the hill above the house. Those rabbits dug tunnels all over that pen and under the fence. I don't remember what we did with the rabbits, maybe that wasn't always chicken that Mom cooked. Those same pens were also used to board some high class bird dogs. I helped with the feeding by opening a can of dog food for each dog. I guess that was just one

way they had of making money. I don't think they ever paid me for helping--maybe I should send them a bill. Pigeons were--and still are--a favorite of my brothers. Full grown pigeons are so pretty but baby ones are terribly ugly. My favorite color was a brown that I called chocolate. I enjoyed watching the flock fly around and land in the chicken-pigeon house. I don't think we ate pigeon eggs or pigeons, I don't know it they ever sold any. Maybe pigeons were just like a lot of other hobbies, expensive diversions that were supposedly fun and time-consuming. I did learn a lot about animals--namely, the fewer around my house the better--and the less work.

70. Roosters do not like each other. We once had a red one and a yellow one. Both of a type called Game. The Game roosters are fierce fighters. My older brothers had paired the two up in a short fight but had separated them before any real harm was done. We had one locked up in a pen and the other had the run of the yard. We accidentally left the gate to the pen open and the Cock of the Walk (Old number one) went looking for the other one. Stout happened to ask where the rooster was and we went looking for him. We finally found the red one dead. He had fought, lost, tried to run and hide but was trapped and killed. We were really upset for several reasons. One was Dad would probably be mad because one of the roosters was dead and it was sort of someone's fault. Of course no one would admit to leaving the gate open. That old yellow rooster must have found a way to get the gate open. Second, we might get blamed for it. Third, we had missed a really

good rooster fight. We really hate to miss special events like that.

71. Setting hens aren't to be messed with by small kids. I was out at the barn one day and saw a little chick and picked it up. It cheeped for its mother and she came a running, flying, scratching, pecking, and hurting. She landed on top of my head and shoulders and proceeded to beat the tar out of me. I ran screaming and hollering all the way to the house. I think she escorted me all the way. Man that hurt like crazy. And to make it worse, Mom saw the whole thing and met me not with sympathy but she was laughing like it was the funniest thing she had ever seen. Maybe it was funny, but not from my perspective. I was so mad that later I took a stick and went looking for that hen. I am glad I didn't find her, I would have hated to have lost round two. I doubt my Mom could have withstood an instant replay.

72. We moved in the middle of the night. Why? I don't know. Dad was often referred to by cousins and in-laws as "curious" meaning he marched to his own drum beat. I was only about 4 at the time but it was one of those significant events that you vaguely remember all your life. We were sitting there and all of a sudden Dad says lets move to the other house. Clem and a cousin hitched up the mule to a large ground sled and started loading the furniture onto it. The other house was only about 150 yards away. I was all excited and was everywhere helping my big brothers. They could hardly do anything without me. They kept saying things like Mom needs your help, or Stout needs your help, or Clem needs your help. I was just indispensable at such an early age. I

remember riding on the big sled and helping hold the reins. If I had been the mule I would have been upset-- worked all day and now half the night. I asked Dad why we moved at night and he claimed it was so hot. But having known him all these years and knowing how "curious" he is (and to some extent, all of us are), I am convinced he did it just because that is when he decided to do it.

73. My Dad shot his finger off when the double barreled shotgun misfired. This was another significant event that I still vaguely remember. Dad, Clem, and Stout were quail hunting and saw a covey on the ground. Dad eased out of the truck, laid the barrel across the hood and cut loose. The barrel was blocked and the shot load came out the side of the barrel and out the barrel. The impact, killed three birds, shot some holes in the hood, (could have hit my brothers) and shot Dad's finger almost off. He said it was dangling by a thin piece of skin, so he took his knife out and cut it off, and wrapped his hand in his handkerchief. Clem and Stout hurried out of the truck, scooped up the birds, and helped Dad. After going to the doctor, Dad came home and said that caps blocked the barrel. I went and got a role of caps for a toy cap pistol and asked if that was what it was. They explained it was the wadding or cap from an earlier shotgun shell. I had a hard time understanding what caps were. We still have that old shotgun and it is now a family heirloom which almost tells its own story. I have often held the gun and am surprised to note that it could have taken his whole hand off instead of just a finger. I have to admire my Dad and brothers. My brothers because they were thinking enough to remember to get

the birds for supper and my Dad for being so tough. If I had shot my forefinger off, I would not have been able to do anything but hit the ground in a dead faint.

74. The Powell's in my family all have bad tempers--the men, that is, because the women are all angels. It sounds sort of strange to say it but we have been known to throw a hammer when it hits our thumb. Would you believe kicking a car when it wouldn't start? How about hitting the side of a barn with a two-by-four? It is sort of a form of physical cursing--words plus action both is a state of almost uncontrolled anger. When the temper flares up we just lose it. It is not a pretty sight-- especially as a boy if I did something to cause Dad to lose it. I usually got out of his way, not just arm's length, but hammer throwing distance too. Few people know that the world record for the hammer throw would have been set in a little town in Georgia--except the barn got in the way. To this day the barn still has a hammer dent on it. Some wonder why the barn leans a little to one side. Most think it was jacked up at one time to get at the rats that roamed around the barn. It was jacked up but the hammer was the jack. (Note: This story is a slight exaggeration.)

75. My parents always wanted us to have a good education. They did very well in life with just an elementary education and I have always been very proud of them. But they wanted more for their kids and did all they could to ensure the opportunities were there. My older brother Clem also encouraged us to get a good education. In fact he "educated" Stout every chance he got. Clem would try to pound an education into Stout,

or maybe he was just pounding him. My sisters Joyce and Brenda did great in school—each was Valedictorian of her class. Brenda would teach me what she learned in school and help me with my homework each night. I really liked school. I guess I was motivated by logging. My Dad logged for a number of years and if you have never been around logging you may have trouble understanding but it is HARD, HOT, SWEATY, TOUGH work. I figured early on that school and books were a lot easier than logging. Maybe the first week of school should require each student to log, sawmill, pulp wood, roof, etc. just to get their attention and get them motivated. And for punishment, make them log, or roof or whatever is really tough. Some bleeding hearts would say that is cruel and unusual punishment--which it is--and would have a court order to stop it. Never realizing that a little proper motivation could do the kids a world of good. Any way, my parents were great and they always encouraged and motivated me to do my best in school.

76. Did your parents ever say "If you get a whipping in school, you will get one when you come home."? I thought the constitution said we couldn't be tried for the same crime twice. I guess it doesn't say you can't be punished for the same crime twice. Ouch and double ouch. I had seen Dad's whoopings first hand (or other part of the anatomy) and believe me I did not want another when I got home, so I was almost always a well-behaved kid in school. Besides, in those days, it was a social stigma to be sent to the principal's office, but more importantly it meant severe physical pain--which I could do without in my life so I did. So far, our kids

have been good and we haven't had to threaten them with the "if you get a whipping in school,,," saying. I wonder if any parents still say that to their kids. (Note: Education should be a joint responsibility between parent and teacher and child. Unfortunately, the parent often doesn't support the teacher and the kids get away with less of an education.)

77. Dad would make us get dressed in the middle of a night time storm. I guess he just wanted us to be ready in case the house blew away or the roof fell in. We would have to get dressed and go get on their bed so we could all be together--and I guess scared together. This is yet another tradition we have not passed on to our children. I told my older son about us having to get dressed in the middle of a night time storm and he said several years ago when he spent the night with Mom and Dad, that Dad had made him get dressed in the middle of a storm and he wondered why and what was going on. So maybe the old ways that I thought were not getting passed on to my kids are in fact being passed on to them.

78. My Dad's grandfather was afraid of Halley's comet. He was afraid the tail would touch the earth and set the whole world on fire. Dad said his grandfather was a scary, nervous person. I wonder if he ever had his kids get dressed in the middle of a night storm. (Note: Dad was born in 1904 and says he remembers the Halley's comet of 1910. But in 1986, you needed a strong telescope to see it.)

79. We saw a big whirlwind by the edge of the road. Dad commented that it would probably turn the car over.

Clem was driving and immediately said lets see. I screamed, "No! Don't do it!" Clem just laughed and turned the wheel away from the whirlwind. I don't know whether he was laughing because he had succeeded in scaring me again (no great feat) or whether it was to hide his disappointment in not being able to conduct a scientific experiment--namely to see if the whirlwind would actually turn the car over. I have always been fascinated by whirlwinds. I have even run and jumped into the middle of them (very small ones of course). They never did lift me off the ground but I did learn something, and that is, you get sand in your hair, mouth, ears, eyes, etc. So, whirlwinds can be very educational.

80. Granddad had a blacksmith shop. I loved to help him do blacksmith work. He needed me to help turn the blower to make the fire hotter. It was fascinating to watch him turn those pieces of iron into red hot metal and pound on it with hammer and anvil and shape it into a horseshoe, ax head, punch or whatever. I loved to hear the sizzle when he immersed the hot metal into water. This was an unusual and enchanting place for a boy to explore and poke into--and occasionally get in the way. Dad said sometimes Granddad would have the furnace going so strong the flames would shoot out the top and it was a wonder that he didn't set the place on fire. We also helped him smooth out the ax handles he had made by taking a piece of broken glass and scraping it until it was really smooth. I don't think we used sandpaper but the glass worked very well. He indulged our assistance and even paid us a whopping 5 cents a handle. Employment at an early age inspired me to make a

fortune--not yet made. But if we could have made and sold a million ax handles, we could have made a lot of money. Of course there wouldn't have been any trees left in Georgia. Anyway, we loved Granddad and we have fond memories of his being with us until he married again. His first wife had died and he later remarried and left us. I hated to see him go but I guess I was happy for him. In researching the Powell family tree, I discovered Granddad's father had remarried too. So when my Dad was about 80 I told him he was breaking a tradition by not having a second wife and he commented without batting an eye, "Don't give up on me yet."

81. Dad loved to fish. He had a very unusual style when he had a nibble. He would try to not just set the hook but also snatch the fish out of the water, over his head and as far up the bank as he could fling it. I can just imagine that little fish's reaction. One second he is biting a tasty worm or cricket and the next he is flying through the air near the speed of sound and crashing onto the ground. They probably died of shock--or a broken neck. Dad let me go fishing--as long as I didn't catch more fish than he did. Once I caught such a big bream that he broke my pole. I think Dad left me at home after that. Just kidding. We fished at Uncle Bo's (Dad's brother) pond. Once someone used a small fish for bait and threw the pole and all into the pond. A little later we saw the pole take off and zip across the water. They paddled out to the pole and pulled out the biggest bass I had ever seen. It was a monster. I was amazed. What a fish. (Probably about a 3 pound bass). I asked Dad if I would catch a big one if I threw my pole into

the middle of the pond and he said something like, "If you don't be quiet I'll throw you in and see what I can catch" (Just kidding).

82. Dad drove a gasoline truck after he quit sawmilling. Of course he needed my help a lot. The truck had five tanks that held 303, 250, 200, 148, or 100 gallons. Back then there were a number of small stores scattered throughout Marion County and we supplied their gasoline, kerosene, or diesel fuel. In winter we delivered fuel to individual homes for heating. That was always extra hectic work because we had to unroll and reroll a 2 inch hose that was about 100 feet long. We sometimes had to climb up onto some kind of platform where the tank was. In addition, in winter I was always cold. So I didn't like to help much. Now in the summer it was OK. Well, OK sometimes. We would deliver fuel to road construction machinery, but we had to deliver it before they started work. Dad would wake me up at about 4 AM and we would go deliver the fuel in the middle of the night. It was a strange experience, the town still asleep when we left and just waking up and coming to work when we got back. We had been up several hours and these sleepy heads were just coming to work. Anyway, we would haul the fuel out to the road site and climb up on bulldozers, scrapers, etc. and fill them up. Some of the tanks were under the seat or behind the seat. Of course I had to climb up there and help and while I was there pretended to drive those monstrous machines. It was a lot of fun climbing all over that equipment. Sometimes we would deliver the fuel at the end of the day and get to watch the equipment work. It was awesome to see what they could do, the

amount of dirt they could move. On one trip we were barreling along through the sandy dirt road with very deep ruts, when the steering wheel suddenly spun around crazily and Dad had no control of the truck. The pin connecting the steering wheel to the wheels broke. Years later I realized how lucky we were to have been in a sandy road. Had that happened out on a normal road, we might well have been in the middle of a spectacular crash and fiery explosion. The Good Lord looked after us that day, for sure. Another time we ran over a huge rattlesnake as he crossed the paved road. He was at least 5 feet long and really sort of mad when we ran over him. Dad got a pole about 20 feet long and finished him off. I know we shouldn't have killed him because he probably ate a lot of rodents and if he had been carrying a sign saying "343 rats killed" we probably would have spared him--who am I kidding, a rattlesnake is a rattlesnake and the only thing that would have kept us from killing him would have been his guardian angel and even then it would have been close. I remember seeing these little ant hills along the roadside and wondered what they were. They were fire ants. Unfortunately, they moved into Georgia in the 1950's and are still here. Maybe if we could teach them to attack kudzu they could get rid of kudzu--or maybe kudzu would fight back and get rid of fire ants. Those are two non-native to Georgia products that I can do without. I guess in 100-200 years all the trees in Georgia will have been smothered by kudzu and all the crop lands will be covered in fire ant hills. Do anteaters eat fire ants? Maybe one more import would solve the problem. Nah, they would probably eat up the goods ants (if there is such a thing) and fertilize the kudzu. (I think some town in Georgia should be named Kudzu City. They could have a kudzu day, make things from it, sell potted kudzu to tourists from up north as exotic plants, maybe cook it, let it cover some roads in the town and call that Kudzu Scenic Drive, etc.).

83. Dad knowingly told a lie--and suffered the rest of his life. When he and Mom got married, she was just barely 14 and he had to lie and said she was 16. He said that was the only time he knowingly told a lie and he has been paying for it all these years they have been married (married 71 years when he died.) I guess that is one case where the punishment truly fit the crime. Except Mom might say she got worse punishment than he did because it is easier to live with a Davis than a Powell. Living with a Powell is easy--take me for example. Anyway, they drove an old model T ford (I think) down to a preacher in Richland and he married them while sitting in the old car. When Dad got to his new In-laws, Mom's Dad said "Tom, I think you have played hell". And for 71 years, Dad agreed that he was absolutely correct. Mom disagrees. They lived in about 13 different houses and he tried farming, sawmilling, and gas truck driver. Mom also worked in a shirt factory in Americus for a number of years. I guess I took their work for granted and never really thanked them for all their sacrifices. An ungrateful kid, yet another penalty for telling that lie.

84. Wringing a chicken's neck is not for the squeamish. But it was part of our chores in growing up in a semi-farm environment. Mom would tell us how many to

wring and we would go out to the chicken pen and grab up the latest victims. Then one by one we would wring their neck and watch them flop around in the dirt. After that we would begin picking their feathers off. Now one day my niece was there during the execution phase and said, "I don't see how you can do that." To which I replied, "It's easy, I just pretend it is my sister Brenda." At that age, brothers and sisters were supposed to hate each other--and I kept up my end of the bargain--but quietly, because if she had heard me she would have boxed my ears again.

85. Having a tooth pulled was a real pain. The dentist in those days was nothing like it is today. Why I even had my dentist tell me recently he didn't want me to suffer. I never heard that when I was a kid. The needles were so much bigger back then--and they always hit me where it would cause the most pain—no numbing cream before the big shot. I always got nauseated and vomited into that little white bowl with the water pouring into it. When he drilled or pulled the tooth, it was murder (in a kid's eyes, anyway). I remember nearly passing out and once I nearly passed out as I staggered out the door. After a few visits, I could get sick just being in the waiting room for more than five minutes. I elevated nervousness and tension to a whole new level. For a kid, the dentist was the worst of all terrors. Fortunately I grew out of it and even visit my dentist regularly-- every five or ten years. ((When grown I mentioned the dentist on second floor over Jake's Drug store and several people remembered him—Dr. Gurr (sp), used a drill turned by foot power—making it more painful and noisy.))

86. Stout and I had our tonsils taken out. I had never had surgery and had never spent the night in a hospital and so I considered it an adventure. I packed up some comic books to read and was all excited. I could go somewhere and do something that my sister Brenda couldn't. Ha Ha. I bet she felt left out. I could really brag about it and be one up on her. I don't remember much about the night before but I do remember the day of the operation somewhat. They told me to blow like I was blowing bubble gum and count backwards. I did and immediately started having one of those dreams I hate where I went round and round and flew higher and higher. Later I woke up and heard the nurses talking to Stout and trying to calm him down. He said he would kill the man who cut his throat. One nurse said she was his girl friend and he should calm down. He opened his eyes and said, "you are not my girl friend and I am still going to kill that doctor." They used ether and it made me sick. I am glad they don't use ether now, and I am sure there are a lot of kids out there that are glad too. Maybe Stout just had a reaction to the ether--or the pain. One trip to the hospital was enough. I haven't been back--as an in-patient (Thank you Lord for good health). Most people would agree, I haven't missed much. When I do go I guess I am too old to take comic books-- besides, my son wouldn't loan me any. ((Update, as of 2013, I have had several colon-scopes, one back surgery, and a minor throat surgery. But am still blessed.))

87. Ricky hid from Dr. Rainy. The family fear of doctors became evident in my younger brother at an early age. One night he went with Dad to the Drug store to get something. Dad left Rick in the truck and ran

inside and came out a few minutes later--but Rick was gone. He looked in the truck and finally found Ricky up under the seat. He confessed he had seen Dr. Rainy coming down the street and hid from him. We equated doctors with shots and pain. I know my kids also don't particularly care for doctors, but we take them so much they probably feel like it just part of a kid's position description. But back when I was a boy, doctors were respected, appreciated, loved, and stayed away from.

88. Clements kept me from being a monkey. He told me many times I should always appreciate him and do anything he asked because if it weren't for him, I would have been a monkey. He said as I was growing up, I had a tail like a monkey and he kept it pinched off so I wouldn't be a monkey. As I think about it now, that is one of the most ridiculous things I ever heard of-- nobody would believe a story like that. I don't know how old I was before I quit believing it was true.

89. I went to church camp. I was a Baptist growing up and belonged to the boys organization known as Royal Ambassadors (RAs) for Christ. There was a week long camp that I got to attend two years near Clayton, Georgia. It was the first time I saw the mountains, and the first time I climbed a mountain. Probably a lot of other firsts, too. The men of the church took us up there and brought us home (there are countless millions who give unselfishly of their time and efforts to help kids like me--I probably never said thanks to the church or the people, but I really do appreciate what they did in helping me grow up as well as I did). It was really a great experience to see the mountains, get away from

home, see parts of Georgia I had never seen, meet new people, and learn some really dumb games like "izzy dizzy". You put your head down on a bat, spin around several times and then try to walk straight--some of these are sadistic. I never played that game again. It should be outlawed. Anyway, the scenery was great. One morning, there were clouds swirling around the mountains and they were so beautiful. My first view from the top of a mountain was special. I still remember a man rowing in a boat and he looked so small. We also took some time out for devotions and tried to get closer to God. I think I did. I did some growing up too. I learned to appreciate home more but also began to 'test my wings' and move a little further from my Mom's apron strings--wonder if she noticed--I didn't--at the time. ((Update: In 2013, I took about 350 used, washed, and dried stuffed animals to Camp Pinnacle for the campers and staff. Just a little way of paying back and saying thank you. Still beautiful.))

90. Our Scouts went to Veterans State Park. We took several trips as scouts, one of which was to the Georgia State Park at Cordele and had a ball. I had never heard of sun tan lotion (I think it had been invented--after all I am not that old). I really had a good time swimming in the neat pool there. I was surprised to find out that my legs burned when I got into the warmer water of the wading pool. When I went to bed that night I moaned and groaned all night with the sunburned legs. Dad, with the typical Powell temper fussed about me getting sunburned. I don't remember what Mom put on the burns but I survived but didn't necessarily learn a lesson. I remember getting burned a number of times after that

painful experience. I know the Scouts give a badge for swimming but I know I would have earned one if they gave one for sunburned--and maybe one for being dumb.

91. Rusty nails hurt when you step on them. Did you know the nail will even go through your shoe? And did you know they hurt a lot? Back then we were so tough we didn't even go to the doctor. (Cost too much and was such an everyday thing--actually I didn't step on one everyday, but often enough that it was a routine accident.) We had home remedies. Soak the foot in kerosene and limp for a few days. Worked every time. You would think we and our parents would think in terms of prevention, like being sure nails were pulled out or bent in all those boards with nails. But I guess the household philosophy was stepping on nails was just part of the process of growing up, sort of like measles and whooping cough. The only difference, we didn't develop an immunity to nails. We could find them with no trouble. You would think we would learn to watch where we put our foot, but being kids, we had heads harder than our feet.

92. Dad got a nail in his eye. Not exactly in his eye, but he was hitting one with a hammer and hit it a glancing blow and it flew up and hit his eye. Thinking back, that was scary at how close he was to losing an eye. Now days, the use of safety goggles is encouraged and had they been invented back then would have been helpful. Dad's eye was red for several weeks and served as a reminder to me to be careful. So I tried to learn to hammer a nail with my eyes shut. Actually did better.

93. Ricky hit me accidentally. We had a pie safe in which we kept pies and other types of food. Once it was off to the side but one of the doors when opened would be in the path way to the kitchen but you couldn't see someone standing at the pie safe. I was going through the safe to see what food I wanted for a snack and little brother Ricky heads for the kitchen. He didn't know I was there but the safe door was in his way. Probably thought someone had left it open so, being a helpful kid, he slammed it shut. The edge of it caught me on the forehead and I probably yelled a little. It was my first introduction to my very own personalized goose egg. I wore that knot around for a long time. Even the principal of the school noticed and asked me about it. I wonder if I ever paid Ricky back--accidentally of course. Another time, we had a couple of hard plastic boomerangs and they were fun. Unfortunately, Ricky didn't understand the concept of being sure everyone is out of the way before you throw. I was walking away and suddenly there was the "whomp" below my shoulder blade. Ouches went through me and I probably gave Ricky a mild rebuke, or two. Can you imagine, hitting your older brother in the back with a boomerang? Wonder why I didn't think of that.

94. I put a BB in my ear. I jokingly tell my kids, it didn't do any harm, it just fell out the other ear. But have you ever done something so dumb as a kid that you are almost too embarrassed to tell anyone? I do not know why I did it. It was a totally dumb thing to do. It scared me and I ran and told my Mom. She didn't know what to do so she called the druggist and while on the phone, the BB fell out. I was so relieved and I guess

Mom was too. At least I don't remember her whooping me as a result. My youngest son said he stuck a red heart small piece of candy up his nose and later in his ear when he was three. (I was a lot older than three when I loaded my ear with the BB). So maybe poking things into your ear is a hereditary trait, maybe it wasn't my fault at all. Maybe I wasn't being dumb but following some primordial survival instinct. Naaaw. I was just plain being dumb.

95. Have you ever played a game called Red Rover? You play by having two teams who get into two lines facing each other with the team members holding hands. The object is to call for a member of the opposite team to try to break through your line. When I was a boy I was always short. We were playing Red Rover at recess and the other team said, "Red Rover, Red Rover, send Donnie right over!" I took off running and hit that line going full speed--only their held-hand-chain was exactly the height of my neck. It was my first encounter with a clothes-line of the worst kind. I didn't break their hands, but I might have broken my head because when I hit them I was flipped onto the ground onto my head. I lay there counting stars for a while but after I sort of came to, the kids were very comforting with such sayings as "Ha, Ha, we showed you. You sure are a weakling. Get up before someone trips over you". Red Rover left a lasting impression on me. That was my last game of Red Rover--I don't even like for my kids to play it. I never even named one of our dogs Rover. Maybe if I had turned my back at the last moment before impact I could have broken through or at least had no injury. No, I probably would have kissed the ground which could

have left a permanent imprint on my face--possibly an improvement. (My wife would probably say that Red Rover might account for some of my strange behavior.) My advice to the shortest kids playing Red Rover and your name is called, is pick out the prettiest girl on the other side and go charge in her direction, stop a couple feet in front of her (her eyes might be closed) and just kiss her. She might slap you but that is a lot less painful than getting a Red Rover Clothes Line.

96.   Crack the whip was another fun game--possibly invented by the Spanish Inquisition. The way we played it was to have all the players get in a line and join hands. The leader would then start the line moving and we would all follow along. The faster the line went the better--unless you are on the end, and being the smallest, I was always on the end. Going in a straight line was fine but the point of the game was to crack the whip and throw people off the line. The leader would turn sharply and everyone would follow. The ripple or whip effect was that the one on the end was usually going about 40 miles per hour and hanging on for dear life. I think the leader got extra points if someone was thrown off right into the side of the school or into a tree trunk. Have you ever been introduced to a tree trunk while hurtling through the air at 40 miles per hour? With such impressions fresh on my mind, I soon wrote off crack the whip. But strangely, most kids thought crack the whip was a lot of fun--speaks well of our intellectual development doesn't it.

97.   Do they still have something on the playground called a flying ginny? I only vaguely remember it--I

think the concussion probably erased the worst parts. The ginny was a long board with a seat on each end, but unlike a see-saw it didn't just go up and down, it was supported in the middle by an upright pole so that it could go around in a circle while going up and down. As I remember it, I finally got my turn to ride and whoever was pushing it must have gotten points for throwing people off because they had it going real fast in no time. They probably thought my screams were of delight--they were not. Anyway, as I sailed through the air, my turn was mercifully over. The landing wasn't too bad. It only hurt when I came to. Obviously, I quickly struck the ginny off my list of playground activities. But I have to admit, our equipment and games were not wimpy--none of this safety stuff for us--safety on the playground was a concept not yet born. The flying ginny has probably been outlawed so, unfortunately, our kids will never know how tough recess really was back then.

98. Do you like the playground merry-go-round? I think the companies that sold playground equipment, field-tested it before considering any safety features. In the old days, kids could climb inside next to the center post. Present-day merry-go-rounds have a metal floor covering that area up so no one can get inside. Anyway, the first time I found out about it was a memorable event. Finkle (called Fink) got inside and started pushing before I knew what was happening and before I could get off. He pushed and pushed and it went faster and faster. I started screaming and yelling for him to stop. The other kids were yelling for him to go faster. Would you believe he completely ignored

me--a close and trusted friend. I don't know what the speed record for a playground merry-go-round, but Fink definitely came close. I thought about trying to jump or fall off but I had seen movies where people were hurt badly when jumping from a speeding train or low flying airplane. The louder I screamed, the faster Fink--my ex-friend--went. I don't know whether I passed out or the bell rang, but finally the ride ended. I jumped off and--being very dizzy--promptly fell all over the rest of the playground. I never got on a playground merry-go-round until I was grown and could jump off. My kids used to think their merry-go-round went fast but they never got to ride the Fink's merry-go-round from heck.

99. Hugh got hit in the head with a rock. Recess was an exciting time. One day the boys decided to play war. Of course every boy who ever played war threw hand grenades. For the first few battles, there were only imaginary casualties and neither army overpowered the other. Dirt clod grenades weren't winning the day. Then one soldier threw half-a-brick-grenade and Hugh--who forgot to wear his helmet--stopped it with his head. He was bleeding when he went running past me--the brick sure didn't slow him down any--never saw him run so fast. They patched him up and sent him back to the front--just kidding. The principal's announcement was something like "don't throw any rocks or dirt clods and the pile of dirt war zone is off limits". Hugh wore his "white badge of courage" bandage for a couple of weeks. I guess the Principal could have had us all go out and pick up bricks and rocks and put them in the trash dump, but he probably didn't want an army all wearing white badges of courage.

100. "Ain't no boogers out tonight, Grandpa killed them all last night", was a ditty we sang as we played a game by that name. When the cousins visited and it began to get dark we would nearly always play that game. Someone would be the booger and try to sneak up on each of the others and get them. Being a natural smart alec, I would yell just as loud as the others thinking I could outrun the booger. It gets a little exciting running around the yard when it is pitch dark (pitch dark is darker than just regular dark). I would be skipping along thinking the booger was somewhere else and not interested in me. It is quite scary and heart stopping when this big cousin booger charges out of the dark screaming and grabbing you. We would sometimes hurt ourselves trying to get away from the booger. Have you ever crashed into a tree or a bush in the dark? It isn't something I would go out and do just for old time memories. It is a little surprising our parents weren't constantly coming out to check on us with all the yelling and noise. Maybe they thought we were OK as long as we could yell, and that they would unlock the door if someone really was hurt and bleeding. I guess that is why we stayed outside as much as we did. Children's games back then nearly always included running and yelling. Now days it is Nintendo and television. It has never been scientifically proven, but after playing Ain't no boogers for so many years, I believe there really are some boogers out there. Maybe that is why I am scared of the dark.

101. We played Gator Pit. When the cousins came, one daylight game was for us to all gather around this shallow hole about 10 feet wide and someone would be

the Gator in the pit and all the others would run through the pit and the Gator would try to tag those running through his or her pit. If you timed it right while the Gator was after one person you could run through the pit. So cousins were good for something, distracting the gator. (Just kidding) Sometimes there would be more than one gator and that would make it tougher to run through the pit. If the Gator was a big cousin gator, we smaller kids were inspired to be honest about being tagged, because if we said we didn't feel the tag and he missed, he would say something like, "I bet you feel it next time." I am sure no one would ever "tag" someone harder than they had to. Of course the older ones knew they could get away with anything short of murder and profuse bleeding, because if we went running to Mother with an injury then we wouldn't be allowed to play with them anymore. Mom wouldn't allow it and the big cousins who got told on wouldn't let us play. We younger kids always wanted to play with the big kids so badly we would do anything they said. We weren't exactly bright but we sure wanted to be with the bigger cousins, even if one of them creamed you in the Gator Pit. As long as you could limp or crawl, you would keep on trying to make it through the Pit. I guess if we had lived in Florida, we would have used real Gators, but then again, real gators wouldn't have been as dangerous so the game might not have been so exciting and real gators wouldn't have lasted long against my cousins. I might not have lasted long against real gators, because, being the smallest, my cousins might have thrown me to the real gators just as an appetizer to get them stirred up.

102. My oldest brother Clem taught me a game called "slap hands". It is still around, but today they call it slaps. The way the dumb game works is the slapper holds both hands out palm up and the slapee holds his hands palm down over the slapper's hands. The slapper then tries to slap the slappee's hand or hands before the slappee can get his hands out of the way. Now I suggest if you are going to play, set a time limit of say one minute per turn. When it was Clem's turn to be the slapper, he would not let me--the slappee--quit until he missed--he never missed. He would keep slapping my hands and arms until they very red and until there were tears in my eyes. But he believed in playing the game, he would laugh and slap, laugh and slap, but he did have a tender heart, because he stopped before I started bleeding--he didn't want to get blood on his clothes. I have to admit, it was a learning experience--a painful learning experience. But after that I was careful about who I played slap hands with and I became more careful about jumping into things without checking them out first. It also helped me be creative. If I told him I had nothing to do and he suggested slap hands, why I would suddenly have a creative thought about something else I had to go do.

103. I jumped off a ladder but my ring got caught and it cut my finger. You would think kids in the tenth (or eleventh) grade would be smart enough not to jump off a ladder--some probably are but I wasn't. We were decorating for a high school dance and I was wearing this silver ring made out of a silver half dollar. There was a fad of taking a half dollar, hitting it with a spoon over and over and rotating it until the edge of the coin

began to flatten out and form a ring. When it was the right width, the center would be drilled out and then you file the inside until it fit. I was cheap the first try. I used a steel washer (hole already drilled) smart, right? I wore out several of Mom's spoons before someone told me steel was too tough to make a ring that way. Silver was softer. In those days the half dollar was mostly silver, not like today's "sandwich" half dollar. Anyway, I was wearing the ring and instead of climbing all the way down, I jumped from about the second step, or at least tried to jump and my ring caught on the ladder and the ring sort of peeled some of my skin off. I got the ring off and headed to the bathroom. Now blood is wonderful stuff--in its place. But when my blood gets out where I can see it, my body reacts strangely--like the brain shuts down and the lights sort of go out. I almost passed out. But after a while I sort of bandaged it up and tried to help decorate, but I wasn't much help. I kept the finger scar, I wish I had kept the ring. It was another of life's little lessons in safety and physics--no rings on ladders and no jumping off ladders and your finger can support your entire body weight for a short period of time if you force it--but there is a price to pay.

104. I got a dime tip. My uncle and aunt owned a cafe and allowed me to work in it--waiting on customers, cleaning up, washing dishes, etc. In a small town it was very friendly and I got to know the customers. I remember one day one customer found a puzzle in the Columbus paper about how to arrange ten pennies in a way so that you have five lines with four pennies in each line. The afternoon was sort of slow so we took ten pennies and arranged them in many different rows and

just couldn't figure it out. So I anxiously looked forward to that customer coming in for lunch the next day so I could find out how to do it. It was simple--but I guess every question or puzzle is simple if you know the answer. Another customer was always nice and one day he left me a dime as a tip under his plate--my first and maybe only tip. I was thrilled. I was doing a good job. A tip. I told my dad and he just smiled. (I hope I thanked the tipper.) I really enjoyed working in the cafe. With no real expenses, it was the only time in my life when I actually had some money in my little bank at home. Ever since I have been in debt--a better tip would have been "don't spend more than you make" or (as I have fruitlessly told my children countless times) "once you spend it it's gone forever". But the dime tip was spendable and therefore more valued--and less long lasting--I spent it quickly. If you work in a job where you can get tips and do get one--a nice one (a dime was a big tip then)--you really appreciate it--and I think tend to leave tips if you get good service. Oh yes, draw a five point star and put a penny on each point and line intersections. Working was good for me--my bank--and learning to deal with people--and appreciate tips--even if only a dime.

105. Have you ever gone to a cattle and hog sale? In Americus every Thursday people brought their animals to sell at a place we called "the Sale" (they still do but I have not attended one in years). We would sit in the stands and watch as each cow or group would come through. The auctioneer would rattle off a bunch of numbers that I couldn't understand and finally say "sold". I remember once, Dad told me to raise my hand

(and bid on a calf) and I asked if he was sure and why and things like that. By the time I raised my hand it was too late. The teen age boys who drove the animals in and out always had sort of a whip but it was about 3 inch wide cloth instead of a leather strip--I guess so it wouldn't leave a mark when they hit the animals. I always wanted a whip like that so the marks wouldn't show when I beat Dad's animals. Then again, if such a whip had been around, my older brothers might have used it on me since the marks wouldn't show. Anyway, I liked going to the Sale except I was scared of those cows and their long horns. So I always kept Dad between me and the cows--just so he'd know where I was and so he wouldn't get run over by me when I stampeded. Do you know how big a cow looks to a little kid? There was one type bull that looked big to everyone, including the boys with the whips. That was the Brahma. They scared me just looking at them. They have these big humps and they are so big--bigger than regular cows--to a small kid, they were huge. Since cows can't climb I always kept an eye on nearby places or things I could climb onto. So when the Brahma came in the boys with the whips stayed close to their protective wooden fence. And there I was about ten feet above the Brahma bull, as safe as I could be, but ready to climb the wall into the auctioneer booth.

106. War news or war stories made my stomach hurt. The war news (or war stories) was I guess from the Korean War. But every night about supper time the radio would tell about the war news and it scared me (everything scared me) and I would crawl up into Dad's lap and tell him my stomach hurt. Now my son has

stomach aches a lot, do you suppose it is hereditary? Anyway, we had this old battery powered radio with a battery that was bigger than a modern day car battery--to a little kid it looked huge (probably about 6" x 8" x 15"). This was before we got TV so we listened to the radio every night. After the TV came, the old radio got put into the storage house and fell prey to the weather, or curious little boys who liked to take things apart. I have often wished we had kept it. It was American made and was still working when replaced by technology--that is the way American products are--they keep on working. You know, as a little kid I wasn't the brightest--instead of listening to the war stories/news why didn't I just turn the radio off or go to another room--especially since Mom could have given me her special Castor Oil treatment.

107. Ricky could get into anything. We had this big bureau about five feet high that I hid my stuff on top of. But before he was old enough to go to school, Ricky could somehow climb up there and get into it. I remember I would save coupons from notebook paper made by Write-Right and Blue Horse. When you had enough coupons you could send in for a prize. I had sent off and received several prizes such as a coin of each President with their picture on it and some information about them on the back. The coins were about the size of a quarter (wonder what happened to them--haven't seen any at antique sales either). I also had received a 4" by 6" silk flag replica of 15 countries. (I particularly liked Sweden and Greece). Anyway, one day I came home and was checking my "stuff" and my flags were all wrinkled up. So I ran to Mom and told

her about it and she confessed that the "climber" had gotten into them and wrinkled them up but she had tried to straighten them up. Needless to say, I pitched a small Powell fit. But Ricky was only about 5 so he didn't see that he had done anything wrong. In fact I am sure I should have complimented him on his inquisitiveness and resourcefulness in finding and getting the stuff--and I would have if he had gotten into my sister's or brothers' stuff.

108. I used to buy U. S. Savings Bond Stamps at school. Every week some older students came to each classroom selling stamps. They sold red ones with a picture of a minute man for ten cents and green ones for 25 cents. After we bought about $18, we could get the Bond that we kept for 7 years and it would be worth $25 dollars. I wonder if kids would buy stamps or bonds now days at school? They collect soup can labels for computers, so why not Bond stamps--except that the government doesn't sell them any more. Anyway, way back then, we anxiously looked forward to filling one up. I remember once I filled one up and my sister and friends talked me into cashing it and getting the $18.75 (a small fortune) instead of a bond. Sounded good so we went to the Post Office to cash it in. The postmaster (and neighbor) listened patiently and said he would be glad to if we got our parents signature on the bond. I don't think we even asked our parents. I also remember I had one that I never did fill up. I wonder if it is still at Mom and Dad's. If so, it could be valuable as an antique. I could never find it--there is so much stuff there. But say--I know an expert at finding stuff--I could either threaten him and dare him to find the

stamps or I could promise him half. Wonder which would be more effective, probably the former.

109. Do you know what a "Croker Sack" is? I think I was grown before I heard them called "burlap bags". I think the name of the company producing the feed was Croker so that was the name on the bag and naturally that is what we called them. I almost sneeze thinking about them. We would store extra ones in the barn loft and they would accumulate dust especially from dry corn shucks. Anytime I got one down for Dad or my brothers, the dust would make me sneeze and sneeze. (If you don't have allergies, you don't know how lucky you are.) We would get cow or hog or mule feed in the Croker sacks so we had plenty of extras. (I am glad Mom never thought of making me a shirt out of one--I would have itched to death--now days it would be in style). It is amazing how many different things for which we used those sacks. We would sack up dried corn--sometimes with shucks still on them or sometimes after we had shucked and shelled the corn using the hand turned corn sheller. I really liked that corn sheller it was so much faster than shelling by hand and it made a lot of noise and it gave us corn cobs with which to start a corn cob fight. We would sack up just about anything in a Croker sack--even little pigs we were selling or chickens. (My wife's granddad supposedly sacked up a bothersome little brother and hung the sack in a tree so the little brother wouldn't bother them.) So anytime we needed a Croker sack, I would volunteer and go running to get them and I would bring them back "just a-running and a-sneezing."

110.   Have you ever planted pine trees?   The Future
Farmers of America (FFA)   or our Vocational
Agriculture class planted pine seedlings for a number of
farmers in the area.   We would go out as a group and
pair off. One would punch the hole and one would plant
the seedling.   The hole puncher used a device made by
the teacher that was a metal pole about three feet long
and with a metal wedge on the end.   The hole puncher
would step on the wedge and force it into the ground
making a hole.   While the planter held the seedling in
place, the hole puncher would punch another hole about
6 inches away and close up the hole around the seedling.
The hole puncher then would stomp the second hole
closed (I don't think the stomper missed the second hole
and stomped the seedling too many times). The land had
been plowed so the trees would be in a straight line but
we were supposed to walk off the same distance
between each tree.   So I am sure they were exactly the
same distance apart.   For most of the boys, it was an
outing and we enjoyed having something to do on
Saturday.   But it was cold and it was in fact work.   A
couple of the older boys finished their work in record
time and just started goofing off (they were never the
hardest workers in the class).   Anyway the rest of us
boys found out they had planted their seedlings
horizontally about a foot deep all in one location.   The
teacher never did figure out why he didn't have enough
seedlings to cover the entire field, but we could have
told him if he had asked.   Shep told us when we were
planting some on his dad's land that the money from
harvesting the trees would be his college money so we
should have been properly impressed with the

seriousness of our work. Shep told us a few weeks later that all the seedlings died and the field had to be replanted. Maybe that is why he went into the Merchant Marine--we killed his college money.

111. Tommy got "caught" stealing watermelons. There are usually a group of "followers" who will jump at any suggestion for excitement, especially in a small, dull town. One night some older boys suggested they go steal some watermelons--a traditional pastime in old B.V. Tommy and some others jumped at the chance. While going to the field, the scene was set by a statement such as, "Mr. Williams is mad about the watermelons that have been stolen, so we need to be very careful tonight. He said he would shoot the next person he caught in his field." The driver let Tommy and several others out to go get the melons. They had gathered several when someone shouted, "You boys get out of my field!" and fired a shotgun. One of the older boys screamed and fell on the ground. Someone shouted "Bill has been shot! Run!" Tommy and the others ran for the woods. After about 30 minutes of laughing the older boys started calling the "followers" in and telling them it had all been a prank. No one was shot. Everyone except Tommy finally got the message and came out of the woods, slightly scratched, still shaking with fright, but sheepishly smiling and saying they knew it was a joke and they just went along to try to convince the others, ha, ha. They couldn't get Tommy out of the woods so they called the police to help look for him. Finally Tommy found his way back to the main highway several miles from the melon patch and just as he finally got onto the highway, he saw a

police car coming, and got so scared about being part of a shooting that he plunged back into the woods. He walked and ran all the back to town and finally arrived home about dawn--very tired, scratched from head to toe by briers, and still scared. He wore his brier scratches proudly for a number of weeks--each time we saw him we couldn't help but ask, "How did you get those scratches, Tommy?" We always were sensitive boys. (I was at home or out of town and fortunately missed out on the watermelon set up. Having a tendency toward being a follower, had I been there, I might have been Tommy's running mate.) I wonder if Tommy has eaten any watermelons since then--probably lost his taste for them.

112. Dad wanted to catch those fishing his pond without permission. Dad owned a pond about three miles from the house and he didn't mind people fishing if they asked first. He wanted to catch anyone who shouldn't be fishing there so he set a trap. He and his number one detective--I--would cut through the woods while my two older brothers drove around and we would have them caught between us. (I probably brought my trusty cap pistol and Cub Scout knife just in case.) So here Dad and I go through the woods and come onto the pond area and, shucks, no one was there. In a few minutes my brothers arrived and we told them we missed this time. Now that I am older, I ask myself, what would we have done if we had come upon a gang of 6 or 8 people--we would have been slightly outnumbered. But generally, in B.V., if you were in the wrong and on someone else's property, you didn't argue too much. So my Dad probably would have scared them

off with just a warning. Speaking of fishing, my Dad had a very unusual way of getting the fish out of the water. When he had a bite and thought he had them hooked, he didn't just pull on the cane pole, he snatched it as hard as he could and the fish would come flying over his hear up onto the bank about 20 feet behind him--from there the no fish ever flopped down the hill back into the water. He is the only one I have ever seen fish that way. Can't you just picture the poor fish--taking a bite one second, then flying through the air, then hitting a tree and/or the ground in a matter of about two seconds.

113. The Cub Scouts made a barometer. When I was a boy in Georgia, apples came in wooden boxes to protect them from getting bruised. (Not cardboard like today.) For a Christmas present to our parents, we were to use the end pieces of an apple box (about 12 inches by 12 inches) and wood burn a barometer onto the piece of wood. We drew and wood burned a picture of a donkey and then wood burned various weather predictions associated with his cloth or yarn tail. For example, "if tail is wet, it will rain; if tail is dry, sun will shine; if tail is gone, cyclone coming. We worked hard on it and finished just in time for Christmas thanks to our dedicated Den Mothers. We wrapped the gifts and I was so excited when they started opening and reading it. Then they started laughing, because the tail was missing.

114. Yankees weren't exactly beloved in B.V. I remember the few times I had any dealings with Yankees, I thought they talked funny and I had trouble understanding what they were trying to say. I probably

wondered why they didn't speak English. My history teacher told us that she was 16 years old before she learned that "Damn Yankees" was two words. Fortunately we don't think that way anymore. We teach our kids early own that they are two words. (Just kidding. We love the yankees and they do bring a lot of variety into our southern way of living.) One of the more colorful locals that went up north was Eddie O. Martin who came back and wore crazy clothes, painted, and told fortunes. I probably thought if all the yankees dressed and acted like that they could just stay up north. I thought he was a nut--wearing a turban and bells, and bright silk shirts and pajama looking pants and wearing a beard. He painted all these crazy things in the yard at his home and in his home and it is really a place that only an artist can appreciate--so obviously I just thought it was nuts and if the yankees have that kind of impact on Georgia boys, I would just stay away from them-- they must be really strange. (You can still see his painted home and surroundings just outside B.V.—it is called "Pasaquan".)

115. We broke the angel's head off. Mom bought a manger scene from Montgomery Ward. The figures were made of plaster of Paris and included two standing angels, one kneeling, three wise men of which one was on a camel, a shepherd, Mary, Joseph and of course the baby Jesus. Through the years the camel got broke and we glued it back together but a couple of small pieces are missing so the camel has a few holes in his sides, but he continues to be a tradition at Mom and Dad's to this day. The set must be at least 40 years old. One year, a standing angel's head was broken off and we were out of

normal, clear colored glue. So being creative, my sister and I used what was available--red finger nail polish. It has held up all these years so finger nail polish is pretty good glue. However, our angel is probably the only one in the world with a permanent red "necklace" around her neck.

116. We hosted a prom-party at our house. It was probably my sister's birthday party and so she had this prom-party and a lot of kids came. It was a bit of an educational experience for me. We would pair off and "prom" around the yard--away from the adults. Now I didn't quite know what to do on a prom with a girl, so we just walked and talked. As we roamed around, I discovered some of the older kids were doing more than just talking. To a young kid like me it was shocking to see them holding hands and even kissing--on the lips no less. So I thought I would at least try to hold hands on the next prom. Wouldn't you know, the girl had her arms folded and I couldn't figure out how to reach her hand without getting into trouble. So, for me prom still meant just walk and talk.

117. My cousin's birthday present was boxes within boxes. He was opening his presents and having a great time. Then he tackled this great big box and we got excited--what could be in the big box? He unwrapped the box and pulled out--another gift wrapped box. So he plunged in and opened it and pulled out another box, then another, then another and so on. He finally got down to the small present--something like a pocket knife. But someone thought ahead and worked so hard so he could have a memorable present--I thought it was

so cool. It was the first time I had seen that and it made an impression on a little kid. You never know what will be remembered. Anything out of the ordinary was exciting in a small town--even boxes within boxes.

118. My brothers went frog gigging. A frog gig is a long handled little pitch fork. They would take a light and gigs out at night to ponds and climb into a boat and go around the pond shinning lights into the eyes of big bull frogs. If they were quiet and careful, they could sneak up on the frog and get within gigging range. They would stab the frog with the gig and drag it into the boat. They would bring all the frogs home, and skin them and Mom would fry the frog legs for us to eat. Tastes a little like chicken. I am told the legs keep jumping while they are being cooked. The legs do not jump once in the stomach. I never was outdoorsman enough to go gigging--I tended to prefer to stay at home, inside away from the mosquitoes, and cottonmouth moccasin very poisonous snakes. They seemed to love it, but it never struck me as being fun. Sort of like the time in Albany when I was grown I took my younger brother to play golf early one morning. There was dew everywhere, so our feet were wet and we weren't playing too well. On about the eighth hole, he looked at me and said something like, "Do you really enjoy this?" I felt the same way about frog gigging (and a lot of other things my older brothers did).

119. We went to the Fair each October. My older elder sister Joyce (the one that is about 14 years older than I) and her husband were so generous and nice that they took us to all sorts of places. Every year the big fair

would come to Columbus and they would take us to it. It was always cold but a lot of fun. Being scary I never rode the wild rides--they tended to make me sick and Joyce didn't really appreciate me being sick in her car. Our Vocational Education Agriculture class along with the Home Economics class would have displays or exhibits each year and compete with other schools. We really enjoyed the exhibits, the rides, the food, the free shows--like tight rope walking and chain saw demonstrations, the trinkets we could buy, the wandering around, etc. The fair was a big event each October and I really appreciate Joyce and her husband Gene taking us. I am sure they appreciated me not being sick in their car.

120. I remember my first trip to the ocean. Joyce and Gene took us to Panama City one summer. Had a really great time. Lost my bill fold with all my money in it, but by retracing our steps, was able to find it (God looks after fools and kids they say). The beaches at Panama City are still some of the prettiest I have ever seen. We played Goofy golf and took pictures that we recreated many years later with our own children--sitting in the monkey's paw, on the paw of the Sphinx, etc. We played in the ocean and dug in the sand. Ageless wondrous pleasures that kids (and adults) have been experiencing for thousands of years. The first trip is always special. Joyce and Gene also took us to Atlanta a few times to the zoo, the Cyclorama and even Stone Mountain. I remember asking Gene what he would do if the mountain started to fall on us, he said "Grab Connie--their baby--and run". I guess I would have just been on my own. Wonder how they would have explained that

to Mom and Dad. "The mountain started falling down and we saved Connie, your first grandchild instead of your fifth child. Couldn't save both." Mom and Dad would probably have said, "That is all right, the grandbaby is much cuter than Donnie was, and a lot less trouble, so you did the right thing. (Just kidding)".

121. I won a week long trip to Callaway Gardens. The Gardens gave high school leaders free vacation trips each year. As president of the Regional Library Club, I received one. We packed up and took off--Mom, my older sister Brenda, my younger brother Ricky, and myself. We were assigned to one of their cottages and I remember Brenda took a quick tour and saw how small it was and was ready to go home. I think there was one bedroom with bunk beds for four and a hide-a-bed sofa in the other room. We worked it out and she settled down. As it turned out we had a great vacation. The Florida State University (FSU) Circus was there and put on a show each afternoon and night. They also helped each of the students learn about circus stuff. I learned the basics of juggling and can still do it today--just 3 balls not 4. I didn't learn how to ride the unicycle or walk on my hands or fly on the trapeze. But we had a great time. I remember they gave us the opportunity to try water skiing. If they gave instructions on juggling, you would think they would give instruction on how to stand up to water ski. They didn't. So when my turn came, the lady gunned the boat and yanked me out of the water--I felt myself falling and pulled on the handle and promptly fell head first into the not-soft-at-all water. Have you ever fell head first into water while traveling about 50 or 60 miles per hour? I tried it a second time

with the same results. On the third time, I was determined not to fall face first--but I did. So, with three strikes, I said try to yank someone else's arms out their sockets for a while--and the boat lady tried. To this day, I have never ever tried water skiing--and don't plan to either. A year later, I saw where one of the trapeze men "threw a triple somersault" a very rare feat. When we were there he threw double and a half all the time.

122. Have you ever pushed a water hose into the ground? The water power will dig a hole and if you keep pushing the hose, in sandy soil, it will just keep on going and going. Another amazing pastime created from the active mind of a totally bored boy. We never said we were bored or had nothing to do because Mom or Dad could always find many chores that needed doing. (Correction, I do remember I did say I had nothing to do when we visited an Aunt and Uncle whose children were grown and had no toys for me to play with. Maybe that is why I always insist our children take toys to play with when visiting.) Anyway, back to the water hose, I don't know what the record is for number of feet of water hose forced into the ground. It is probably recorded in the Guinness Book of world records. We may not have set the record but we surely had fun. Try it sometime, even as an adult, I still find it a lot of fun. Oh, I do vaguely remember a kid in California did the water hose in the ground thing and surprisingly when she stopped pushing it, it just kept going on its own and I think they couldn't pull it out. I don't know whether they turned the water off or not, but if they didn't, after all these years the hose should be nearing China by now.

123. Do you remember taking aptitude tests? I remember taking one in the first grade in which the teacher told us to draw a line under a certain thing. To one with an active imagination, I heard the word "lion". So there I am, no artistic ability, trying my best to draw a lion and I am not even half way through when she goes to the next question. I keep rushing back to it between questions and wonder how all the other students were able to draw their lions so quickly. I was in the front row, so when she turned to the next page, I looked at her booklet and noticed she had the answers on hers and she had a "line". So now, between questions again, I frantically try to erase the lion and draw a line. I don't know how I did on the test but it was certainly traumatic. Years later, I had a chance to see my permanent folder and got to see that test and I could see the outline of the erased lion. I wonder if the teacher ever noticed.

124. We had a lot of nicknames. For some reason the older generation seemed to all have nicknames, including my Dad. His name is Roy Alto but his nickname is "Tom"--I think because his Dad's name was W. Thomas. Elijah Eugene was "Bo", Harvey was "Pete", and the other nicknames included "Rag", "Bim", "Shim", "Tink", "Bunch", ""Hub" and so on. I have no idea where the nicknames came from but I have to admit they are unusual and interesting. One problem was when I went to look them up in the phone book, there were no nick names and I had no idea what their real names were, so I had to ask. Another problem was some stranger would ask for Roy Powell and no one would know who that was--but most people could

reasonably deduct that Bo is a natural nickname for Elijah--right?

125. I ate a persimmon. A persimmon is a little plumb-sized fruit that grows naturally on the persimmon tree. My Dad said when the fruit ripens, really ripens, it would be sweet and tasty and that opossums and raccoons really loved them. So, being my usually gullible self, I asked if they were ripe. He looked at them and said, "Maybe, why don't you try one." So I took a great big bite and gave about one-half of a chew. It was the bitterest, sourest taste I had ever tasted. My mouth turned inside out, I spit and spit but I couldn't get that horrible taste out of mouth for a long time. If that one was ripe, I would hate to have bit into a green one. I recommend persimmons as an unusual treat--but only for the animals.

126. Most of the stores closed on Wednesday afternoon. They were open all day Saturday, because that was when most people came in from the rural area and did their business. The store owners were very customer oriented--or a little greedy. Now days, doctors take off on Wednesday to play golf--just think little old Buena Vista, was a trend setter. Another thing many stores did back then was to allow customers to "charge" things as a convenience and also to make them more competitive with other stores in town who would allow charging. Unfortunately, there were people who charged to the limit and then skipped town. That is probably one of the reasons the small stores have become such an endangered species. The store owners knew their customers by name and also knew something about

them. You surely don't hear modern stores call anyone by name--they don't know mine and I don't know theirs--even though I may go there 5 or 6 times a week. Back then, it was heart warming to be in a store and hear someone say, "Hello Hub, how is Bunch?"

127. We were going to make a fortune collecting pine cones. The Forestry Commission would pay $5.00 for a bushel of green pine cones. They would then remove the seeds and plant them for next year's seedling crop. Several of us got together and decided we would harvest the crop and make a fortune. One of the older boys, Boyce, volunteered to climb a tree and knock out the pine cones. Being a ground person, that was fine with me. Now danger is seldom something kids think of but in looking back our little group of moneymakers was a prime candidate for an accident. Boyce could have fallen out of the tree from 30-40 feet high and really been hurt. He could have fallen on top of me and I could have really been hurt. But what actually happened is one of the pine cone missiles hit his younger brother right on top of the head. The sharp points on the cone left several bloody stripes on his scalp. (In later years he probably told the girls those scars were from his fighting a bobcat bearehanded and headed.) Any way, as I think back on the incident, I wonder if it was just a coincident that his younger brother was the only one hit. (I can almost hear Boyce up in that tree saying "Darn, missed him again".) As with so many get rich quick schemes, this one turned out to be a bummer--too much work, too little money for the effort (do you have any idea how many pine cones it takes to make a bushel?--hundreds, thousands, maybe even millions), and very little

pleasure. (Of course Boyce might have gotten a little pleasure out of his brother getting accidentally hit in the head.) Years later, Coneheads became popular, but little old Buena Vista had the original cone(d) head.

128. Have you ever helped trim a mule's hooves? Just about anything my big brothers did was always interesting to me and, in my mind, they just couldn't do it without me there to help. I remember helping Clem trim the mule's hooves and I think put horse shoes (mule shoes) on the old mule. I had to get up real close as he used these giant pliers-type clippers. Being up close I got a good whiff. Wow. Those hooves stink like crazy when cut or trimmed. I don't know how Clem kept from passing out but he did and just kept on working. I kept on helping and watching--from about 100 feet away. When putting on the shoe, I asked if driving those nails into the hoof hurt the mule and he said no but my goodness how could it not hurt. He said it was just like cutting a toe nail and the hoof had no feeling so the nails didn't hurt. But I wasn't convinced. But in thinking back, I guess if it had hurt the mule would have spoken to Clem by kicking him into the next county. (Come to think of it, Clem's wife is from the next county--maybe that is how he met her.)

129. A hand-turned corn sheller is a neat invention. Ours was anchored to a wooden box that would catch the shelled corn. As a youngster, it was fun to shuck the dried corn and drop the ear into the opening and crank the handle. This forced the corn to be forced up against a metal wheel with little cone-shaped teeth about a half inch long. The teeth would shred the kernels of corn

from the cob as the ear rotated and went down the chute. With practice you could feed one ear after another and keep the kernels continuously falling. It was indeed great fun--for about 5 or 10 minutes--and as long as it was optional. If I had been required to shell a barn full of corn I am sure my memories would have been very different. After shelling the corn, we had a very useful by-product to discard--corn cobs. I never made a corn cob pipe but others did. I collected them to add to my arsenal for corn cob fights. I also practiced by flinging the cobs at various targets, like the side of the barn (which I could hit, usually), cows, pigs, dogs, chickens, and generally anything that looked promising. I never hit my sister Brenda with corn cobs because it just would not have been gentlemanly, would have been contrary to my southern upbringing to hit a girl, but mainly because she could throw cobs harder, straighter, and faster than I could. (I may have been dumb at times, but I wasn't stupid.)

+++++++++++++++++++

BoyInGA130-138

130. I had to block Jon in sandlot touch football. A group of us would gather each Sunday afternoon and play football. No equipment but lots of exercise and fun, until someone got mad and wanted to play tackle. I never wanted to play tackle. Anyway, Jon was a couple

years younger but tall for his age. In one game for some reason on one play, I noticed that he seemed upset or something. He was to rush the quarterback and I was to block him. He was spring-loaded, set to explode through me like a rocket, his fists were clenched tight, he was reared back ready to strike, he had a glint in his eyes, his jaw was clamped shut tightly. I said to myself, "Wonder what is wrong with Jon. He is going to knock me all the way to Ellaville. He is going to kill me. My goodness, what am I going to do?" When the ball was snapped, Jon charged like a runaway freight train. I was doomed. I took half a step--and since he wanted my side of the field, I just stepped aside and let him have it. Since I wasn't there to slow him down, he completely lost his balance and, as I glanced over my shoulder, he proceeded to claim my side of the field. I saw elbows, knees, legs, arms flying everywhere as he tried to regain his balance for about 10 or 15 yards. He dug up quite a trench and while he was excavating, the quarterback completed the play untouched. Best job of blocking (or not blocking) I ever did. When Jon came back to the line of scrimmage, he smiled and said something like, you got me that time. On the next play he was a lot more under control and I couldn't fool him, so he only knocked me half way to Ellaville.

131. My aunt sulked or pouted. Clem tells of the time he visited a cousin whose parents started arguing quite heatedly. She got so mad she went out and sat on the wood pile sulking and/or pouting. After it began to get dark Clem began to get hungry and suggested they go visit another nearby aunt and uncle but the cousin said "no, no, we don't have to do anything when they are

arguing." (Clem used those manners he often kept well hidden because he knew it would be bad manners to just go into their house and help himself to some food.) Clem then was hoping Dad would come by so he could go home where there was some food, but Dad didn't come by. Finally the uncle called out to our aunt to come on inside it was getting dark, but she was still mad and continued her resolute stand (or sitting) on the wood pile. Finally, quite a bit later she came in (uncle probably apologized--Powell men have a long history of knowing how to--and when to apologize--so I am sure he did----NOT.) Clem said he was really glad to see her--or more appropriately, the food she put on the table.

132. Ronnie was tough. Ronnie was so tough he charged where others feared to tread. He wasn't superman but he might have tried to stop a speeding train or leap tall buildings. Not really. Here is what actually happened. On the playground he was running really fast but without looking where he was going and ran right into the path of another student (Andrew?) who was swinging quite high. Ronnie--whether intentional or not--apparently tried to stop the swinger's feet with his jaw. Unfortunately, either Ronnie wasn't superman, or else Andrew's shoes were covered in Kryptonite because he lost a few teeth (ouch). The principal's announcement the next day was something like "be careful around the swings and watch where you are going and those of you swinging don't swing so high and try to stop if someone is in your way". (The principal got to make a lot of announcements.) (Note: As I reviewed these stories, I was surprised how many accidents occurred and how many things on the

playground were dangerous. I sure am glad things are safer now.)

133. Clem made a sling shot. Both my brothers made lots of flips from forked or "Y" shaped branches off trees and rubber strips from inner tubes from tires. In the old days before tubeless tires, all the car tires had rubber inner tubes that were always developing holes so there were lots of old inner tubes around because you could only patch them so many times. Anyway, flips were common and surprisingly, most of us still have both eyes. But one time Clem decided to make a sling shot, like the one David might have used against Goliath. He cut the tongue out of an old boot, punched a hole in each corner, tied some cord to the holes, put a knot in one of the cords, loaded up a rock, swung it around his head, released the non-knotted cord and watched the rock sail away. Now Clem was shrewd, he tested it out in the middle of a field so no windows were broken or parents' heads hit either. So he let me try and after a while I didn't do too badly, but I never ever came close to being in David's class.

134. The bank was robbed. Yep, in broad daylight a couple of robbers entered our little bank, stole the money, locked the people in the vault, as they were about to leave, encountered my brother Stout. They escorted him to the back of the bank and then hit him over the head with a gun. Fortunately, he had (or has) a hard head and recovered quickly. I shudder to think what could have happened. They caught the robbers and I think recovered some of the money, but their gun probably still has a dent in it. Stout had another

situation when a drunk started bothering him and so Stout slugged him in the head. Not a great idea because he sprained his hand and the doctor wrapped it up for him. Another time Stout ran into the city police chief (force of 2)--literally. He was driving and had a fender bender with--of all people, the police. I am not sure, but I think he got a ticket. Come to think of it, he was driving a pick-up truck one day, went to sleep and had a wreck (flipped over). Thankfully, he was not hurt. Also Clements had a wreck and cut up his hand pretty badly but did recover fully. Joyce saw the blood and did what I would have done had I seen it, she did a great impression of a woman fainting. Cars and trucks and Powell's just seem to go together like oil and water, water and sodium, etc. Thankfully, no serious problems.

135. A horse introduced Clem to a telephone pole. I think the horse was in a bad mood that day and Clem should have backed off, but he is as stubborn as a mule. (Mule rides horse??). Clem knows how to guide a horse but in this case the horse had other ideas. He headed straight toward the pole and when Clem leaned to one side to avoid hitting the pole, the horse quickly changed directions and whopped Clem into the pole before he could get out of the way. I think he fell off and knowing Clem, he was probably smart enough to call it a day. Whether then or later, when he put the horse up, I would bet he gave it a love pat or two with a 2" by 4", just to show him there were no hard or injured feelings. The Powell's are always very forgiving like that.

136. Ricky fell off a horse. He had a slight concussion, which was very scary. He could remember what had happened. Since he had disobeyed Dad by getting on the horse, he was scared, but also addled by the concussion. Another time he was chinning on a metal pole Stout had put up to build up his arm muscles. He fell and hit his head again and it left a bloody mark on him which really upset Dad who tore the pole down. Later when Stout saw his pole torn down, he shouted "Who tore this down?" To which I replied, "Dad" and his calmed response was "Oh", Stout was quick on that one. Fortunately, we are blessed with hard heads and so there was no lasting harm done (I think).

137. Clem hiked from Butler to Charing (about 12 miles). He was going to school in Atlanta to learn how to repair televisions. He would hitchhike or ride the bus as close as he could and then, call for someone to pick him up. But being a Powell, he was slightly prone to be impatient and had a reputation for starting to walk if we weren't there by the time he hung up the phone. The argument still remains unsolved at home to this day. Dad says he told Mom not to go through Ellaville (which would have been about 15 miles out of the way) but Mom swears he said do go through Ellaville. By the time we got through Butler via Ellaville, Clem was not at the bus station. We asked around and found out he took off toward BV. So we headed for home and finally saw him coming out of a store at a little town called Charing. I think he was glad to see us but I don't think those were his first words--probably something like, " What took you so long". Just think, if Dad had said don't go through Americus, he would have been home

before we found him. Wonder what he would have said if that had happened.

Boy-In-GA-138++typed2013

BOY IN GEORGIA, by Donnie Powell

137 A. RACCONS. Dad tells about the night he, Stout, Clements and cousin Jerry Davis went coon hunting with new coon dogs and a new squirrel dog (Joe). The hounds took off and Joe ran off a little ways and started barking. Clem got onto the dog, said un-nice things about poor old Joe. When they flashed their lights into the tree, Dad counted 14 eyes. So at least seven coons were up there. They got only 5 because they ran out of bullets. Don't know how many were up there, some may have had one eye closed.

137 B. GASOLINE TRUCK. Dad drove a gasoline truck (had 5 tanks total of about 1000 gallons) for Wight Motor Co., in BV. I rode with him a lot. We filled up road construction equipment before the drivers came to work. So he'd get me up at 4 or 5 am and we'd go. I'd help handle the long hose. Looking back, I enjoyed it. Once we were barreling through sandy road and the pin broke on the steering rod and he couldn't steer. But deep sand kept us from wrecking by stopping us cold when the wheels suddenly turned. (I hate to think what would have happened on a hard road. The Good Lord looked after us.)

137. C. CASTOR OIL, ETC. Dad and Mom believed in castor oil, Vicks vapor rub (we called it salve), soak foot in kerosene if you step on a nail, and other home remedies. Dad had his own weather forecasts—three

109

foggy mornings and then a rain, if ground spider webs are covered in dew it will rain, etc. Mom and Dad would warm up the castor oil. Used a very huge (10-gallon) spoon. Mother would say, "Take it all in one swallow". She gave it to us outside on the front steps. (no cleanup). King Kong couldn't take it all in one swallow. She also always said, "If you throw it up I'll give you another." I did and she did. After getting it down we wanted to keep it down more than anything else on earth. But....Even after all these years, I have trouble swallowing, like right now.

137 D. . SHOTGUN.   Dad bought a doubled barreled 12 gauge shotgun in 1928 (used—from ?Welch). One day in about 1948/49 while hunting, he saw some quail, he stopped the truck and got his shotgun. Clements and Stout stayed in the truck. Dad laid the gun across the hood of the truck and fired. One of the barrels was clogged up with the cap or plug or top of the last shell and the barrel exploded out the side shooting off his left pointer finger, shot holes in the truck and killed three birds. His watch stopped. I think he wrapped his finger in a handkerchief and drove to the doctor (Clem and Stout too young to drive.) (He was tough—I would have passed out.) (I guess there are 2 morals: First, always keep a hanky handy. Second, never shoot birds on the ground.) I think I remember when it happened because when they said it was caps that clogged up the barrel, I got some caps for a toy cap pistol and asked if that is what clogged it up. (We were living in the "shacks" at the time.)

137. E. DAD AS BOY. Dad (Roy Alton "Tom") said his brother Harvey ("Pete") used to beat up on him and "Bo" (probably named after E. E. Foster, maternal grandfather, Civil War Vet.) So Tom and Bo made a pact that if Pete jumped on one, the other would attack Pete. Together they could handle Pete.

Dad said he was sick a lot (with ? heart dropsy) and when he finally got well he just ran and ran. Ricky said Clements said he and Dad were out in the woods and they started racing and Clem looked over his shoulder to see how far behind Dad was and found out that Dad was way ahead. ((Although I (Donnie) jogged in a couple 6.2 mile Peachtree Road Races, I never was fast—took me over 55 minutes.))

138. BIBLE SCHOOL. Vacation Bible School was fun. I remember at the Baptist church, I always attended their VBS and loved it a lot. There was singing, Bible stories, refreshments, games, etc. I also remember we always lined up each morning and someone got to carry the American Flag, the Christian Flag and the Bible. I always wanted to get called to carry one of the flags but never did. Maybe it was because I was so small they were afraid (probably rightly so) that I wasn't strong enough to carry a flag. I can just imagine me being asked to carry a flag, and being able to just barely get it up the steps and inside and then when holding it for the pledge begin to weaken. I suppose it would have been slightly irreverent to have yelled "timber" as the flag went crashing down—so maybe it was just as well that I didn't get selected. I remember once at the Methodist VBS they were talking about Moses at the burning bush.

The teacher asked what happened next and I said God told Moses to take his shoes off because he was on holy ground. The other kids burst out laughing because they thought that was the dumbest answer they had ever heard. I noticed even the teacher could see the humor in the answer. (By the way, God does indeed have a sense of humor.) I probably never thanked those wonderful teachers and helpers but they helped shape me and made me a better person. I hope to have the opportunity to thank them in heaven—maybe there I will be strong enough to carry the flag or Moses' shoes.

139. HI NEIGHBOR. Columbus had "Hi Neighbor" Days (or something). Somehow, I got to go on a trip with other kids to the Hi Neighbor festivities which included visits to a number of locations and businesses in Columbus. We visited Tom's candy and peanut plant and I was amazed at the way peanut butter candy planks were made by starting with a big blob of candy, twisting it on a machine, and feeding it down to a smaller and smaller continuous strip until it was the right width and then the machine cut and wrapped it. Naturally, we got some free samples. I could have saved the samples and given some to my sister Brenda Jane or I could have just eaten it then and there. She didn't miss it. We also went to the Royal Crown (RC) bottling plant and they were bottling Nehi orange. It went through this long clear tube, over and around, then into the bottles and capped off. There were no plastic bottles back then, just glass—tasted better too. We also got to go to Fort Benning and ate lunch. Also saw an attack dog demonstration. Always being a little afraid of big dogs, I was courteous and offered my front row seat to someone else and

promptly moved way up in the bleachers. Think the band played the Colonel Bogey March??. At the end of the day, we ate at the fairgrounds and had some entertainment, but the only ones I remember wee Lester Flatt and Earl Scruggs playing banjos and guitars or whatever. I guess I was a little disappointed they didn't invite me on-stage to sing; most folks have not don't that consistently so my singing talent remains (mercifully) undiscovered. We had a great time and developed some lifelong memories and I really appreciate the friendly people who put it together and let me go and to the organizations who hosted us; but being a kid, about all I really appreciated at the time were the free samples and supper. Sorry Brenda Jane, I looked after me first.

140. THE GOURDS. Clements tried farming early by planting some gourds along the fence near the barn. He pampered those gourds and carried water to them (he might have even given each a name). So one day when he came home he was shocked to see all the gourds gone. He probably immediately jumped to the conclusion that Stout had done away with them. So he rushes into the house hollering something like "where's Stout, I am going to pound him." So he comes into the kitchen and there's Mom and through gritted teeth, says, "Where's Stout—on second thought I'M hungry" (even revenge took second place to Clem's stomach—and besides revenge is better on a full stomach.) After Mom gave him something to eat he sadly told Mom of the demise of his gourds, probably even shed a tear or two (yep—Clem could get real emotional about things he loved like hound dogs, bird dogs, horses, and of course

gourds.) Then, Clem got the shock of his life when Mom confessed she had picked the gourds and was cooking them for supper. (Mom is a good cook and will cook just about anything, including watermelon rind pickles, pear preserves (umm) ,etc.) I don't remember whether we actually ate them or not, probably not, gourds would have to taste terrible. But if budding farmer ever planted gourds again, he kept it a secret from all of us, especially Mom.

141. STOUT'S GUITAR. Stout got a guitar from somewhere and for some reason. Why? Never have found out why. None of us knew a note of music and couldn't carry a tune if we had to. On second thought. Brenda and I (maybe Ricky too) learned a few notes playing the "training flutes" in the fifth grade. So maybe we could have learned the guitar. Anyway, we would play it when he wasn't around and had fun seeing what kind of strange noises it could make. If you played it up near the skinny end it sounded like what we called Chinese music. We also had fun trying to get things out of the round hole in the middle. We would drop something like a penny inside and then flip it over and shake it until the money came out. It would make a funny noise when it hit the strings coming out. In the comic book story about Nancy and Sluggo, Sluggo played ping pong with this violin. If we had had a tennis ball, we could have used the guitar as a racket and really powdered the ball. Oh well, lost opportunities. Needless to say, with such tender loving care, it is little wonder that the guitar joined a host of other items that the Powell's sent on to their respective

hunting grounds. Just think, if Stout had stuck with it, he might have been another Elvis P.

142. "BEAR" WEATHER. When Dad was logging and the weather was hot, the brothers and "hands" would say "that old bear is going to get you today." I always took everything literally so I thought they were talking about a real bear—like grizzly. Scared me half to death. I didn't want to go into the woods, the bear would not only get me he would eat me up—after all I couldn't run as fast as the grownups. (Seems like I remember them saying the "Bear" got Stout one day. Naturally, I was surprised to see he wasn't even scratched up or chewed up at all. Stout must have been a great fighter to beat off a bear without a scratch. Clem better watch out.) Finally, someone explained that it was just a saying that meant it was so hot the workers might get heat exhaustion and pass out. (I was reminded of the "bear" saying the other day when it was 100 degrees plus and I was just standing outside and "something" almost got me. I made it back into the air conditioned house, and I swear that bear laughed.)

143. SNUFF. Most of my uncles smoked. (I think most died fairly young of lung cancer) and some of my aunts "dipped snuff." You could sniff snuff or put it inside your lip (like inviting cancer to come in), but most had it in their mouth and had to spit. (This is gross.) Snuff is dumb. In fact, does the use of tobacco in any form, make even a little sense to any objective thinking person? I remember nearly every smoker told me many times, if you don't smoke, don't ever start. They regretted smoking but refused to quit. Fortunately,

my brothers convinced each other to quit smoking (thankfully they didn't dip snuff or chew tobacco, yuck.) Have you ever seen some used tobacco and thought, "someone had that in their mouth?" Anyway, snuff and tobacco were just one of the things we accepted back then—not too bright, I guess.

144. LAND JUDGING. In about the 10th grade, I made the Land Judging team. We would go out and study a field or gully and rate it. The score was from 1 (the best) to 8 (the worst), with 5 being swamp land. I remember our teacher said #8 was like Stone Mountain. He also said Marion County was between the plains and the plateau so we had many types of land on which to practice. We did pretty well and went to a regional competition in way-off Tifton, GA and came in second. I remember our teacher pointing out the work being done on Interstate 75 and said it would go all the way to Ohio and not have a single stop sign or red light on it. I thought and thought and couldn't figure out how that could be possible. (Quite an engineering feat when you think about it.) If we had won first place, we would have gone to Kansas City for the national competition or something. (Being a home body even then, I wasn't too disappointed to have come in second.) Now to the uninformed, land judging might seem about as exciting as watching paint dry, but it had its points—the best I guess, was the free trip to Tifton.

145. BUZZARD WITH A COW BELL. Clements and Stout were often very innovative and creative in finding diversions to keep themselves entertained. On one occasion they decided to capture a buzzard and tie a cow

bell to it. What would possess two normally sane fellows to do such a thing? No one knows, but once the idea was hatched, they did not hesitate to put it into effect. They planned it pretty well. They devised a sort of harness so the buzzard could not get the bell off. Then they captured one near an old dead animal. (Bet the buzzard boys smelled great.) They wrestled the unfortunate captive to submission and strapped on the old cow bell. They say Dad was very angry, not at their goofing off instead of working but because they lost a good cowbell. (Maybe he should have complimented them on their resourcefulness.) They also said that for weeks after that they could hear a "clang clang" in the skies and they would just laugh and laugh. (Just imagine a poor, hapless sick animal with that buzzard descending for a meal, thinking, "This is serious, not only is this one coming in but he is ringing a dinner bell for all the others to come too.")

146. RESUSCITATING A MULE. When Clements worked as foreman for Uncle Pete in the sawmilling business, things often happened. His telling it (with a few embellishments) is much funnier than reading about it, but here goes. One day down in the woods, the mules were pulling ("snaking") logs across a beaver dam. Everything was going well until one of Uncle Pete's favorite mules got tangled up and fell into the beaver pond. By the time they got the truck skidder over there, hitched the mule to it, and pulled him out, he had died. Uncle Pete rushed in and took over. He told the workers to lock arms and jump up and down on the mule while he opened the mule's mouth and pulled out the tongue. Then they rolled the mule over and tried it from the

other side. Poor Clements, the foreman, was anxious to do his part but the sight (reminiscent of the Keystone Cops saving a mule) of those grown men doing a trampoline act on the mule was too much for him—he totally lost it and just fell down on the ground laughing and laughing. Uncle Pete rushed over, pointed his finger in Clem's face, and said something like "Get up and help save this mule!" That just made him laugh harder. To this day, tears come to Clem's eyes when he tells this supposedly true story. Don't know if the tears are from his sadness that they lost the mule, that he disappointed Uncle Pete (and probably got fired), or more probably, that it is still one of the funniest things he has ever seen.

147. MORE LOGGING TALES.   Logging was a very hot job in the summer. One day, it was so hot and humid down in the swamp that the "bar" got cousin Bim and he claimed to have gone blind for a while. Now being sensitive people, no one ever mentioned going blind to Bim—unless he was within hearing range.

Uncle Bill (as told by one of his sons) had a severe case of the Powell temper. One day, he fired the whole sawmilling crew, told them to get on the truck and go back to town. Then a few minutes later when he saw them on the truck, he said a few (dozen) unprintable words, asked what they were doing, and politely asked them to get back to work. Now that in itself doesn't sound too bad, but according to Billy Mack, he did it 6 times in one day. (Probably the only truck in Marion County that was brand new up front and completely worn out in the back from the workers getting in and out of it.)

The man Uncle Bill sold his lumber to wrote him a letter and complained about the boards they were cutting. Uncle Bill didn't take kindly to the criticism and told his foreman Clements (as he was trimming a stout stick) that Clem was to go get Uncle Bill's wife and come down to the jail to visit him because he was going to kill that lumber buyer. Later Clem saw Uncle Bill in a store drinking a number of cokes—about 6 or 8 at a time—he really did love cokes. Clem asked him about the lumber buyer and fortunately Uncle Bill had reconsidered—cokes to the rescue again.

One time Clem and Uncle Bill were riding down a dirt road to check out some timber they were going to cut the next week. A man with a shotgun (possibly a moonshiner) stepped out into the road and asked what they were doing there. Clem told the man who they were and why they were there and the big old man told them to go on down the road but to stick to their logging. Clem drove on and about 100 feet later, Uncle Bill said he would take that shotgun away from that man and whip him. Clem stomped on the brakes and started backing up. Uncle Bill asked what he was doing and Clem said he was taking Uncle Bill back so he could beat that man up. Uncle Bill hollered for him to put the truck in forward and get them out of there. (Clem gets a bit of a tear in his eyes on this one too.)

148. ROMAN CANDLE COW. A neighbor's cow wandered over to our house a number of times and always fertilized the front yard. Finally, Clem and Stout decided enough was enough. So they took the cow to the barn, tied a roman candle firecracker to her tail,

pointed her toward home and lit the candle. When that candle went off, the cow took off like she had—well a firecracker tied to her tail. She was mooing and the last they saw of her was when she turned the corner at the mail box heading toward her house.

149. FIRE BUZZARD. Catching a buzzard the first time was so much fun, they decided to do it again. This time they simply tied a lighted torch to it and turned it loose. The buzzard instead of soaring high into the air, flew straight into a neighbor's barn. Buzzard catchers instantly turned into firefighters and fortunately got the fire out. (So far there have been no more stories about capturing buzzards, so that fiery episode may have cured them.)

150. COW RIDING AND HUNTING. One cousin was hunting with a group of friends one night. He had a torch in his hand, and was a little lit himself, when he stumbled over a cow just standing up. The cousin lost his balance, wrapped his arms around the cow's neck, and somehow managed to put the torch under the cow's nose. The cow didn't need many sniffs to get it in gear and tore off through the woods with cousin hanging on for dear life. The cow ran under a tree limb and nearly took cousin's scalp off. So the group took him to the doctor to get his scalp sewed back on. But undaunted, cousin then said, let's go hunting.

151. LAW OFFICERS. One time Uncle Pete was helping the city police try to capture a suspect, but he got away. However, the man's dog was still there, so they captured the dog, locked him in the jail and

demanded bail from the suspect and if no bail then the dog would have to serve his time.

Another time they were trying to capture a moonshiner who took off running wearing rubber boots and carrying two five-gallon cans of moonshine. Either the officers were rather slow or the moonshine was really (quite a man) because he escaped.

Another fast one was a woman that two officers couldn't catch and simply said, "She could run."

One officer was discussing a suit against himself with the city attorney. When the officer explained that the attorney was also named in the suit, the lawyer said, 'Well, let's get us a good lawyer."

152. BILLY'S FIRSTBORN. Billy tells of the time he was showing off his firstborn son to Uncle Rag Davis. Billy was so proud, bragging on him and just beaming. Until Uncle Rag asked, "well, Billy, are you going to try to raise him?"

153. DIAPERED CAR. Joyce and Gene took us to the fair in Columbus many times. On the trip, Mom brought Ricky who was about 4 to 16 months old and still in diapers. Mom always liked to take along something to eat and a Mason jar of good old Marion County water. A few miles out of town, she discovered the jar of water had leaked out and wet all the cloth diapers. (There were no paper diapers back then.) So our only choice was to hold one or more out each window and hope the wind would dry them as quickly as possible. Everyone that saw the car must have thought we were trying to look like a sail boat at full mast or that we were just very

121

strange. Now days, we could just buy some paper diapers or just hold them out the window and the passerbys would just think we were on our way to some football game and would flash us a V for victory sign. Being just a kid myself, I was just embarrassed by it all. When we got to the fair, we had a great time as usual. But I remember a boy about 12 came up to Mom and said Ricky was so cute could he hold him. Mom (as with all mom's) was glad to let someone else hold the baby a few minutes, eagerly passed him off. The boy instantly took Ricky to show his parents what he had won at the fair. When asked where Ricky was, Mom said some boy had just took him. Several tense minutes later the boy came back with a baby. Mom was so relieved that I wonder if she checked to see if she got the right baby back. Maybe he was switched. Why my real brother might just be somewhere in Alabama. Come to think of it, Ricky sometimes seems different from the other Powell's. Why sometimes he actually loses his temper and he is the only one to ever do that. I believe he is moody and pouts a little sometimes too—clearly not a Powell trait. And he sometimes talks lowly or mumbles as he is walking away from you—something none of us would ever think about. The real clincher is that he is balding—none of us brothers have any problems with balding, as long as we can comb the hair over the bald spots. So there, the evidence is clear, Ricky just might not be a Powell. But then again, if he isn't, he is doing a great impression.

154. LOST WASHCLOTH. According to Billy and Billy Mack Powell, there is a well endowed—extremely well endowed—woman who had to go to the doctor. In

the course of the examination, the doctor lifted one of her breasts and found a washcloth. The woman commented, "I wondered where that washcloth was." (I should have asked but didn't, I wonder what the doctor found under the other one.)

155. ILLNESS. Someone said he knew a woman who was ill a lot. Finally, the doctor was able to diagnose the illness—distemper and mange ((diseases unique to dogs??))

156. SKIM MILK. They said Clements and Stout hated to milk the cows. So they would milk enough to cover the bottom of the milk bucket, let the calf in to finish "milking" the cow, and fill the bucket up with water. They said Mom wore out many electric churns trying to get butter out of that watered down milk. They invented skim milk.

157. BEING THEMSELVES. Billy Mack said that Powell's can't help being themselves—charming and good looking. (I am sure some of the wives could add a few choice adjectives.)

158. RICH AND FAMOUS??? Billy and Billy Mack were on television to tell about the grist mill, how it works, when it is open, etc. Billy Mack started—on national tv, mind you—and said, "I'm the famous Billy Powell, and this is the rich and famous Billy Powell."

159. CROSS THAT LINE! Billy Mack said they would draw a line in the dirt and dare Clements or Stout to step over it. Just you do it and see what happens. Clements of course would step over it without

hesitation. And just as quickly, Billy Mack would draw another line, and another and another.

160. ANSWERING EVERY QUESTION. Clyde and Clements were not only cousins but close friends that played together a lot. Supposedly, whenever Clyde (or anyone else) asked a question Clements would answer authoritatively and without hesitation. It was many years later that it finally dawned on Clyde that while Clem always had an answer they weren't always the correct answers.

161. AUNT CLARA'S DRIVING. Whenever Aunt Clara drove to our house, the boys would gather around and make bets on how many times she would choke the car down while trying to drive through the sand bed. Hubert would yell and distract Aunt Clara and she would choke it down again, and again, supposedly as many as 100 times, much to the delight of the hillside of betting boys.

162. BILLY'S SON. Billy and Billy Mack are together a lot and it seems to really "thrill" Billy when someone asks him if Billy Mack is his son.

163. BILLY'S BIRTHDAY PRESENT. Billy just loves to get birthday presents, especially when Lavern (his wife) spends a lot of his money. She was thrilled to have found an antique corn sheller on a wooden box for the amazing price of only $250, but she craftily talked the seller down to a mere $180. Billy was speechlessly thrilled—or at least speechless.

164. FLYING HAMMERS. When asked if their Dad's (Uncle Bill and Bo) also believed in trying to teach

hammers to fly when they lost their tempers—Billy and Billy Mack agreed that the trait was not limited to just my Dad (R. A. "Tom"). Hammers have apparently been flying in the Powell family for several generations, and more often than not, the training of the hammers included some colorfully explicit expletives. (Maybe that is why dad's sons are each in various stages of baldness (or as my daughter said when she was small "he wears his hair on the back of his head"—I like that better. Baldness implies we don't have hair. Her way of saying it is that we have hair, it is just at the back of our head, not on top.) Maybe those verbal blast during the temper tantrums had nuclear or microwave type properties that killed our hair roots. But that is not a valid theory because we would not have any eyebrows.) Anyway, teaching hammers to fly seems to have been one of the things Powell's did (or do).

165. SWEET POTATO HILL. One way of preserving crops such as sweet potatoes was to dig a hole, cover it with pine straw, and put the potatoes in the hole and cover them with straw. This preserved them through the winter. I remember Mom telling me to go dig out some potatoes from the potato hill. It was an adventure, like going into a foxhole or digging for treasure. I also remember that it was cold so I probably only found a few potatoes—but since I did not like vegetables, I gladly gave mine up. Even then, I knew that all that healthy food was bad for you.

166. GRANDDAD CHEWED TOBACCO. Granddad Powell lived with us a few years and one thing I remember was that he chewed tobacco. Sometimes

when riding with Dad and some of us kids, Granddad would have to spit. Unfortunately, sometimes he would not notice that the window was rolled up and, and---well you can imagine the brown streak on the window. I sure did love my Granddad—but not his tobacco. ((He had a blacksmith shop which I enjoyed playing in—when he wasn't around. Enjoyed turning the bellows to blow air into the fire to heat up metal. He was also supposed to have been able to used a forked stick (?peach?) to "water witch" and find water.))

167. HIGH-LIFE HORSE. Clements Powell says when he was young, about 9 or 10, some older cousins, Bob Jernigan and Clark "Monk" Powell conducted a scientific experiment. They had a horse in the barn and decided to see what the horse would do if a caustic substance called "high-life" was applied to the horse. Clements being young (and quite smart) ran outside and climbed a tree. Just as Bob applied the high-life, Monk ran outside and shoved the door open so the horse would run out. But the wind blew the door shut and trapped the horse inside with Bob. The horse screamed, hollered, kicked but most of all tried to bite Bob. Bob had to jump from rafter to rafter to keep the horse from getting him. I wonder what Bob's version of this would be—probably that they were taking good care of the horse, feeding it, petting it and the HORSE accidentally knocked over the high-life and then went crazy and chased a very innocent Bob into and across the rafters. (Note: Wonder what the horse's version would be? Although he was quite young, it is still hard for me to believe my brother Clements was so completely innocent—maybe at that age he was just an

"apprentice". Clements (laughing hard) painted a rather comical picture of the horse trying to bite the not-too-innocent Bob as he tried to be "Tarzan of the barn rafters.")

168. TREE FALL NEAR HOUSE. Clements and brother-in-law Gene Henson were cutting a large tree for Johnson Henson in his yard. They tied a cable from the tree to another tree and started cutting. It fell close to the house and really rattled the ground and the house. Johnson came running out and asked Clements "weren't you scared?" Clements said, "No, it is not my house."

169. I CAN'T LOOK AT THE TREE CUTTING. Uncle E. E. "Bo" Powell asked Clements to cut a big, pretty tree near his house. Clements got the cable tied, "boxed" the tree (cut it on one side so it would fall in that direction) and started cutting. Uncle Bo tapped Clem on the shoulder and said he had changed his mind and not to cut the tree. Clem said, it is too late, I have cut too far and it has got to come down now. Uncle Bo said could you wait a few minutes till I get in the truck and drive down the road; I just can't stand to watch you cut it down.

170. SAINT & MOM'S SCHOOL DAYS. My Mother is Mina Davis Powell; she was married to Dad, Roy Alton "Tom" Powell for 71 years when he died in 1997. We have a saying "if you are married to a Powell for 10 years you are a candidate for sainthood". Mom is a saint 7 times over. I asked what grade she completed in school and she said the sixth. She said the teacher would just move you up to the next grade when she thought you were ready. They had no report cards.

((She and Dad were remarkable, wonderful, talented hard-working good, good people.))

171. Mom's father Shadrack "Shadie" Addison Davis, in 1920's carved some wooden letters used to write on concrete slabs in cemeteries in Marion County, GA. This is documented in "Bulletin of the Association for Gravestone Studies" Volume 34 Number 1, Winter 2010, pages 12-14. Letters were used to write on his own grave. (His father Jonathan D. Davis was a War Between the States Veteran guard at Andersonville as a teenager. His Grandfather Addison William Davis was also WBtS Vet. Shadie's maternal grandfather Christopher Pearson also a Vet. All buried at Smyrna Cemetery (in Church Hill area) about 12 miles south of Buena Vista, GA on Ga. Highway 41.)

172. Mom made quilts—my favorite being family tree quilts for each of her 6 children. Took many hours of talented work and love. Her interview about quilts was written in "The Tri-County Journal and Chattahoochee Chronicle", July 1, 2009.

173. Mom's uncle Stephen Davis was a policeman killed in the line of duty in 1910 in Irwin County, GA. His name is on the Georgia Public Safety Memorial in Forsyth, GA.

174. Dad was very innovative—could fix just about anything or make a contraption to do something. He nailed a can horizontally onto end of a stick to pick up pecans. He used gasoline for a number of things including killing wasps. (I do too, and yellow jackets at night, and bushes/trees—drill hole in tree and pour in

gas.) Watched him take generator (?) apart and replace the brushes. Loved to repair tractors—and lure Ricky in to repair it if he couldn't. At about 80, climbed pecan tree to string electric wire. He loved having electric lights—ran line to shelter, another to the barn, one across front yard. After moving to the home place, Mom met new neighbor who said, I know you, yall keep those electric lights on all the time. Guess coming from no electricity (lantern light is not very bright) to electricity was just something to celebrate with electrical display. He showed me how to cut the bottom off a glass bottle to make a funnel. He would cut a can at an angle, add a short handle and have a scoop to scoop feed or seeds. To cut a walking stick, he bent it way over and then cut it—much easier. Once as a kid, I was with him when he was driving through the woods where there was no road—he would turn and twist the truck to avoid the big trees but enjoyed knocking down the smaller ones— I was a little concerned but looked at him and he was laughing and having a good time. Mom said as kids they would go into the woods, climb a small tree, lean over, bend it down and ride it to the ground—then bounce on it. To get rid of rats in the chicken houses at the Murray place, he filled 5 gallon bucket with water and put a circular wooden cover over them with a nail on each side so if the rat walked across the board it would tilt and drop the rat into the water. It worked. Speaking of the Murray place, it was not home and I did not like it. It had white fence with horizontal boards on top which we walked without falling off. At the home place, Dad would tie yokes to the dogs to keep them from going through the fence into the neighbor's property (I would have been unsuccessful in trying to do that but he did it.)

175. Tennis net monster. One summer (about 1961), several of us guys decided to learn how to play tennis. We ordered tennis rackets, repainted the old court, and tried to teach ourselves what to do. In retrospect, I am reminded of an old Little Rascal movie where they were playing gold with "clubs" being a weed-cutter sling, a hockey stick, etc. We might not have looked like good tennis players but looks can sometimes be deceiving—in my case they weren't. One player Travis, was so competitive that he always gave it his best. When he played the net against me, it was as if he had some magnetic force that just drew my shots to him and he promptly creamed it so hard that it bounced over the screen. So insult to injury, I had to go find the ball. Once he slammed one hard and I called it out. He came running over and said it couldn't be out. We looked and sure enough, it was both in and out. The skid mark showed it was in when it first hit, but he hit is so hard it slid or skidded about a foot on the smooth concrete and it came up outside the line. If I had been smart I would have tried to team up with him more often and maybe would have won more games. Anyway, we had this dumb—I mean really dumb—tradition of jumping the net to congratulate the winner. I got lots of practice jumping the net and got pretty good at it. But you know, when you do something dumb, it only takes one mistake—99 out of 100 is ok for some things but the one you mess up on is the one that really makes an impact. One day, I didn't quite clear the net, my foot got tangled up by the net monster, and landed on my

tailbone. Ouch. I limped a number of weeks, but I learned something (landed on my brain?), don't do dumb things that can hurt your body. I learned my lesson well, to this day I haven't jumped a tennis net and have thus stayed from the tennis monster that lives in every tennis net..

176. UNCLE "RAG" by Donnie Powell Jan 2018 Uncle Rag was a bit of a character. His son Bo told this story. Bo was dating girls some distance away and his dad said, "Why do you date girls so far away—don't you know that takes a lot of gas and gas is expensive. You should date girls close by—why don't you date local girls?" Bo said, "It's because the local girls--and their dads--know you and your reputation and they won't date me." For once Uncle Rag didn't have a thing to say.

177. Bob Jernigan said as a child they rode their bikes on Uncle E. R. Jernigan's frozen mill pond one winter. Went back later in the day—sun had melted some of the ice—and they fell in but were able to get their bikes and themselves out of the pond (same one where I almost drowned.)

178. Dad/Mom sayings. He would say and "boot" when talking about trading for something (meant extra money or items added to make the trade even). The US mail brought bills to be paid—Dad called them "duns". Mom would say "wrong side outwards"—we say "inside out". Think I remember a peddler coming by the house selling things.

++++++++++++++++++++++++++++++++++

++++++++++++++++++++

SECTION III   MEMORIES OF MOM

MEMORIES OF MOM----MINA POWELL   By
Donnie Powell   April 2009 (updated family members
June09)

As Mother's Day approaches, an idea emerged to
give Mom a present of memories—though long
overdue,(she is 97 on 19 May 09) finally putting them in
writing helps me honor her and perhaps will help other
family members also list some of their memories.

These questions/thoughts are just memory
joggers and can form an outline for each of us to capture
our thoughts. Most people will have better ideas but
these thoughts might be a starting point.

I have the best Mom in the world!

BACKGROUND-- MOM'S CHILDHOOD/FAMILY

Mom is Mina Myrtle Davis Powell born in
Marion County, Georgia, on 19 May 1912 (died Sep
2009), the youngest of 10 children. Her parents were
Shadrack "Shadie" Addison Davis and Malissa Jane
Cosby, good, honest hard-working farming parents. Her
grandfather Jonathan D. Davis was a young guard at
Andersonville during the War Between the States.
Jonathan's father, Addison W. (or W. A) Davis, was a
Confederate States of America (CSA) veteran--father
and son both CSA vets—as was Jonathan's father-in-
law, Christopher Pearson. Malissa's father (William H.

Cosby) was also a CSA vet. Though Mom remembers Jonathan (called him "Grandsa") talking about the war when she was a child, she does not remember any of the stories. One thing her father did was to help dig graves for family and friends and place a cement slab as their tombstone. He carved some wooden letters and words to use to write their names on the cement slab to make a professional looking remembrance. He caught pneumonia while digging a grave and died—as a tribute, the wooden letters were used to write on his own grave.

Mom completed about the sixth or eighth grade in school.

In 1926, at the age of 14, she married Roy Alton ("Tom") Powell. They always were honest, hard working good neighbors all their lives—for many years farming, later Tom got into logging followed by driving a gasoline truck in the local area for Wight Motor Company, in Buena Vista. Mina worked about 17 years in a shirt factory in Americus, GA. They raised 6 children--with only one bathroom. They were married 71 years when Dad died in 1997—have always said, "living with a Powell for 10 years qualifies you for sainthood"—Mom is a saint 7 times over. Their marriage encompassed many amazing changes— imagine, horse and buggy days, dirt roads, no electricity, almost totally rural Georgia, segregation, the Great Depression—or "Hoover Days" as they called it--World War II, radio but no television till about 1954, almost no divorces, farming with mules but no tractors, almost no Hispanics, no computers, most mothers did not work outside the home, no washing machines till about 1950, no clothes dryers until about 1960, no social security, no Medicare, and on and on.

MOM AND ME

FAMILY MEMBERS

Mom and Dad had six children—

(1) Joyce was born in 1930 (lives in Buena Vista)—married T. E. "Gene" Henson (died in 1968)—two children.

(A) Connie (John) Dent (in Marion County)

(B) Peggy (Scott) Miller (in Columbus) with one child Lauren.

(2) Clements, 1934 (lived in Marion County, died May 2010), married Weone Fussell (she died 2008)—three children,

(A) Leta (Randy) Welch (in Marion County) (with two children, Mitch (Samantha) Welch with one child Talan Davis Welch—he's fifth generation to Mom and Dad), and Matt.

(B) Alton (Becky) Powell (in Marion County) (with two children, Clint and Kinsey)

(C) Nenia (Edmond) Bassett (in Marion County) (with one child Jason)

(3) Stout, 1938 (lives in Sumter County) two children (with Shirley Hall)

(A) Rhonda (Frank) Davis (in Columbus) (one child (with Robbie Wells) Travis—who has two

134

children Irelynn and??—another fifth generation for Mom and Dad).

(B) Danny (Died 1987), one child (with Bonnie Chapman) Shannon, who has two children Kason and Sophie —another fifth generation for Mom and Dad. Danny had one child Gage with Christy.

(4) Brenda Jane, 1943 (died in 1981) one child Billy (Erin) with Dr. William Smith in Atlanta.

(5) Donnie, 1944 (lives in Warner Robins) married Delores Lightsey--three children

(A) Richard (Natalie) Powell (in Snellville, GA)

(B) Sharon (Tommy) Hancock (in Warner Robins) with two children (I call them my "grand-darlings), Rylee Jane (after Brenda Jane) and Haven (born in 2004, a hundred years after Pap) ((They call us O-MA and O-PA—named by Rylee who shortened "Oh Grandma" and "Oh Grandpa".))

(C) Ben Powell (in Warner Robins)

(6) Ricky, 1953 (lived in Buena Vista) (Died Apr 2012). I was so glad when he was born because Mom couldn't call me her "baby" any more. It is still amazing that they raised a family this large, and did such a good job of it. Dad came from a large family of 8 children, so any type of get-togethers had lots of Uncles, Aunts and cousins—lot of kids with whom to play.

Mom and Dad had 6 children, 11 grandchildren, 10 great-grandchildren and 5 great-great-grandchildren (or fifth generation). Truly blessed!

2. MY EARLY CHILDHOOD MEMORIES (INCLUDING CHRISTMAS)

Mom tells the story that I was about 3 or 4 and said "I want a drink of water". She said my name is Momma or Mrs. Powell, to which I said "Mrs. Powell, I want a drink of water." Some of my early memories are of Mom cooking, cleaning and doing the required multitude of household chores, which through the years got easier as we acquired appliances. She dispensed the dreaded Castor oil—not just a tablespoon but a spoon I called "the 10 gallon spoon". She would heat it up and tell us she'd give us another dose if we threw it up—which I usually did, regrettably. We stayed close to home after being dosed. She had a foot-powered peddle Singer sewing machine—later replaced by electric one—which she used to sew many things for the family. She made me some shirts out of 25 pound flower sacks—which also provided us some sheets.

She enjoyed planting and growing flowers of all kinds—she even fertilized them with manure from the barn.

She endured a husband who enjoyed buying, raising and selling pigs and other farm animals as well as automobiles and Ford tractors. She also put up with her two older sons' love of hunting and fishing, raising dogs, having pets of squirrels, rabbits, etc. Why, they even invaded her kitchen to cook cornbread for their prized hunting dogs. I remember Uncle Roy Daniels gave me a little dog whom I named "Rusty"—he was a beloved companion—but not sissy enough to be an inside dog—our dogs would have been insulted had we brought them inside.

Christmas memories are wonderful. It was only later that I realized how much they sacrificed to provide gifts for us. I usually wanted a gun-and-holster set (always too big for me) and Brenda wanted a doll. We got many more toys and gifts including oranges, apples, grapes, Brazil nuts, English walnuts—all of which were treats usually reserved for Christmas. Mom and Dad were amazingly patient at Christmas because we'd wake up about midnight to see what Santa had brought (unwrapped) and then we would stay up all night "quietly" playing with our treasures while they tried to sleep. Firecrackers added to the Christmas season— miss them but still have all my fingers. One thing I never liked was my 6 December birthday led Mom to say of my birthday presents, "now this is part of your Christmas" (thought I'd never say that to my children, but I did). Made me wish for a June birthday.

3. SCHOOL DAYS MEMORIES

I loved school—studying was so much better than manual work and chores. My family always encouraged me to get a good education. Mom would listen to me read and helped me with my homework— how she found the time I'll never know. Sometimes my sister Brenda would also teach me the next day's lesson.

In the second grade, Mom was my "Grade Mom" and helped when needed, especially with parties. When she came to school, I remember thinking how pretty she was—so much prettier than the other grade moms.

She was available to help at home or school when needed and attended all our school plays and programs, clearly showing how important she felt education and extra curricular activities were. Her proudest moments were probably when all six of us graduated—my sisters being Valedictorians. Brenda and I were privileged to go to college—with scholarships—and Ricky to technical school, but we would not have been able to go without the emotional and financial support of Mom and Dad. I often think the three that didn't go to college/technical school could have easily met the academic requirements, given the opportunity.

4. MOM'S COOKING

We all loved Mom's cooking—relatives always stayed for supper when visiting. She cooked way too much food—the table was covered. She used lots of shortening or as we called it, lard—but that just made it taste great.

She cooked on a wood stove for years until it was replaced by an electric one. She was a wonderful cook and enjoyed cooking for family and friends even into her 90s. Some of the great things she cooked included, fried chicken (straight from the yard), chicken pie (Brenda always wanted the heart) with the thinnest dumplings, hamburgers (Clem and Stout could eat about 10 each), rounded-over thin biscuits (brown for me and others and "white" ones for Dad), fried sweet potatoes,

138

sweet potato biscuits, sweet potato pie, chocolate pie, pecan pie, oyster stew, lemon pie, butter-roll pie, apple pie, peach puffs, sweet whipped cream, crackling corn bread (which we crumbled into a class full of butter milk—sometimes added chopped onions), pancakes at supper (about 3 inches in diameter—we ate stacks of them), bacon, sausage, eggs, fresh meat from home slaughtered pigs, syrup-biscuit (poke a hole in the biscuit top and fill it up with syrup), Irish potatoes in lots of juice, baked sweet potatoes with lots of real butter (which she churned for a number of years), hoke-cakes fried on top of stove, roast beef, roast pork, fried side meat, fried ham, corn on the cob, cream corn, turnips, squash, okra, rice, grits (never cream of wheat), chocolate cake, German chocolate cake, lemon cake, coconut cake, home made ice cream, ambrosia (oranges, coconut, pecans, so good), and on and on (my mouth is watering). Cooking was one way she showed her love for her family—and we returned that love by eating as much as we could as often as we could. In addition to feeding us, when someone died she would prepare covered dishes and take them to the family.

She canned many things by cooking them on the stove and putting them in mason jars—such items as figs, peaches, pickles, pears, watermelon-rind pickles, peas (we shelled seemingly tons of peas) butter beans, corn, tomatoes, snap beans, and on and on.

Clements tells that Mom even tried cooking gourds—but only once.

5.   SPECIAL   OCCASSIONS/FAMILY   GET TOGETHERS

139

Mom liked family get-togethers and always brought many covered dishes—think some even would make a special request for chicken pie, butter roll pie, etc.

A strange thing happened at these get-togethers. All the women would be sitting in one room and every one would be talking at the same time—somehow they perfected talking and listening at the same time. Maybe they did not get much talking/listening time from Dad and the other husbands. But they had a wonderful time and so did all us kids.

6. MOM WHEN I WAS SICK OR HURT.

When I was sick or injured, I always went to Mom who somehow made it better. Came in from flying kites with older kids with my hands so cold I almost cried—Mom made it better. I had asthma all my life and many nights when I was wheezing and had trouble breathing, she would sit up with me and rub me down with Vicks salve (now called Vapor Rub). When we stepped on a nail—a pretty frequent happening—she would soak our foot in kerosene—this was before the time when kids were rushed to the doctor for such events. Kerosene also seemed to help when we got ground itch. When my foot got stuck in the spokes of a bike which peeled my shoe, sock, and skin off, she was there to treat it and console me—I sort of liked having people feel sorry for me—but I especially liked Mom's attention—she was always there for me.

7. VACATIONS/TRIPS

140

About the only trips we took were to uncles and aunts—always enjoyed those trips—such visits may be a lost art—we talked instead of watching TV. We took a few trips to places like Macon to check on some of Dad's sawmilling equipment. Sometimes we went with Joyce and her family to Americus or Columbus shopping or to the Columbus annual Exposition or Fair—loved going there. Joyce and family even took us to Atlanta a few times as well as other places.

Only vacation Mom ever took (I believe) was in summer of 1961 when Callaway Gardens awarded us a week-long vacation in one of their cabins. (Callaway's was very generous to do this for us and many other academic achievers.) Brenda, Ricky and I had a great time swimming, seeing the FSU circus, playing games, meeting other kids our age, etc. Don't know what Mom was doing (need to ask her), probably some cooking and cleaning but bet she had a ball. (Think Stout and his family joined us a couple of days.)

8. CHURCH/SOCIAL EVENTS/SPORTING EVENTS

Though Mom did not attend church regularly— too busy cooking for the family—she was very religious. Remember going with her and some other relatives to "all day singing" where we had dinner on the grounds (not "ground" as I thought).

Our social events were usually family related including wedding, funerals, birthdays, reunions. Mom's sisters gave her a surprise birthday party once (maybe twice) at our home (about 1956 and 61)). Each had great turnouts and good visits.

9. MOM'S TALENTS/CRAFTS/HOBBIES/ETC.

Mom was very talented in sewing, knitting, tattin', making quilts, etc. She gave each of her children about 6 quilts each. I have some with airplanes, flowers, girls in long dresses, but my favorite is our Family Tree Quilt (completed in 1985, when she was 74) with all the uncles and aunts and their children on both Dad's and Mom's sides of the family. She stitched each name and the trees or flowers and I still marvel at how much time it took and how much love she put into each of them. Joyce and I compared ours and found some differences but both are remarkable. She even made some baby-sized quilts (mine for my cold feet) which I use daily—one has a mini-family tree. She made them using quilting frames which she suspended from the ceiling in the living room, the only room big enough for the frames. I appreciate all she did but really cherish the family-tree quilt.

She was always sewing or making things for the grand and great-grand children. She made a number of dresses for the grandchildren. We had some old Indian powder rocks from which she made some things, gluing eyes on them, gluing some rocks together, etc., to make items that looked like certain animals, etc. She could look at something and figure out how to make it—such as certain type dolls, decorations, clothes, place mats, etc. From a picture, she sewed our son Richard an Ultra man outfit.

She (sometimes with Dad's help) made stitched pictures, nameplate by driving nails into a board, a checker board table, a checker board cloth mat with cloth checker men, and on and on.

10. GRADUATION AND BEYOND

When I went to college I suddenly had to do my own washing and ironing and missed Mom quite a bit. To boost my morale, Mom wrote me a letter every week keeping me up to date on happenings back home and she included much appreciated money—both were appreciated.

After graduation and moving away from home, my relationship with Mom and Dad changed. But they were both always thinking about all their children, proud of us, and there to support us when needed. Mom came to help with the household chores when our children were born. She would come when she could when any of us were in the hospital or needed her—she was a tremendous help.

After I became a parent, my opinion of and respect for my parents went up tremendously—we survived three teenagers—they survived six—amazing. (And we had two bathrooms and barely made it at times. Just kidding, we have great children.)

Visits back home were great but all too short— they always wanted us to stay longer ((I now understand that))—especially when our children were born. We tried to cram a week's worth of visiting into just a few hours.

11. MY MARRIAGE/WIFE AND MOM

My wife Delores and I were married in her home church of Clyattville, GA, about 170 miles from Buena Vista. Mom, Dad, and Ricky rode together. It was (I think) the only time Mom and Dad stayed in a motel room. Wedding was nice and very hot. On the way home, Dad drove very fast on I-75. Mom said she started snacking some to calm her stomach and nerves. The faster he drove the more she ate. She said by the time they got home, she had eaten up everything in the car. She said she had no idea why he drove so fast—passed everything in sight—made her glad to get home.

One of the biggest reasons for problems in a marriage is the in-laws. We were fortunate in that Mom and Dad never interfered but always supported us in any way they could. (Maybe they were afraid if we divorced I'd move back home and they did not want that.) Mom and Dad never said negative things about their children in laws—they always tried to help. Great Dad and Great Mom.

12. OUR CHILDREN AND "GRANNY"

As grandchildren were born, Mom and Dad became (and I still say) "Granny" and "Papa". They often babysat the grandchildren for working Moms—a feat at which I still marvel—especially when we keep our energetic but wonderful grand-darlings. How did Granny and Papa have the energy?

They kept our two older children a few times over night or several nights and developed strong bonds.

13. OTHER THOUGHTS/MEMORIES

144

I remember Mom saying when Joyce was just a little girl, she would lift up the edge of the bed and set it down on Joyce's dress sash so she could play while Mom worked in the fields.

+++++

TO MINA MYRTLE DAVIS POWELL AND ROY ALTON (TOM) POWELL

CONGRATULATION ON YOUR 65TH WEDDING ANNIVERSARY ON 22 MAY 1991!!!

(Note: When Dad died, they had been married 71 years!!)

You have been married 65 years and have seen and done many things. There have been good times and sad times buy you have stayed together through it all. You have raised six fine children to be (like yourselves) honest, hard-working, good citizens who believe in God, who were and are eager to learn, who are goo and helpful neighbors, patriotic Americans, loving, caring, loyal and on and on. You taught us by doing and being a good neighbor, citizen, etc. You encouraged education and can be proud that all six of us have graduated from high school and have continued learning. You have 11 grandchildren and 6 great-grandchildren. By all standards you have lived a successful and productive life and have shown you are a good team.

You have lived through the most amazing times in history. You have gone "from" and "to" such things as the following:

FROM   TO

145

Horse and buggy and model T   Jet planes, and men on the moon.

Early radio   Color TV, VCR, computers

No telephones Phones in home and Car, and wireless phones

Mules   Tractors

Mostly rural/small farms Mostly urban/ no small farms

No fire ants   Many, many, fire ants

Segregation   Integration

Wood stoves   Electric or gas stoves

Most moms in the home Many moms working outside the home

Small local restaurants/stores McDonalds,K-Mart, Coca-cola, IBM, etc

Much cotton in Marion County No cotton grown in Marion County, GA

Ice boxes   Refrigerators

Fountain pens   Ball point pens

Much polio, small pox   No polio, small pox, for fatal pneumonia

Depression ("Hoover Days")   The New Deal

American Cars & Products	Japanese cars, China products
World War II, Korea, Vietnam	Peace (In short intervals)
Out houses	Bathrooms (Yeah!)
Well water	Running water inside (Yes!)
Lanterns	Electric Lights (Thank you Lord!)

You have seen and done many things and have helped many people. We could always count on you. I am very proud of you and I love you. I could not have had better parents or a better home life. "It's a Wonderful Life" and I thank you for the life you gave me! I THANK GOD THAT YOU ARE MY FATHE AND MOTHER!!! I LOVE YOU. Donnie P.S. There is one thing I would have changed—no castor oil.

++++++++

14. COMMENTS

I have always respected, admired, and loved Mom and Dad so very much. I had the best Mom and the best Dad in the whole world!

(Note: Proverbs 31:28 Her children rise up and call her blessed… She is a great blessing to her relations. Think the writer of Proverbs knew my Mom (and probably ate some of her chicken pie while wrapped in one of her family tree quilts.))

End.

++++++++++++++++++++++++++++

SECTION IV. EULOGIES—MOM, CLEMENTS, AND RICKY

Granny-Eulogy-Sep09   Preacher's comments

EULOGY--MINA MYRTLE DAVIS POWELL— also known as "MOMMA", "GRANNY", "GREAT GRANNY", "AUNT MINA" "MRS. POWELL"

...

Preacher: Reference "Hymn of Promise"

+++++++++++++++++++

Preacher: Now I'll read what her children wrote which expresses the feelings for all. This shows among other things how much Mrs. Powell loved her family.

(In some language somewhere, the name "Mina" must mean "love of family".)

Mina Davis, the youngest daughter of Malissa Jane Cosby and Shadrack (Shade) Addison Davis, was born on May 19, 1912 and was only 14 years old when she married Roy Alton ("Tom") Powell on May 22, 1926.   During their 71 years of marriage they had 6 children—Joyce, Clements, Stout, Brenda, Donnie, and Ricky. All of these children were born at home without any kind of pain medication.   They now have 11 grandchildren, 10 great-grandchildren, and 3 great-great-grandchildren—the first one's middle name is "Davis" in he honor.

Before getting married, she was raised in a family of 8 siblings. This was during the horse and buggy days when you washed clothes by hand, drew water from a well or carried it from a spring. They cooked on a wood stove, went to the fields to pick cotton, stack peanuts, pull corn; they raised their own vegetables in a garden and chickens in the yard. They killed hogs on very cold days, milked cows and did many other farm jobs. She walked to school even with ice frozen on the sides of the dirt road.

Then Daddy married her and whisked her away to--well, more of the same. They were a great team— they had to be. They lived through the Great Depression or, as they called it, "Hoover Days" and World War II. They lived by the slogan "use it up, wear it out, make it do, or do without". When we children came along, we learned never to get sick, or act like we felt bad because we knew we would get a BIG, HUGE, LARGE dose of castor oil. It was so bad, each of us said we would never give our children castor oil.

All of her children and grandchildren had to have quilts to keep warm. So she spent many, many hours piecing together scraps and then quilting them. Each of us also received a unique "Family Tree" quilt where she had embroidered names of all her siblings and their families, plus Daddy's families, as well as each of our families—these are treasured heirlooms. She had a talent for making many other things including "Western" style shirts, special outfits for grandchildren, etc.

Through the years, she spent a lot of time babysitting her grandchildren and great-grandchildren, loving them and always letting them do things her own children were not allowed to do. She always welcomed new in-laws into the family and never said anything negative about them.

We were lucky to have her as a grade mother. This involved helping 3 or 4 other mothers serve goodies and drinks for parties, such as Christmas, Valentines, Easter, etc. She attended almost every school function including plays, programs, graduations, etc. She supported all of us children and strongly encouraged us to get a good education.

After her youngest child started to school, she got her first paying job at Manhattan Shirt Company. They carpooled to Americus, and between the 4 or 5 women riding together, we're sure they had some very interesting gossip—Momma was very friendly and loved to talk.

Her family always came first—she loved each and every member dearly. She did without many, many things for herself but was very generous in giving to her family; she was totally unselfish—and she never complained. Somehow they managed to always have bounteous Christmases whose memories we   still cherish today.

We think her favorite passion was cooking. She always cooked big meals each Sunday hoping her children and their families would come. Anybody else that came was always welcome. No matter when you went to see them, she always wanted you to eat. This was her way of showing love. Some favorites were chicken pie, cakes, pies, biscuits, peach puffs, sweet potato biscuits, vegetables, fried chicken, cracklin' corn bread (crumbled into a glass of buttermilk), hoke cakes fried on top of the stove, fried side meat, home-made ice cream, ambrosia, butter-roll pie, roasted pecans, and on and on.

She endured many heartaches during her 97 years—the death of her parents, all her brothers and sisters, her beloved daughter Brenda Jane, a son-in-law, her husband, a grandchild and a daughter-in-law.

Proverbs 31:28 say, "Her children shall rise up and call her blessed".

Today, as we her children, other family members, and friends, say our final goodbye to her, we give thanks to God for this special lady, her love to us, and her blessings of 97 years. Lets us not just mourn her passing but celebrate her most remarkable life.

(Written mostly by Joyce (Powell) Henson).

((Note: Another thing Mom did was to write handwritten letters to her children away from home in college, the Army, etc. She was very faithful in keeping in touch with her family. Handwritten letters are increasingly a thing of the past.))

++++++++++++++

HYMN OF PROMISE   BY NATALIE SLEETH, 1986

1. In the bulb there is a flower, in the seed an apple tree

In cocoons, a hidden promise, butterflies will soon be free

In the cold and snow of winter, there's a spring that waits to be.

Chorus: unrevealed until its season, something God alone can see.

2. There's a song in every silence, seeking word and melody,

There's a dawn in every darkness, bringing hope to you and me.

From the past will come the future, what it holds, a mystery

Chorus: unrevealed until its season, something God alone can see.

3. In our end is our beginning, in our time, infinity

In our doubt there is believing, in our life, eternity.

In our death, a resurrection at the last, a victory.

Chorus: unrevealed until its season, something God alone can see.

((Note: We put some items in Mom's casket that had special meanings. For example, needles, thread, a big spoon (castor oil and cooking), a small corner cut from a quilt, pictures of family, etc.))

((Note: When Dad died, she said her last goodbye by caressing his cheek and saying "Good bye Tom." It was a holy moment that opened the floodgates. I followed her example in saying goodbye to her.))

+++++++++++++++++

Clem-eulogy-May2010

EULOGY--CLEMENTS ALTON POWELL   (Born 2
Dec. 1934—Died 9 May 2010)

Clements Alton Powell was born in 1934, during
the Great Depression which helped make him tough and
strong.   Having an older sister Joyce who beat him up
also helped. He was the second of six children born to
R. A. "Tom" and Mina Davis Powell. He was raised in
Marion County, Georgia and lived almost all his life
here. He and his brother Stout were born in the home
now known as "High Pine Lodge".

Living in a rural setting, he developed a life-long
love of animals. He loved hunting, especially quail and
coon hunting and enjoyed training and working with
hunting dogs. He and Stout were known to go frog
gigging. As he grew up, he had many chores such as
milking a cow and even plowing behind a mule.

He also developed many talents, one of which
was being positive and convincing, so much so, that one
cousin said he was grown before he realized all those
things Clem told him were not necessarily factual. He
was an early hero to younger brothers who believed
everything he said or suggested--like bite down on these
crossed smut grass stalks and I will show you a trick--
Clem jerked the stalks and the trick was a mouth full of
smut grass.   Or, don't put a buffalo nickel in your

pocket, the buffalo will do-do in your pocket--little brother Ricky always declined those nickels.

His advice was often good, such as when he told younger siblings to study hard and get a good education. Then again he told one younger brother he had a long tail and Clem kept it pinched off to keep him from being a monkey. When he first heard younger sister Brenda's name, he said "Brindy", that is a cow's name" and he often called her Brindy Cow.

Clem and his cousins could get into things alone but were worse when together. Someone lived on a red clay hill which was easy to drive up in dry weather. When having a gathering there, the cousins would draw well-water and pour on the red clay road and sure enough the late arrivers could not get up the red clay hill. One commented that there could be a drought all over the county but when they came here, that road was always wet and you couldn't get up the hill. Another time the cousins were riding a goat. They challenged one cousin to hang on--the goat ran under the house and the cousin hung on--could hear his head hitting the support beams under the house--bam, bam, bam.

He had many jobs and skills including working at the local "box factory", supervising catching chickens, working in sawmilling for uncles and at a young age for his Dad, running the chicken-feed mill for Dent Poultry, being self-employed as general maintenance worker at Chase Farms, and earlier he served a couple of years in the U. S. Army, and was called back during the Berlin Crisis. He self-taught himself many skills such as carpenter, welder, plumber,

154

electrician, and on and on--he could fix or repair just about anything. He had lots of common sense, good judgment and a sense of fairness throughout his life-- which served him well when he was on the Grand Jury-- he would have made a good judge.

In his early years he enjoyed dating, dancing, partying and so forth. He once remarked "if these shoes could talk, I'd have to burn them up". It was at one of these in Webster County that he met Weone Fussell and he was smitten--they married in October 1954. They lived with or near his parents for a few years until they bought their home near Draneville which was their home for over 45 years. They were blessed with three wonderful children Leta, Alton, and Nenia and later with wonderful children-in-laws Randy Welch, Becky Miller, and Edmond Bassett. Clem adored his grandchildren Mitch and Matt Welch, Clint and Kinsey Powell, and Jason Bassett, and one great-grandchild of Mitch and Samantha, Talan Davis Welch.

Their home gave Clements room to really expand his collection of animals. He now gathered increasing numbers of pigeons, goats, horses, game roosters and hens, ducks, dogs, cats and on and on. The home gave him plenty of room to accumulate stuff and things like lumber, junk cars filled with stuff, cross cut saws, disassembled feed bins, and on and on-- surprisingly, he could always remember where to find a certain item.

Clements always loved children and would take them with him whenever he could and spend time with them. He taught them many of his skills--especially the grandchildren. Somewhere along the line the Grands began calling him "Snuffy" like in Snuffy Smith--he just loved that name.

He loved to tell stories (with a little exaggeration) and pull pranks on people. Here are some examples.

1. He said when in elementary school, there was to be a class play or program. The teacher said, "Clements you are Shadie Davis' grandson I know you can sing--get up there and sing". Clem did. Next day when practicing the program, the teacher had deleted Clem's singing.

2. As told by Clem and his Dad, they and some cousins went coon hunting. They were surprised when a new dog barked up a tree close to the truck. They shined their flashlights in the tree and counted 14 eyes--so there were at least 7 coons--could have been more if some covered up one eye. Ran out of bullets, only got 5 that night. Even Clem's Mom couldn't stomach that tale.

3. Clem and Stout were with their Dad when he spotted a covey of quail. Dad laid the double barreled shotgun on the hood of the truck and fired but a barrel was jammed and it fired out the side shooting off Dad's left forefinger. Dad wrapped his finger in his handkerchief and, so the story goes, noticed he had also shot holes in his truck and killed 3 birds. We still have the shotgun verifying part of the story.

4. Clem was riding a horse who decided to go close to a telephone pole. Clem leaned one way and the horse did too so that Clem crashed into the pole and got a few scrapes and bruises. Don't know if later he had a " two

by four" discussion with that horse but, in spite of that, he kept riding horses all his life.

5. After high school, Clem went to school in Atlanta to learn how to repair televisions. He would ride a bus or hitchhike and call us to come pick him up. Once he called from Butler. Dad told Mom "do not go thru Ellaville" (about 15 miles out of the way). Mom said he told her to GO thru Ellaville (issue never resolved). When finally arriving in Butler, Clem wasn't there--had started walking home. Some say he was a little impatient--he'd call for you to pick him up and if you weren't there when he hung up the phone, he'd start walking. Mom finally caught up with him after he had walked, carrying a suit case, about 12 miles, at Charing. His first words were "What took you so long?"

6. Clem also liked growing things. He had some pretty gourds that he discovered missing. He rushed to find the culprit, only to discover Mom was cooking his prized gourds--after tasting them, she never cooked gourds again.

7. Clem and Stout were quite inventive and talented. Somehow they managed to trap a couple of buzzards at different times. They tied a cow bell to one and for days after you could hear the clang, clang up in the air--which was very funny until Dad discovered the missing cowbell. The other time they tied a Roman candle to the buzzard, who promptly flew into the barn and set it on fire. Fortunately they were able to put out the fire. That ended the buzzard capers--however, it was not the end of fireworks. A neighbor's cow kept coming over until finally Clem decided to do something about it. He

pointed her toward home, tied a Roman Candle to her tail, lit it and turned her loose. Last he saw of her she was giving wild "moos" and headed for home.

8. Clem and Stout did not like milking cows, so they invented skim milk. They would get a couple of inches on milk in the bucket and then fill it up with water. Supposedly, Mom wore out electric churns trying to make butter.

9. When working in sawmilling with an uncle, a mule was dragging a log across a beaver dam and somehow they wound up in the lake underwater. When they got the mule out using the skidder, he was not breathing. The uncle pulled the mule's tongue out so he could hopefully breathe and got the "hands" to jump up and down on the mule trying to resuscitate him. When Clements came on the scene, it struck him so funny that he fell down laughing. The uncle came up and shook his finger in Clem's face saying you ought to get up and help save this mule. Clem said it was the funniest thing he had ever seen and he couldn't even stand up let alone help resuscitate the mule.

10. Another sawmilling story occurred with a different Uncle when they were driving around scouting trees for sawmilling. A large armed moonshiner stopped them asking what they were doing. As they drove away, the uncle said I should have taken that shotgun away from him. Clem slammed on brakes and started backing up. Uncle asked what Clem was doing, Clem said, "I'm going to let you take that gun away from him." Uncle ordered Clem to get them out of there fast.

11. While in the Army, Clem was a tank mechanic. Once while test driving he managed to turn the tank over, a feat not many can--or would--boast about. Also, while in the Army, Clem and a buddy got into an argument with some soldiers from another unit. Fisticuffs followed and fortunately a Sergeant arrived and broke up the scuffle--after Clem and his buddy had laid out 13 of them.

12. Clem had one sergeant who was a bit of a challenge so when he went into town one Saturday night, Clem and his buddies took a jeep apart and reassembled it in the Sarge's room. When he returned, he opened his door, looked in, went back outside to check the building number to be sure he was in the right barracks, came back inside and told all the "sleeping" soldiers, "OK, I get the message, I'll straighten out but when I get back in 2 hours that jeep better be gone."

13. Clem could figure out ways to make life easier. To help pass inspections, he had his locker covered with posters about reenlisting and making the Army a career, after which he passed all inspections. When his enlistment was almost up, a sergeant came running up with papers in hand saying Powell you've got to reenlist. Clem removed the posters and said, I am NOT reenlisting, I'm going home to Georgia.

14. On the way home, they were on a big boat--an ocean cruise all paid for by Uncle Sam. The ship ran into a terrible storm, all the soldiers got seasick. Clem would add lots of unpleasant details which we will omit. The voyage was rough enough to break a hole in the ship. But he gladly endured it to get home.

And so he finally got home to Weone and saw his first born Leta for the first time--what a homecoming.

Being a father did not slow down his sense of humor or his jokes/pranks. One example of this happened when his children were grown and they were all at a Christmas gathering at Granny and Papa Powell's. He started laughing and laughing. When asked what was funny, Clem said "I called out "Hey Ugly" and my wife and both daughters answered".

Another fairly recent example shows how convincing he could be. He rushed into a local store and told the cashier, "Quick give me two $10 bills for this $5, hurry, hurry". She did and he returned a couple minutes later returning the two $10, laughing, and asking if she realized she gave him two $10 bills for his $5. She said, "I thought something wasn't right but you were just so convincing."

Clements and Weone worked hard all their lives to provide for their children, and for several months generously even cared for children of a relative. They loved their children and were so very proud of them.

It wasn't all hard work because Clements and Weone enjoyed going to yard sales, flea markets, "mule days" and on and on. He commented that after retirement, he particularly enjoyed being able for the both of them to go pretty much anywhere they wanted. He even participated in a mule plowing contest at one of the mule days events. He and two other cousins came in first, second, and third--though there was some discussion of who should really have won. At one auction, he bid on some chickens by raising his hand behind Weone's head. When the man said sold to number 17, Weone said, "Wait we didn't bid on that". After hearing Clem's laughter she realized what had happened--and as always, she was a good sport about it.

Clements and Weone also enjoyed fishing. When she wanted to talk he would tell her "sh-h-h you will scare the fish away". He said one reason he liked fishing was he could tell her to be quiet and get away with it.

If any of you have Clements stories or pranks, please share with family members after this service.

In closing, Clements was an honest, hard-working, man devoted to his family whom he loved so much. Some family members like to think that right now, in heaven, he just might be having a great reunion with his wife, parents, sister, uncles, aunts, cousins, grandparents and on and on. He's probably already been asked to repair some things up there, found out where the flea markets are held, and had a great big meal, helped with "feeding up" the animals, and maybe, just maybe, everyone is gathered around him asking him to tell some of those stories--starting with the one about resuscitating that mule. (End) Good bye my hero, my brother Clem.

++++++++++++++

Ricky Powell Eulogy Apr2012

EULOGY-- Ricky Powell was very smart and did well in school and at the Americus Technical School. He worked in Ford Motor Parts section in Americus and Columbus and helped in Buena Vista parts stores also.

When he was little, he often watched TV with his brother Clements and wife Weone who lived about 100 yards away. Just before he started home in the dark, he would call and say "Watch me home"; then he would run very fast and hit the screen door going wide open. One night brother Donnie came in, latched the screen door, and went to the bathroom. The phone rang and a few seconds later Ricky hit the latched screen door, which flung him about 10 or 15 feet back into the yard. Then he crept up to the screen door and yelled for someone to open it. After that, when he called, he would say "Watch me home, and unlock the door". Ricky was always a fast learner.

In his early years, his Mom, Mina Davis Powell, went to work in the Americus shirt factory and Ricky often stayed at the Ford place with his Dad, Roy Alton "Tom" Powell until quitting time. He enjoyed riding with his Dad on the Gasoline truck delivering gas all over Marion County. He was a quick learner and learned how to do many tasks on the Gas truck and around the Ford place, where he got his first paying job.

He was dealt a tough hand with his back surgery in 1973 and resulting problems through the years

Ricky could fix just about anything. Even to the end, he would find a way to do things that others of us who are less talented, would have to call a plumber, carpenter, mechanic or whoever.

He liked working on cars and left several projects he planned to get to one day soon. He liked guns and target practice. He once had a dune buggy that provided lots of fun to him and other family members to ride "up on the hill" and into the woods. He would even let young nieces and nephews "drive" with his close supervision.

Ricky was always honest and kept his word--he was a good friend to many and was generous and often bought things for others.

He loved his parents and brothers and sisters Joyce, Clements, Stout, Brenda Jane, and Donnie and extended families. He was a devoted Caregiver to his Dad and later to his Mom. For example, he visited Her in the nursing home many times, often bringing her things to eat and he would sometimes read cards and letters to her. He put a knife in his Dad's pocket in his casket because "Dad always had a pocket knife on him". Later, this triggered other family members to place special items in their Mom's casket.

Ricky was definitely his Father's son as he was blessed with a liberal dose of Powell stubbornness or lets call it determination. He wanted things done his way. He also was one of the top Powells in the area of being "Curious" (unusual, eccentric). When asked why he did something "unusual", he always had a logical (to him) reason for doing it that way. He also had another Powell--or maybe Davis--trait, if it was not his idea, forget it. He liked westerns and doing crossword puzzles in ink--but not just any color ink, it had to be blue ink from a certain kind of pen.

He recently said, "Dad said "keep something 7 years, if you have not used it, keep it another 7 years". Ricky believed in that--and would probably say "then keep it another 7 years".

Ricky, some family members believe you are now having a great reunion with your parents and other family members and all the other friends and relatives who have gone on before. The remaining family members want you to give them a great big hug from them and to really enjoy your Mom's wonderful cooking of biscuits, chicken pie, fried chicken, pork chop, sweet-potato biscuits, peach puffs, pies, cakes, and on and on. And they want you to help your Dad with some of his many projects like repairing Ford tractors, and to enjoy some of those wonderful stories and jokes they all loved to tell.

In closing, Ricky, you were a kind and generous person who was also a very good person, and your family and friends will miss you. May God bless and keep you as your heavenly family has "watched you Home" for the final time.

++++++++++++++++++++++++++

+++++++++++++++++

SECTION # V.   CHILDHOOD CHRISTMAS MEMORIES

Here are some old memories of Christmas. Shared these with some of my classmates.

+++++++++++(Positive Powell)+++++++++++++

Christmas-Memories-BV-Dec2010

((Hello fellow/former BV-ans. Merry Christmas to everyone. Addressees/families are I hope--Dennis Parker, Donny Finkle, Brenda Henson, Mary Burgin, Annell Powell, Buddy Powell, Benny Hudson, Billy Moore, Rex Harris))

1. Do you remember in the early days (like before computers, and even color tv, cell phones, cable, etc) we were allowed to pop firecrackers. Businesses sold lots of firecrackers at Christmas. It is a wonder I still have all 8 of my fingers. (Just joking).

2. Remember how crowded the city square/businesses were on Saturdays.

3. Mrs. Cleo provided FREE cartoons--nothing but cartoons-- on Christmas Eve morning and we got a free gift--like ice cream or something. I know all the Moms and Dads appreciated her doing that--got us out of the way for an hour or two.

4. The city decorations were lights strung around the courthouse square.

5. We drew names and exchanged gifts at school. Remember I shopped at the Dime Store. One year I gave 2 little glider wooded planes to someone.

6. Remember sometimes in elementary school teachers would cook good smelling popcorn and some kind of syrup and make popcorn balls for the students--so good. They had to be sticky but we loved them.

7. We would go to auditorium and watch a black and white version of "Christmas Carol"--don't think I understood that movie till I was much older. (The ghosts probably scared me).

8. Seems we would be out for Christmas for about 2 weeks or more.

9. Donny F, seems I remember you once got a neat cowboy outfit you wore to school--think I was a little envious.

10. Think our church youth went caroling a few times-- they probably asked me to just lip-sinc the words.

11. Remember one Christmas play --Moms had to make the costumes--where I was lucky to be a toy soldier and someone made wooden rifles for us soldiers. After the play I got to keep my rifle--fought many battles with that gun. (Update--Donny F said he was also a wooden soldier and Mr. Olin Burgin made the wooden guns-- maybe indicating it was first grade since Mrs. Burgin was my first grade teacher.)

12. We would ride around and look at outside decorations. One I really liked was at the end of the street Brenda Henson/Bill Brady lived on. It was in dark blue and think a light shone thru the cut out words of "Holy Night". ((Update: Donny F said the house belonged to Emerson and Eunice Bryson.)

13. Remember if one light on the string on the tree went out they ALL went out.

14. Mom bought a nativity set made of plaster of paris (I think). The wiseman/camel got broken but we glued them back together--mostly. One of the angels got her head knocked off--only glue we had was red fingernail polish. That angel has a "red halo" around her neck even today. When Mom died I got the nativity set and still cherish it today. Gee it must be at least 55 years old.

(Might have gotten it from Montgomery Ward??)

15. We must have had some Christmas programs at church but can't seem to remember any. I do remember Ms. Jessie Belk always gave us (good kids?) a small box-like container of life savers--I liked most but some of the peppermints did not taste good--but I loved getting a present. That was so nice of Mrs. Jessie--hope I thanked her.

16. Think stores decorated their windows.

17. Wells and Welch was open till about 9 pm on Christmas Eve. We would exchange and open presents(not Santa) on Christmas Eve and my sister in law worked at W&W and we had to wait and wait until

she got off work. Later we changed to exchanging gifts on the Sunday before Christmas.

18. As a kid, I liked having many Christmases--one at school, one at church, Christmas Eve, and of course, Santa on Christmas Day.

19. Santa did not wrap presents for us. Santa did wrap presents for my wife when she was little. So--as you might expect--Santa wrapped presents for our children. One year he didn't wrap and our children let us know they wanted Santa to wrap in the future--which he did.

20. Popsicle stick baskets. Somewhere/somehow I learned from someone how to glue popsicle sticks together to make a basket. I would collect them from the playground at recess, wash them and then glue them together to make the basket and painted them--may have even given them as a Christmas present to some unsuspecting family member. Do not remember where or how I learned this--was it at Scouts, or a school project or one of many things learned before/after school bell rang or at ecess/lunch/between classes--that would be a good title for a book--think we could all come up with items to contribute. Paper airplanes, paper hats, etc, --tips about girls, think "sex ed" was handled during those times,

21. My sister Brenda learned (maybe in Home EC???) to use the old paper/cardboard quart milk jugs to make candles then decorated the outside. Think she made a number of candles.

22.(Not a Christmas memory) We would take a half dollar (more silver in them then, so softer) and use a table spoon to tap, tap tap and rotate until edge flattened. Then file out the middle and you had a nice silver ring. (Washers wore out the spoon.) ((Saw "Cool Hand Luke" and a convict was making a half-dollar ring). Was wearing mine when decorating for Jr-Sr prom, sort of skipped the last step coming down and jumped off the step ladder but the ring caught on the ladder and my 120 pounds was held by that ring and my finger for just a second until it came loose after cutting into my finger (still have a little scar). Seeing my own blood made me woozy. Ever since, have been more careful with ladders.

23. Other crafts you remember?

24. I learned how to make pot holders with the little square loom. Can still buy them today. I gave pot holders for gifts. Mom suggest they be thicker so I used double loops--double difficulty in keeping them on the loop frame. But was. fun.

25. (Just added--a Valentine memory). Each class would get a hat box (does anyone remember what a hat box was?) from stores selling hats or from home and would decorate. Think there was a contest to see which was best decorated and it was displayed on the stage (or maybe all were displayed???).

26. Mom would buy me something--like a jacket--for my birthday and would often say "this is part of your Christmas". Made me want a June birthday.

+++++++++++++

SECTION # V—A--- AUTOBIOGRAPHY—HIGH SCHOOL—DONNIE POWELL   Written 1961 and typed 2018   (This was the draft—cannot find the final version or the Senior year Autobiography.)

On the night of December 6, 1944, Dr. B. T. Rainey, delivered a brown-eyed, healthy, handsome, boy to Mr. and Mrs. R. A. Powell. He was I. I was the fifth child of a growing family. My brothers and sisters were Joyce (14), Clements (10), Stout (6), and Brenda Jane (1 and one half).

I was probably making indistinct sounds before my first birthday. But I have been told that I took my first steps a short while before my second birthday. Lazy wasn't I.

Late one night, we moved from the house in which I was born to the one in which we now live, the house which I call "home". I was still small but I did my share, probably by staying out of the way. It thrilled me to move.

In 1948, Joyce married Gene Henson, but I do not remember it. On July 25, 1949, I became an uncle. Connie Henson was my first niece. She was born in an Americus hospital and I remember visiting her.

Many of my pre-school playmates were cousins of mine. There would be parties, reunions, or just Davis or Powell gatherings and I always enjoyed these a lot.

Brenda Jane started to school a year before me and I was left without a playmate. (She will graduate a year before I do, but I won't mind that.) I often waited for her and was usually glad to have her home.

I visited an uncle of mine and he gave me a shy feist dog that I had made friends with. I named him Rusty and he helped fill the vacant moments. We were the best of pals. One morning he didn't come when I called. I discovered that he had died. Stout buried him but many a day I mourned for Rusty and I kept flowers on his grave but gradually other things occupied my time and I found other companions.

Christmas was one of the big events of the year. We would go to see the cartoons at the theater and spend the long day waiting for night when Santa Clause would come. Then one Christmas Day, Brenda Jane told me that she had not been asleep when Santa had come. Knowing this took a lot of fun out of Christmas, but it is all a part of growing up.

Another big event was the family Fourth of July barbecue, which was held at one of my uncle's house. After lunch, everyone went swimming. I remember that I was playing in the pond where the older boys were swimming. I got too far out and Stout yelled for me to watch out because there was a deep hole there. Well, I heard him but he was just a little late because the next thing I saw was bubbles in front of my face and muddy water all around me. Fortunately, Clements went under water and came up with me. It only took a second for me to get my lungs filled with air again and when I did, I let everyone know that I had been scared "half to death". I stayed away from the deep water the rest of the day.

I have little memory of my grandparents because they were all dead , except for Granddaddy Powell, before I was old enough to remember. His wife had died and he married Mrs. Pleona D. Pierce, a widow. I remember seeing the car with the tin cans and signs on it. Granddaddy Powell was very kind. He would let us help him do things and he would give us coins for helping him.

When Granddaddy Powell became ill, we went to stay with him late into the nights. Then one morning, Brenda Jane told me that he had died. I could not believe it.

It was very difficult to attend my Granddaddy Powell's funeral. I had one last look at the last of my grandparents. He was a very dear friend and he had departed leaving a vacant spot to be filled by my family and friends.

For several years, I attended the Frist Methodist Church of Buena Vista. When Stout joined the First Baptist Church of Buena Vista, I left the Methodist church and attended the Baptist.

Most people start to school at the age of six but since my birthday is in December, I started when I was five and I suppose I was the youngest in the class. My first grade teacher was Mrs. Burgin. Our class was the first to begin in the new school building.

Teaching me to read was probably very difficult because even today my reading is slow and careless. I also learned to print in the first grade.

During this year (1950), Mother and Joyce gave my class a surprise party which we all enjoyed.

About this time I had asthma attacks. To prevent the attacks I was given short by doctors. They helped but did not cure. I began to fear doctors and dentists because often they gave shots. Only recently have I partially overcome my fear of dentists and doctors.

My second grade teacher was Mrs. Cook. It was her difficult task of teaching me to write. She made it easy by telling little stories about each letter and thus we could remember the letter by the story. ((Just remembered one—the letter "r" was a man with a bag on his back.))

We were allowed several parties, which we enjoyed more than the rest of school. This remained true for the rest of Elementary School.

The summer months were short and now forgotten but they helped build enthusiasm for the next year as was true for the rest of school.

The third grade had but one teacher, Mrs. Singleton, so naturally she was my teacher. I remember very little that happened in the third grade.

On June 4, 1953, Ricky, my little brother, was born ending about eight years of me being the youngest in the family.

My fourth grade teacher was Mrs. Moss. In this grade, I took my first six weeks tests and mid-term tests.

One day a friend offered me a ride on the back of his bicycle. I accepted and after we got to going pretty fast my foot got hung in the wheel. The wheel skinned my foot, but I thought it was just terrible. It hurt pretty badly but I got over it and I am not afraid of a bicycle.

In those days if a person had an average of at least ninety in a subject, he would not have to take the Final Test in that subject. I was exempt from most if not all my subjects and when the tests were being given, I was allowed to be absent.

In Sunday School, I was promoted to the Junior Class with Mr. Bob Swint as my teacher.

I passed the summer as usual, by swimming, working a little, fishing, and reading. I read mostly adventure stories, animal stories, sports, especially football, and biographies of famous people. I enjoyed reading even though I was slow at it.

Mrs. McCorkle was my fifth grade teacher. There were two fifth grades in 1954/55 because the County Schools had been consolidated. Because of this, I met George Grier and we have been friends ever since. Ernest Hart and I were always close and so we three became close friends.

It was till customary at the Halloween Carnival to have Kings and Queens (of High School) and Prince's and Princess's (Elementary School). A King and Queen and Prince and Princess of the Carnival were chosen.

Diana Brannon and I were chosen to represent the Fifth grades in the carnival. Even though we worked very hard, we did not get enough votes to become the Prince and Princess of the Carnival.

On October 24, 1954, Clements married Weone of Webster County. I attended the wedding but knew very little about what was happening.

The Easter Egg hunt of Mrs. McCorkle's Fifth grade was held at my house. I was very glad to have it at my house.

In the spring, there was a revival at my church and I joined. I was baptized on Easter Sunday of 1955.

Mr. B. G. Moores, band director gave us flute lessons. Having no musical talent. I made the first "C" (70-80) I had ever made on a report card. Because of this, I did not consider Mr. Moores as one of my favorite teachers.

During the summer of 1955, I learned how to swim. The year before I had been able to swim a few strokes by in 1955 I was able to swim much farther— say twenty feet.

I was assigned to Miss Brady's sixth grade. The boys were allowed to go to the gymnasium if they wanted to I went for a short time. I thought Coach McGlaun too stern and so, like a baby, I quit. Maybe the asthma attacks were partially to blame.

Asthma made me miss at least one day every year. I would be sick with it all night and be physically unable to attend school the next day.

In 1956, we moved to a chicken farm about two miles outside the city limits. There were three chicken houses and we raised chickens for market. Since the dust caused me to have asthma attacks, I could only work with the chickens until they were about three weeks old.

I disliked the farm mainly because it just was not home. There was a pond near the house and I often went fishing.

In Sunday School, I was promoted to Intermediate Class with Mr. Ed. Brooks my teacher for two years.

My Seventh Grade teacher was Mrs. Wooldridge.

On Jan 6, 1957, Stout married Shirley Hall of Marion County.

February 14, 1957, (Valentine's Day) is the date of my second niece's birthday. Her name is Peggy Joyce Henson, daughter of Mr. and Mrs. T. E. Henson.

Previous seventh grades were allowed to go to Atlanta and visit Stone Mountain and Grant's Park. But when I came, the rules are naturally changed. We got to go to the Little White House and Ida Carson Calloway Gardens. Since I was involved, it did not rain, it poured. Even so, we enjoyed trip.

Clements entered the United States Army in March 1957, for two years. We missed him very much. He occasionally got to come home a week-end until he was sent to Germany.

As the end of school year approached, the two Seventy Grades presented plays as a sign of farewell to Elementary School. Everyone in Mrs. Wooldridge's section participated and at the end of our play, the valedictorian of our class gave a speech which Mrs. Wooldridge had prepared. By much hard work which resulted in good grades, I was given the privilege of presenting the speech. But at the time, I didn't consider it a privilege, but rather a task. I received a perfect attendance certificate, breaking a six-year losing streak.

Since we would start having one hour classes, in Junior High, we had to arrange a pre-school schedule for the next year.

In the summer of 1957, the Royal Ambassadors (R. A.'s) a Baptist boys organization was organized in our church. I joined and will never regret joining.

In Junior High, as in the rest of High School, we had home rooms and hour classes and not in one room all day, as in Elementary School. Naturally, confusion resulted. My schedule went at follows. First period—Study hall in the Library   Second   period—Study hall in Miss Lovelace's (Science teacher) room. Third period—Arithmetic under Miss Lancaster. Fourth period—English under Mrs. Benson. Fifth period—Health under Mrs. Benson. Sixth period—Vocational Agriculture under Mr. Beard.   I really had it easy with a schedule like that, but I did not realize this until the next year.

Rhonda Powell, daughter of Mr. and Mrs. Stout Powell, another niece to me, was born October 15, 1957.

The eighth grades elected a Who's Who just like the seniors. I was elected "Best Student" and "Most

Likely to Succeed" and "Most Courteous. This was a great honor at the time.

In the eighth grades, I tried for the F. F A. Land Judging Team but failed to make it. Our team got second in the district.

I joined the Boy Scouts during my eighth grade of school. Mr. Beard was the Scoutmaster. I was not an active Boy Scout and I learned little.

The FFA and FHA Chapters attended the FFA/FHA Camp above Covington, GA in July 1958. I was in the group that went. This being new and different, I enjoyed it. There was dancing, sports, handcrafts, and many other things.

Since Brenda Jane was at the time better than me at playing checkers, and the best we had at camp, she played for our chapter and won. We were good only at checkers as is shown by the fact that we were second from the bottom in sports.

On July 24, 1958, I attended Youth Rally Day in Columbus. We had a lot of fun. We toured Fort Benning, Tom Houston peanuts, Royal Crown Cola bottling company, and Well's Dairy. We also went to a movie and then returned home.

Verinda Leta Powell, daughter of Mr. and Mrs. Clements Powell was born on August 2, 1958 while her father was still in Germany. Leta is my fourth niece.

I was elected Ambassador in Chief (Same as President) of the Intermediate Royal Ambassadors.

Mrs. Pryor was my Freshman home room teacher. I was elected class president. I did my best but I just did not have the ability to be president. My subjects were: First period—Algebra under Coach McGlaun. Second period—Vocational Agriculture under Mr. Beard. Third period—Geography under Mr. B. G. Moores. Fourth period—General Science under Miss Lovelace. Fifth period—English under Mrs. George McGlaun. Sixth period—Study hall in the Library.

I was a member of the Library Club, FFA, and after Christmas, when the Co-Ed-Y was organized, I joined.

The dislike or fear of Coach McGlaun and Mr. Moores was still within me. But after having classes under them, I admired and respected them both. I did not want Mr. Moores to leave.

When time came to pick the Land Judging team, I put in an extra effort and go on the team. We won second in the district, missing first by one point. ((Competition was in Tifton at ABAC.))

Clements returned from Germany and was dismissed from active duty in the Army in March 1959.

To my joy, we left the chicken farm and returned "home" in April 1959.

In the summer of 1959, I again attended FFA and FHA Camp at Covington, GA. This time I could best Brenda in checkers so I played for our Chapter. I won the championship but again we were on the bottom with points. Checkers took up most of my time and I had little time to make new friends.

Members of the Royal Ambassadors of our church attended Camp Pinnacle at Clayton GA. Joe Alexander, the pastor's son, and I were the two Intermediates that went. We played volleyball, basketball, softball, went swimming, climbed Mount Pinnacle, descended into Tallulah Gorge, made new friends, had religious inspirations, and we did many other things. ((That was my first trip to the mountains and I am still awe struck by them; on my last trip from top of Blackrock Mountain, I said "Wow! God. Wow.")

That summer of 1959, we went to Camp Friendship, between Buena Vista and Americus, for an overnight camping trip, a time or two. ((Slept indoors on bunks.))

Miss Lovelace was my Sophomore home room teacher. I was elected class reporter. Sponsors were Miss Lovelace and Mrs. McGlaun. First period—World History under Mrs. Lowe. Second period—Algebra II, under Mrs. Lowe. Third period—Study hall in the Library. Fourth period—English under Mrs. Garrett. Fifth period—Typing I under Miss White. Sixth period—Biology under Miss Lovelace.

I was a member of the Future Business Leaders of America, Coed-Y and a Library Assistant and in the Library Club.

Cheerleading ((for basketball)) looked easier than I thought, and I just had to go see the off games and I gave it a try. By "hook or by crook" I became a cheerleader. I was often and rightly called a "sissy" because only a "sissy" would take those insults.

I saw our boys lose only five out of twenty-six games and our girls lose only four out of twenty-six games. Then our boys entered the tournaments. They won three straight, the last being an upset over Richland. The game that decided whether or not our boys would go to the state tournaments in Macon, GA was played against Lee County. Our boys lost by three points. It was heart breaking.

Our girls won two games and a shot at trying to go to the state tournaments. They played Fort Gaines. They played their hearts out and perhaps their best game of the season but luck was with Fort Gaines so our girls did not get to go to State either.

Typing was one of my favorite subjects, I suppose because it was new and different. But I could not make ninety or better in it.

When quail season opened, I went along with my brothers a few times and "got the fever". I bought a 16 gauge Ithaca pump shotgun on the installment plan ((from the old Western Auto Store)). Though I did not kill many quail, four to be exact, I still enjoyed hunting very much.

In December, our Pastor moved away, and Rev. Moore became our pastor. I met Billy Moore in Sunday School and we have been good friends ever since.

During football season, boys from town would play games of football on vacant lots. Being much enthused about football, I seldom missed a game.

On January 28, 1960, my first nephew Alton Powell was born to Clements and Weone.

We played basketball and baseball during their respective seasons.

When summer came after a very long school year, Billy Moore and I attended Camp Pinnacle. It was a lot of fun because there was a lot more organization. ((When Billy's Dad and brother Tommy came to pick us up at Camp Pinnacle, Tommy announced that the school had burned.))

The summer passed all too quickly. Time was passed in the usual way. Only this year, I overcame my fear of a baseball and tried to play. I had a fear of thunderstorms, large animals such as cows and horses, which my Father had produced. He would read things caused or done by the above incidents in which a person had been killed or hurt. Well it has taken me a long time but I am gradually overcoming that fear.

((11th Grade)) Mr. Simpson, the new Science Teacher and Mr. Moss were my Junior sponsors. The subjects I took and the periods are: First period—American History under Mrs. Lowe. Second period—Plane Geometry under Coach McGlaun. Third period, English under Mrs. Garrett. Fourth period—Business math under Coach McGlaun. Fifth period—Chemistry under Mr. Simpson. Sixth period—Basketball Manager under Coach McGlaun.

I joined the FFA—Mr. Moss said I could join one year without taking Vocational Agriculture. I also joined FBLA, Coed-Y, which I served as the Inter-Club relations Committee Chairman, and the Library Club in which I served as Library assistant whenever called upon. I was "tapped" in assembly by the Senior Beats which offered me membership in the club. A person at any school has to have an overall average of ninety and be a Junior to be eligible for membership. I was initiated into the Beta Club, along with the rest of the Junior Beta's. I had to come dressed as a cigarette girl and I had to sell candy cigarettes at a pep rally held that day.

Since I had a free period in my schedule, I tried out for the boys basketball manager and being the only candidate, I became the manager. It is a big undertaking for one person but I thought I did a good job. ((At end of year, Coach complimented me by saying I was the best manager ever.)) I received a basketball jacket and transportation to all off games including the tournaments.

Our boys had the greatest team in the history of our school. We lost only one game during the regular season. Then won three straight in the tournaments. We played Jakin, the winner would go to State. We won, but were not satisfied. We won first place in our region by beating Edison the following night. We went to Macon for the State Tournaments on March 8, 1961 and played Yatesville, winning by about eight points. The next day we played Midville, again winning by about eight points. Then we met "lucky" Ludowici. We were "off" and they were "hot". Even so we gave them the game of the tournament, losing by one point. This was a heart breaker. We should have won but the luck was with Lucowici. We left Macon, Saturday morning. When we got seven miles from town, there were cars all over the place with horns blowing and people shouting they were just as proud of team as they could be. I almost cried for I had called them unloyal supporters which they definitely were not. I feel that I had a small part in their accomplishments.

The girls had a rather poor season losing about eight games. But they did fine in the tournaments. They played their best game against Leslie and upset them. Then were unable to beat the Lucky Lee County team. Our girls were not "hot" but Lee County was. Despite this, we gave them one tough fight losing by three little points. And missing another chance at State.

In November 1960, I was elected Third District West President of the Georgia Association of Library Assistants. I thought this would be a great task but now I am looking forward to it as a challenge to my ability. I am sure I can handle the job with help from the other officers of our district.

In January 1961, I passed my Operator's License Test (I got my Driving License), which made me very happy.

Since I was sixteen, I had to purchase a hunting license so that I could go hunting, quail mostly.

I was elected Chaplain of the Co-Ed-Y Club for the school year 1961-1962. I am looking forward to giving this office the best I have.

On May 5, 1961, Danny Lewis Powell, my second nephew, was born to Mr. and Mrs. Stout Powell. Now all my married brothers and sister have two children each.

The big event of Junior year is the Junior-Senior Prom which will be held May 12, 1961. Our theme is "The Old South". ((I will have the privilege of escorting Joyce McCorkle.(this was struck through for some reason).))

I am looking forward to my Senior year. I intend to take Senior Math, English, American Government, Physics, Study Hall and Typing II. I will have a lot to do but with God's help I can do it.

Donnie Powell

++++++++++++++++

SECTION # VI. BASKETBALL MEMORIES
Basketball-Memories-1960s-Dec07

BASKETBALL MEMORIES OF THE 1960'S—DIM AND DISTANT---by Donnie Powell—Dec 2007

Background: The following are some dim, distant, and vague memories (not in any order) of basketball in the early 1960's in Buena Vista, Georgia a rural, small town. Please pardon if memory got the facts wrong. This was before integration and also when the world was simpler and more trusting and sportsmanship reigned. Our tiny gym was built in the Great Depression by the Workers Progress Association (WPA). Our classification of teams was "C" or smallest towns back then. When there was to be a game in town, it was "the" event and the gym was packed. Back then smoking was allowed and the gym was not air conditioned so by game time, it was very smoky and hot. But the teams were well supported and cheering often "raised the rafters". The memories below are usually either 1961 or 1962 seasons.

1. In 1961, I was the team "manager" (water boy) and got to see a number of things "behind the scenes" not otherwise available to fans. The team was Marion County High School, with colors of Black, Red and White with a mascot of Red Foxes. (Marion County is named after Francis Marion a Revolutionary war hero known as the "Swamp Fox"). In 1961, Marion County High went to the State playoffs for the first time— awesome experience; they lost in the semi-finals. In 1962, they won the State Class C basketball championship.

2. One game in BV in 1961 (I think against Talbotton) , Coach George McGlaun, substituted all 5 of those playing whenever someone made a mistake. It was total substitution 5 in and 5 out. It was difficult for the team to develop a rhythm or get on a streak—but they won anyway. Afterward, one key player said something like, "Boy, we really stunk and showed our rear ends tonight".

186

3. In a game in Georgetown, a fairly weak team that year, at the end of the first quarter, we were ahead so Coach sent the first team to the showers to dress and then watch the rest of the game from the stands. The second team was quite good too and was able to keep or even extend the lead.

4. In one game, we had a slight lead and Lanier Roberts missed a couple of shots instead of "freezing" the ball. Although we won, Coach told Lanier he should not have taken the shots but froze the ball. In a later game in Butler, a similar situation arose and Lanier took and made a couple of shots that put the game out of reach. After the game, Coach went over and shook Lanier's hand, in effect saying this time Lanier was right.

5. In the sub-region playoffs of 1962 in Preston/Webster County, we were behind Preston and then the Foxes "got hot" and really played great. During one time out, Mrs. Jessie Belk jumped on the edge of the court and did a little dance waving her arms in the air. We finally got ahead in the third quarter and stayed ahead. In the finals against Richland the Foxes finally got hot in the fourth quarter and won the game I believe by one point. There was standing room only and they had us packed in everywhere, even on the stage, where I was. Leading by one point, we got the ball but believe it was Barney Miller who at first was going to throw the ball in and then put the ball down to let someone else throw it in but the ref gave the ball to Richland who got off one last shot that just missed—whew. We went wild. In the trophy ceremony, the Principal for Webster County said, "For three quarters last night, they (Marion

Co) almost didn't do it and tonight for four quarters, they almost didn't do it"…But we did do it.

6. In the 1961 regional playoffs, we played Edison for the championship (I think in Edison). At a 15 year reunion, Coach said he told Arthur Powell (my cousin) on the bus going to the game, that he would have a difficult time guarding Edison's center, that he was very good. He said Arthur played a great game. Years later, Arthur told me that in the Edison game, Coach had told him their center was good and Arthur said "But I got him". He played a great game and it was close all the way with Marion winning by, I think, 45-39. Our last 2 points were when Brownie Benson was at the free throw line—he looked up at the score board and had a big smile—and sank both free throws. I was saying don't smile, they could get the rebound and get a quick shot—but even I smiled and yelled when he sank the free throws. This team went to State for the first time ever. At the end of the semi-final game, we were behind by one or two points, when our player was fouled while shooting. He missed the first shot and the Ludiwici coach called time out—first time I ever saw the time out used to "ice" a player—it worked, we lost. In the locker room, there were a lot of tears. On the way home, between Butler and BV, I noticed Myron Wells and someone in a car on the side of the road and they passed us. Realized later, he beat us to town to let everyone know we were coming. There were a lot of people around the town square clapping and shouting to greet their team. (No cell phones back then for Myron to use.)

7. In 1962, our boys again went to state in Macon. I was in Atlanta at a Beta Club meeting but along with Billy Moore, got a ride home with Mr. Arthur J. Benson, the Superintendent who went to the game on the way home. Forgot who we played but we won. One picture in the Macon Telegraph –Atlanta Constitution showed Bobby Wooldridge, a guard flying through the air and blocking an opponent's lay-up—a great picture of a great block. Another play, was when the first half clock was about to expire, and Brownie shot from beyond mid-court and made the shot but the ref said he "traveled" or took one too many steps before shooting (ref wrong again). That was the year Perry, in Class B, won I think about 35 games in a row—we could have beaten them. When the team returned home, there was a brief celebration in the gym and Mr. Benson dedicated the new gym to this 1962 Championship team. What a great victory for our team, school and entire community. ((For my 50th class reunion, I went to Mercer library and found some write ups and the above picture which I put in a notebook to our classmates. Bobby and John saved the trophies that had been thrown away.))

8. In 1961, we played in Vienna (Class B) and we trailed. We got to within 7 points but could not catch them—one of the 1 or 2 games we lost that year. After the game, Brownie said, when we got to within 7 points, I thought we were going to catch them.

9. In 1959 or 60, in the sub-region playoffs in Lumpkin (?) against Lumpkin, we were in a close game. Our center, Boyce Miller, had 4 fouls and Coach put Freshman or Sophomore Brownie into the game and he

did great. At the second half tipoff, Coach put Calvin Brown (he is about 6 foot 5 inches) in to jump the tipoff. Good thinking. Brownie went back into the game shortly. We lost the game but was a good game.

10. Do not remember any of the sub-region playoffs being played in BV. Maybe their gyms were bigger?

11. In 1961, as the team manager, one job was to keep the players' valuables in a gym bag. Everyone just put their stuff in and later took it out—honor system. At the end of the first game, one player said I'm missing some money—someone must have taken too much. After that, instead of just dumping their valuables in the bag, I had them put their stuff in separate paper bags with numbers written on the bag (later put the player's number on their bag). Stapling the bags ensured nobody would lose anything. Had to buy a lot of paper bags, but never had any more missing items.

12. In 1961, once at practice after school, Bobby Wooldridge stayed for extra practice and he'd shoot one ball and I would throw him another so he could get in lots of shots. He finally got tired saying "my arms are about to fall off". Someone once asked Bobby if the game noise bothered him and he said he did not even hear the noise. He and the other players were so focused they didn't hear the racket. ((At our 50th reunion, Bobby said he and close friend John (both guards) would confer at mid-court. Everyone thought they were discussing plays but often would share something like— did you see that pretty girl on the second row.))

13. In 1961 or 1962 practices, Coach ran a "full court press" drill, because we had lost to a full court press the year before. That drill was something. The second team pressed the first team as hard as they could, with no fouls being called, it was an awesome workout. It worked, because the press never worked on the Foxes after those drills.

14. In 1960 or 1961, in Harris County (Class B), the Foxes started playing very well in the second half. Their lead grew and grew. On the bus, Arthur Boyette said, Coach said, if the lead gets down to 10, call a time out; later he said, if the lead gets down to 15, call a time out, etc. On the bus, Coach told the team they had played a great game.

15. In Plains, the Foxes were playing well and near the end of the game the Foxes were approaching 100 points. Plains decided to freeze the ball to keep that from happening—one of the few times the losing team freezes the ball.

16. In Leslie/DeSota GA, their Union High School, had a brother and sister (Watts) who were the stars for their respective teams (I believe she could have played on any boys team). The Marion girls won their game and that was one of Union's girls teams few defeats. When they came to Marion County, they had their game faces on and played great, defeating our girls—one of our rare losses. In one game in Marion County, she missed one free throw on purpose to try to get the rebound. In a boys game at Union, they set up a double screen play for Watts to shoot over and it was practically impossible to defense. Think we won. Watts later played for

Georgia Southwestern (Junior) College in Americus and he was good in college.

17. Our school Annual (The Vistan '62) said the school was closed due to flu epidemic from 19-23 Jan. 62. Seems we lost a game just before that and had to cancel or delay a game, which was good because the Foxes were down at the time—and some team members were probably sick.

18. In those days, the girls team had 3 guards that played only defense and 3 forwards that played only offense. (I am not making this up.) They each played on only half the court. When one team scored, the other team got the ball in the center of the court. In one game, with time almost out for a quarter, Nell(?) Welch got the ball right after the other team scored, she had no time so just flung it at her goal, and rang it, but score did not count because she had to pass the ball first—but what a shot. In one game, Marion's girls were so far ahead that Coach swapped the guards and forwards—not much scoring from players who never practiced shooting.

19. My sister, Brenda Powell, was about 5 feet 2 inches tall but very, very competitive. When shooting free throws, she would line up away from the foul line and then "launch" herself and the ball at the goal with a long follow- through. She practiced a lot and was quite good. She wore number 30 and to psyche herself up for games would sit in front of her mirror and say "Number 30 is going to be hot tonight"—and she often was. (Somewhere, maybe at camp, the Principal from Preston told her he remembered the way she lined up to take her

free throws. She was surprised he remembered her.) She loved the game.

20. On the weekend, Coach would give some of us the key to the gym to go play some basketball. It was great to play in the gym. One time we found some pipes frozen with water spewing near the back door. We told Coach and he fixed it while we played—guess he was also the plumber. A classmate Travis Watts was not on the team but was good and had an unusual jump shot above his right shoulder. I sometimes guarded him but could never block his shot. He had a habit of getting the rebound (we played half court), dribbling to the corner, whirling with hardly a look around and firing his shot at the goal. One time when guarding him, I timed it perfectly and jumped to block his shot just before he whirled around. In mid-air he realized I would block his shot and he was such an athlete with such quick reflexes that he passed the ball off in mid air. Shucks, I wanted to block that shot. Not being tall, I didn't get a lot of rebounds. When an opponent got a rebound, he usually dribbled the ball; so I rushed behind him and often stole the ball away. I could not shoot very well but I hustled.

21. Coach had some warm-up exercises for the boys to do before practice. One was to jump rope—just like boxers. It was funny watching the boys learning to jump rope, which they did quickly—I had learned as a kid. Another exercise was to do pushups on their finger tips to strengthen their hands and fingers to hold on to the rebounds. The exercises seemed to help. At the beginning of the season, he would have the boys and

girls run the bleacher seats—up and down, up and down, really strengthened their legs and stamina.

22. Donnie Comment: Those were the days when basketball was basketball and sportsmanship was almost universal. No dunking and dancing like today. A return to real basketball could occur if the goals were raised to say 15 feet—this would negate the requirement to be giants—all would have to be able to shoot not just dunk.

23. Manager duties included having about 10 practice or warm up basketballs (carried in 2 green canvas bags) available for the team. Forgot where we stored those 2 bags on the school bus on away games, probably in the overhead shelf. Another duty was to have water in a quart jar for the players during time outs and between quarters. Everyone drank out of the same jar back then—it's a wonder everyone didn't get sick. After the team got hot and scored a lot of points in one game, a man asked what I had in the jar. Another job (not sure it was as manager or just a "helper") was to chart the shots. Each time someone shot, we would list his number in the approximate place on the chart, which had a diagram of the basketball court. If he rang the shot, we circled it. When the games got exciting it would be difficult to list all the shots. Don't remember anyone having 20 points on field goals with only 3 shots but am sure some shots were not recorded.

24. My older brother Clements Powell graduated in 1953 and I believe he was a manager one year. I do remember he played in a playoff game that my Dad took us to—we were way ahead and he got to play. The next

night we lost and Clem did not get to play—bet we would have won if he had played.

25. The "Vistan '62" said there was a donkey basketball game Dec 9, 1961. The donkey game is a rather dumb concept where people ride a donkey while trying to also play basketball. It was quite a fun spectacle. Donkeys do not always do what you want or go where you want them to. There was a good turnout and lots of laughs.

26. The BV Methodist Church played the Baptist Church—seems only the older members played—do not remember who won. As a Baptist then, we had analyzed the various players and were convinced we would win easily. However, we had not counted on the effects of age and lack of practice—our Baptist oldsters did pretty well but they weren't spring chickens as we thought. We all had fun and good fellowship (maybe we did win.)

27. In 1961 (or maybe 62?) , John Dent was one of our better players but broke his right hand (perhaps playing touch football) and could not play in a number of games.

28. In about 1958, in one girls game, I noticed an opposing player had her foot on the foul line as she shot. I shouted out, "her foot's on the line". The ref did not see it on the first shot but when I shouted it for the second foul shot, he did notice and waved off the point. So in a way, I prevented the opposing team from scoring a point, not as a player but as a fan. Oh, when the ref waved the point off, the opposing lady glared over in my direction—you should have seen that look. I was glad

she did not know it was me—could have been someone around me. Whew.

29. One day some of the players were horsing around after practice and one broke the one and only light bulb in the dressing room. He immediately said, "Don't tell Coach I will fix it." When the next home game (at night of course) rolled around, Coach came to the manager (me), gave me some money, and said go get a light bulb for the dressing room. He asked, "Did you know about the bulb being out?" I said (remember I'm scared of Coach), "Yes, but Calvin said he would fix it." He sent me on my way without a public beating. Before he could put the new bulb in, he had to get the old broken one out, without getting shocked, which he did. Didn't realize Coach had to be such a handy man. Also learned that sometimes people either lie or forget (or both) and that things do not fix themselves. When I confronted Calvin the next day, he said, "Oh it is fixed now"—he didn't seem to mind that I was in trouble with Coach— another lesson learned—if someone is in trouble, no one cares, unless they are the ones in trouble.

30. After the game has progressed and finally a foul is called on an opponent, a favorite yell of a fan is "He's been doing it all night, ref". The boys game started with a jump ball and one night our guy was fouled while getting the tipped ball. Being somewhat of a smart alec, I yelled "He's been doing it all night ref." (Well, the game was only 2 second old, he had in fact been doing it all night.)

31. Sometimes the band would be at the game. I do not remember if they played at half time or what. I

remember them being there because (before being a manager), I had a special seat near the concession stand where I would sit to avoid as much smoke as I could, and when the band was there, the drummers stored some of their instruments in my seat and I did not outrank a drum.

32.   The concession stand was a money making proposition for the class or group that worked in it. Usually things were donated by the class so all the money taken in was pure profit. It was a very busy place and quite crowded—but those were some of the best hot dogs.

33.   The cheerleaders were great. At half time they would lead in the singing of the Alma Mater. Still remember some of it—"On a hill in western Georgia, wind the corridors, boys and girls of Marion County...) That was the only time the gym got quiet during the game. There were often two maybe three or more generations of Marion County graduates in the gym singing the song. (Once, the band leader, Mr. Morse, heard me "singing" the Alma Mater (or something) and suggested I lip sync—having heard myself "sing", I have to agree with him—and to this day, often just move my lips.)

34.   In one home game with Preston visiting us, they were ahead late in the game. We almost never lost at home. Finally, the Foxes got hot and pulled the game out by only a point or two. One of the Preston player's parting shot in the dressing room was, "we'll see you in the playoffs". After he left, one of our players said, I hope not.

35. Another Manager's duty was to use a wide (about 4 feet) broom, mop to sweep or clean the court. I learned how to do that pretty quickly—Coach was quite a motivator. But strangely, never could learn how to sweep at home.

36. In 1961 at the State playoffs in Macon, we stayed in the Dempsey Hotel which was probably the first Hotel for several of us. One manager task after each game was to take the first team uniforms down the street to a cleaner. (Guess the other options were to wear dirty uniforms or wash them out by hand in the Hotel—think the Dempsey would have frowned on the latter). The uniform in those days was about 6-8 inches above the knee, unlike today's uniforms which are 6-8 inches below the knee. Don't know where the money came from for the hotel, cleaning bills, etc.—probably from the generous people of Marion County.

37. Coach (as state champ?) named Brownie to the South All Star game in 1962. When asked, Brownie suggested player (Peek??) from Edison also be named. Later Brownie said Lee Martin from Perry was very good, especially at passing; said after a couple of practice games between first and second team, some changes were made because the second team won both games. Do not know if he got to play much in the all star game but it was quite an honor for him.

(22 Dec 07—that's all for now.)

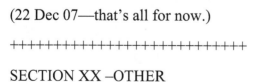

SECTION XX –OTHER

.1.   LIFE-CHANGING EVENT BY ONE OR MORE
TEACHERS   By Donnie Powell   June 2012
(Powell-life-changing-June2012)

Marion County High School, Buena Vista GA, Class of
1962 just had its 50th reunion which prompted a lot of
reminiscing, thoughts, stories, etc. After the reunion, it
dawned on me that one or more teachers had a hand in a
life-changing event for me.

My academic grades were good and I had
dreams of college but my parents were not financially
able to pay for my college education.

In the mid 1960's, to help alleviate a teacher shortage,
the State of Georgia provided scholarships which paid
for room, board, books, etc., as long as the student
maintained a B average and paid back the loan by
teaching in Georgia for three years.   Do not remember
how I learned of this scholarship but I am sure some
teacher took the time to get an application form,
encouraged me to apply, and probably gave me a good
recommendation.   I happily received the scholarship,
completed 2 years at Georgia Southwestern (then) Junior
College and graduated from Georgia Southern in 1965
with a teaching degree in math.   I taught math for 3
years in Albany, Georgia and then obtained a civil
service position in civilian personnel.

In looking back, I realized without that teacher's
scholarship, I would not have gone to college,

not become a teacher, not met my wife, not qualified for
the civil service position in civilian personnel which
resulted in a good career, not have been the father of my

wonderful children, and so on. What job(s) I would have landed without college is only speculation but would not have been as rewarding, and whom I might have married (if any) I cannot guess.

The light bulb came on. Some wonderful teacher(s) went out of his/her way to help me go to college—a life-changing event that I only just recently recognized. Wish I could remember who and I hope I thanked them.

++++++

NOTE: I want to thank Dennis Parker whose tribute to one of his teacher's got me to thinking about the impact on my life of un-remembered teacher(s) who steered me toward a teacher's scholarship and how different my life would have been had this not happened. Though my experience is far less dramatic than Dennis', it was still a life-changing event. I suspect many classmates have been shaped and helped by our teachers, often in un-remembered ways.

+++++++++++

+++++++++++

2. MR. MOSS AND STOUT

Mr. L. K. Moss was the Vocational Agriculture teacher for many years. One of his favorite sayings was "I said all that to say this". When my older brother Stout got married in the middle of his senior year, he dropped out and started to work. Mr. Moss went the extra mile--he pulled Stout's records, came to Mom and explained that Stout had enough credits to graduate and get his diploma—all he had to do was complete a test (or something). Stout did and got his diploma which may well have helped him in future jobs—certainly it helped his confidence and feelings about himself. Mr. Moss did not have to do what he did, but he, like all our teachers, was not just a good teacher but a good person who cared for his students and helped people. I say all that to say this, "Thank you Mr. Moss for being a good, caring teacher and a Christian who put his faith to work in helping Stout."

++++

3. BRENDA JANE POWELL—MEMORIES OF HER By Donnie Powell (written in 11/81 and retyped Jan 2018)

((Some of these are in my "book" "When I Was a Boy in Georgia" and from these memories of Brenda came the book.))

.1. She and I both went to FFA/FHA camp two or three times. She was one of the few girls ever to win the checker championship. She was also good at ping pong. She surprised many boys by beating them at their own game.

2. One time she had two dates on a Sunday afternoon. When she got back from the first date, her second date was already there waiting on her—and waiting and waiting.

3. Another time, one of her boyfriends (or a friend of someone) broke a yoyo of mine but bought it for 35 cents before he told me he'd broken it. As many boyfriends as came out to the house, if I'd been smart, I

could have made a lot of money selling that broken yoyo each time (by letting them think they broke it.) ((Added: One date had a convertible, and as he drove down the dirt road to our house there was a spot where the dogs were on a little hill which was higher than the car. Dogs could have jumped into the car—think it startled him.))

4. Brenda Jane would study till 100 am or 200 am so her grades would be high. She was very competitive—determined to be the best. She was the Valedictorian in high school (Marion County GA High School Class of 1961), and in top 10% in her nursing class at Georgia Baptist. She was smart enough to figure out Papa (our Dad)—few people can make that claim. Whenever we asked if we could go somewhere or do something, he would always say "NO". Well Brenda Jane just went ahead and did it without asking him (and never got into trouble). But I never did catch on.

5. She and I never double dated and she never fixed me up with a blind date. I don't know whether she thought I didn't need any help or whether she tried and it was just hopeless.

6. When she was in the first grade and I was still at home, each day she'd bring me a "goody" from town as he walked home (about one mile). I really looked forward to her coming home. ((When I did go to school, she would help me with my homework. My 4th grade teacher Mrs. Moss told us that tomorrow we will study thus and so. I said I'll get Brenda to show me how to do that. She said no, wait I'll teach you tomorrow. Brenda was a good teacher.))

7. She had asthma until one night in the third grade, she was in a play and had it really bad. But after that night, she didn't have it any more. (Per Grannie/Mom)

8. When I was initiated into the Beta Club as a cigarette girl, she loaned me a bra. We had to give peanuts to those already in the club and I rubbed a pod of hot pepper over my peanuts. (Don't know why I was so mean.) I fibbed and said they were near the pepper and must have absorbed it. (If they believed that they shouldn't have been in the Beta Club.) When I got home, Mom asked how they liked the hot peanuts and Brenda overheard. Boy was she mad. Said I was in a lot of trouble. But I never heard any more so I guess she forgave me. ((Update: Those being initiated wore their costumes to school and at half time of the basketball game had to parade around. Ball game exceptions included players, cheerleaders, and managers which let me out. But I still had to wear costume at the girls game until time to do my duties for the boys game. Forgot my game shoes and got a family member to go home and get my shoes. I waited at the entrance. Mr. Tom Hollis heard me speak and said "I thought it was a girl, it's just a Powell." (probably thinking and what an ugly girl.) Later in life, accidentally got some Cajun or hot peanuts—not good—but maybe I invented them and the Cajuns took credit??))

9. She and I fought a lot. Rather she fought, I lost. But like everything else, she played to win and usually did. One day, I got her down, with Clements refereeing and coaching me, I was actually winning. She gave me a sob story and I let her up and I turned around and started

toward the house. Next thing I knew, I was face down on the ground and she was beating the tar out of me. She'd tackled me from the rear, and now she had the upper hand. She'd played on my sympathy to let her up—she was always able to do that to me—and then clobbered me. She taught me a good lesson.

10.   In Monopoly she bought everything and nearly always won using the tall white token/piece. Even when I was winning she'd give me this sad story and I'd trade some property or make some other stupid deal and she'd pounce on it and then get the upper hand. She did that one time, and she convinced me how poor she was, no monopolies and she looked so sad.   I had all the monopolies and so I swapped her some property so she could have some.   Then she pulled out hundreds of dollars she'd stashed just waiting for me to take the bait—and of course she won again.   (When I told Richard and Sharon about this, they started on a two day Monopoly game, broke the bank like we used to do and stashed some money all over the house.)

11.   One night Rxxxx was to bring Brenda Jane home from church. I'd gone to church and had been home a long time before she finally came home. I said I bet you've been out to the loop. (A lovers parking area). Is that where you've been? She wouldn't deny it and just left the room as I told Mom/Granny all about the loop (not first-hand experience). After a while, when Brenda got me alone, she said something like "You shut your mouth about where I've been!!   It's none of your business. Mind your own business!" She really fussed at me—probably her fist reinforced her point.

12. She was number 30 on the girls' basketball team as a forward. (Back then there were three forwards (offense) and three guards (defense) and they played on opposite ends of the court never crossing the center line.) Peggy (niece) said she overheard Brenda saying "#30's going to be hot tonight." She practiced long and hard and sprained her ankles some. She had the longest follow through in shooting foul shots. She'd follow it through till she almost touched the floor.

13. She used to scare me the way she drove. Not reckless, just fast. Richard and Sharon told me that when she and Joyce took them to Panama City, Brenda got a ticket for speeding. Richard said nobody said a word after that...not even a word.

14. On that trip, I found out later, that they let my little Sharon (about 5-7) ride those swings that go around so fast they swing way out. At age 8, I still don't let her ride those things.

15. I remember the times Brenda would come help with Richard when he was sick. She'd stay up with him and try to get liquids into him every 30 minutes. ((He would dehydrate and wind up in the hospital to get IVs for several days. Happened about 20+ times. Fortunately, he outgrew it, whatever it was.))

16. We went to Vacation Bible School, Sunday School, school clubs, etc. I guess it was pretty tough always having a little brother along.

17. One summer (1961), Mother, Brenda, Ricky and I went to Callaway Gardens on a free trip. ((Callaway's gave one week in small cabins to many students and

their families—to me because I was the District Library Club president.))   When she saw how small the cottage was, she got mad and was ready to go home.   But of course we stayed and had a good time.

18.   She and I each had a pet Easter chicken.   (One drowned in the commode I think.)   ((We each had pet pigs but sent them to the "Sale" for money.))

19.   Granny said Ricky once brushed his teeth with Brenda's "eyeball" brush.   I don't think she particularly liked that.

20.   Connie tells about how Brenda would stay in the bathroom (only had one) until nearly time to go to school and the minute I got in there, Brenda would bang on the door and say "hurry up Donnie or I'm going to leave you."

21.   Brenda told me about Santa (otherwise I might still be expecting gifts.)   She told me when Granddaddy Powell died.   She and I used to use broken glass to scrape axe handles that Granddad had made.   He'd pay us for each handle we smoothed.

22.   Bill and I play chess and he wins about 90% of the time.   One time in the middle of a game, Brenda came over and sat on Bill's lap and started loving and kissing him and whispered in his ear.   He made a careless mistake and I was able to win.   Wonder what she told him?

23.   She won a $500 scholarship in 1961.   She was on tv receiving it and a picture of her is in the high school

annual. ((She used it to pay for her nursing school at Georgia Baptist in Atlanta.))

24. Her high school autobiography tells how she got her nickname from Granddaddy Powell. He asked what her name was and when told it was Brenda, he said "Brendy, that's a cow's name." Clements laughed and dubbed her "Brindy Cow" after that.

(End of memories of Brenda Jane)

+++++++++++++

"Other" continued.

++++++++++++++++++++++++++++++++++++++

+++

YB. Memories-Joyce-Nov2014

From Joyce Powell Henson to Donnie Powell   20 Nov 2014

Hi- Thanks for birthday wishes. My day was fine--if you call spending $175.00 at dentist office. Reg cleaning, x rays, gum treatment --all here at Christmas. Went to lunch with Scott and Peggy and then to Front Porch indoor antiques and stuff. Connie was sick all night, vomiting, hot then cold. She is some better now-- guess it was a 24 hr virus. Hope I don't get it.

I remember Mom drying clothes inside if it was raining- or waited till sun was shining. We really had it good compared to what our parents had to do. Vegetables from garden, chickens from yard, which included wringing necks and getting all feathers off, cutting them up before cooking. And of course that awful hog killing time which had to be a very cold day; always a mess in house when this was going on. Ironing with old irons heated in fireplace, getting up ashes; cleaning lamp chimneys, bringing in wood to cook with and heat house- and somebody had to cut wood up. Drawing water from well (early years of their marriage went down to creek to wash clothes)   I remember going to my granny's house and backing up to fireplace, burning your legs and still be cold; but no wonder because cracks in the floor let dust and wind in--chickens were under house scratching and made so much dust. Mom said when I was little, she put the bottom of my apron(these were short dresses) under the leg of table and left me to help daddy in field right across the road. Today DFCS would take child out of home for this. So glad we and our children grew up in better times than kids today. We are blessed to have good parents with good morals. Thanks again for thinking of me. Love to all   .

On Wed, Nov 19, 2014 at 8:16 PM, <dd66rsb@cox.net> wrote:

Hey,

Made a list of some of the things am thankful for--added Clothes Dryer. We can do laundry day or night rain or shine.

That made me try to remember what Mom did on rainy days/weeks. Guess she hung them up inside the house--

or maybe we just wore dirty clothes a few extra days? I just couldn't remember.

++++++++++++

Have used some left over mashed potatoes--mixed with egg and flour --to fry into small pancake-sized (I guess potato cakes).   Have done it several times and just not as good as Mom's--guess nothing is ever as good as Mom's.   Mine taste ok and I like them but could be better.

+++++++++

Happy Thanksgiving. Hope to see you then.

Love Donnie and Delores

+++++++++

YC. UN-ANSWERABLE QUESTION   Also cannot un-ask it once asked.

Here is a magic button XX that can go back in time and prevent slavery in the United States (and Caribbean) .

QUESTION: Do you press the button and eliminate slavery or do you not press it?

PRESS: If you are against slavery in US in old times, you press the button----however, that would mean all the Blacks in the US would have been born in Africa—that there would be very few Blacks in the US—no Martin Luther King, no Jackie Robinson, no Obama, etc etc. Today's Black US citizens would be in Africa hoping for a chance to come to the land of opportunity and freedom.

DO NOT PRESS: To not press the button means you favored slavery in the US. How could anyone be in favor of slavery?

++++

Now that the question has been asked, we cannot just walk away and not answer—to not answer is to answer. You are either against US slavery of old or in favor of it. (I suspect politicians would say I don't answer hypothetical questions—in which case they voted in favor of slavery.) (PS—I don't know how to answer the question either. Perhaps it is a trick question similar to "Do you still beat your wife?")

+++++++++++++++

+++++++++++++

YD. QUILT—FAMILY TREE QUILT BY MINA DAVIS POWELL

From "The Tri-County Journal" & Chattahooche Chronicle, July 1, 2009, Page 1, by Kendall Prevatt. Had picture of Mom holding a quilt she had made.

Mina Myrtle Davis Powell was born in Marion County, Georgia on May 19, 1912. She currently resides in Magnolia Manor of Marion County. To celebrate her recent 97th birthday, a few of her children put together a booklet of memories of her childhood, family trips, Christmas and her most appreciated and beloved hobby, quilting.

Mina Powell says she learned to sew by hand from her mother who stressed she sew small stitches and insist she rip out and redo ones she claimed were too large.

With this skill, Mrs. Mina has gone on to hand sew numerous quilts including a baby quilt and family tree quilt for each of her six children. Also she has sewn many more for her grandchildren as well as more for her sons and daughters and others. Mrs. Mina, having a daughter who suffered from cancer and also being a cancer survivor herself, once mad a quilt to donate to The American Cancer Society to be raffled off for cancer research funding.

Of all her quilts, Mrs. Mina's family tree quilts are definitely the most memorable. On each one are large quilt squares often made with scraps from dresses and other clothes that she sewed. These squares are filled with beautiful hand sewn embroidery and hundreds of family members' names sewn in Mrs. Mina's very own handwriting. When asked where she came up with the idea for a family tree quilt, Mrs. Mina said she "just needed something to fill up the square."

Each of Mrs. Mina's quilts are very unique, memorable, and very much appreciated by the family members and the friends who own them. With her amazing talent and creativity, she has sewn heirlooms that are sure to be passed on throughout the family for many generations to come.

Mina Powell is the daughter of Shadrack "Shadie" Addison Davis and Malissa Jane Cosby, and the granddaughter of Johathan D. Davis, who was a young guard at Andersonville during the War Between the States. She was blessed with six children: Joyce Henson, Clements Powell, Ricky Powell all of Buena Vista, Stout Powell of Sumter County, Brenda Jane Smith of Atlanta, and Donnie Powell of Warner Robins.

++++++++++

YE   BLANK

++++++++++

YF.   MEMORIES OF TEACHERS AND BUENA VISTA (2011)

Only teachers that I can think of that might be still living are Ms Lovlace (we had her for 9th & 10th grade science), Mr. Beard (8th grade ag & Boy Scouts) and Mr. Simpson (11th grade Chemistry and 12th grade Physics). Haven't heard any news from B.V. in a while. What's going on there?

Subject: Memory of Mrs. Garrett

Hello Buena Vistans,

1. Saw part of black and white movie "A Tale of Two Cities" on tv.

Remembered Mrs. Garrett talking about that book in class--even told of the mean

woman who would get the blood of executed all over her hands and arms (and maybe

face). On the test she asked the name of that woman. I had no idea but would not leave a blank on the test. So I guessed--"Bloody Mary".

 She marked it wrong--naturally. Hope she at least got a chuckle out of it.

2. Wonder if she ever wrote a book--could have included my answer as one of the

dumbest.

3. Remember one year I was scheduled to have 3 classes in a row under Mrs.

Lowe--one was French. I dropped French--she was not happy--do remember learning

one French word ""LaRue" which means "street" (Not Lash LaRue). Think Billy

Moore also dropped French.

4. When Marian McGlaun died, I heard she was living with her mom. Are any of

our other teachers still living? They were great and helped shape me in a

positive way. We were so lucky to be born in and raised in BV--it was a

"Mayberry era and Mayberry type town".

Better hush. Share some memories   Take care. Donnie Powell

+++++++++++++++++++++++++++++++++++

1. Do you remember in the early days (like before computers, and even color

tv, cell phones, cable, etc) we were allowed to pop firecrackers. Businesses

sold lots of firecrackers at Christmas. It is a wonder I still have all 8 of my

fingers. (Just joking)

2. Remember how crowded the city square/businesses were on Saturdays.

3. Mrs. Cleo provided FREE cartoons--nothing but cartoons-- on Christmas Eve

morning and we got a free gift--like ice cream or something. I know all the

Moms and Dads appreciated her doing that--got us out of the way for an hour or two.

4. The city decorations were lights strung around the courthouse square.

5. We drew names and exchanged gifts at school. Remember I shopped at the

Dime Store. One year I gave 2 little glider wooded planes to someone.

6. Remember sometimes in elementary school teachers would cook good smelling

popcorn and some kind of syrup and make popcorn balls for the students--so good.

They had to be sticky be we loved them.

7. We would go to auditorium and watch a black and white version of

"Christmas Carol"--don't think I understood that movie till I was much older.

(The ghosts probably scared me).

8. Seems we would be out for Christmas for about 2 weeks or more.

9. Donny F, seems I remember you once got a neat cowboy outfit you wore to

school--think I was a little envious.

10. Think our church youth went caroling a few times-- they probably asked me

to just lip-sinc the words.

11. Remember one Christmas play --Moms had to make the costumes--where I was

lucky to be a toy soldier and someone made wooden rifles for us soldiers. After

the play I got to keep my rifle--fought many battles with that gun.

12. We would ride around and look at outside decorations. One I really liked

was at the end of the street Brenda Henson/Bill Brady lived on. It was in dark blue and think a light shone thru the cut out words of "Holy Night".

13. Remember if one light on the string on the tree went out they ALL went out.

14. Mom bought a nativity set made of plaster of paris (I think). The

wiseman/camel got broken but we glued them back together--mostly. One of the

angels got her head knocked off--only glue we had was red fingernail polish.

That angel has a "red halo" around her neck even today. When Mom died I got the

nativity set and still cherish it today. Gee it must be at least 55 years old.

(Might have gotten it from Montgomery Ward??)

15. We must have had some Christmas programs at church but can't seem to

remember any. I do remember Ms. Jessie Belk always gave us (good kids) a small

box like container of life savers--I liked most but some of the peppermints did

not taste good--but I loved getting a present. That was so nice of Mrs.

Jessie--hoped I thanked her.

16. Think stores decorated their windows.

17. Wells and Wells was open till about 9pm on Christmas Eve. We would

exchange and open presents(not Santa) on Christmas Eve and my sister in law

worked at W&W and we had to wait and wait until she got off work. Later we

changed to exchanging gifts on the Sunday before Christmas.

18. As a kid, I liked having many Christmases--one at school, one at church,

Christmas Eve, and of course, Santa on Christmas Day.

19. Santa did not wrap presents for us. Santa did wrap present for my wife

when she was little. So--as you might expect--Santa wrapped presents for our

children. One year he didn't wrap and our children let us know they wanted

Santa to wrap in the future--which he did.

  Donnie Powell

+++++++++++++

YG. GENE HENSON MEMORIES   2009 by Donnie Powell

Connie asked for any memories I had of her dad. Have lost a lot of memory cells so those listed may be vague and sketchy at best. (Connie, you may want to ask Joyce for more accurate details on most of these things, like where they lived, cars, jobs, etc.)

.1. Joyce and Gene took Brenda Jane and me many, many places. They took us to Atlanta at least once. Seems I remember a big mountain—think it was Stone Mountain—where we picnicked. I asked Gene what he would do if that mountain started to fall on us, he said he'd grab Connie (a baby) and run. (Guess the rest of us were on our own). Think we also went to the zoo at least once. ((2018—a bit of a memory—think they entered baby Connie in a baby beauty contest in Columbus???))

2. Joyce and Gene took us to the annual Columbus Fair every year. ((May have called it the Chattahoochee Valley Exposition??)) They even let us bring a friend along—took Ernest Hart at least once, mainly because he said he did not like to ride the wild rides like everyone else did. I never could (still cannot) ride those wild rides—always told our children they could ride when they were big enough to ride them by themselves. Still remember the great exhibits there from all the high schools in the area. On one of the trips to the fair, Granny (My Mom Mina Davis Powell) went and took Ricky too*. He was in diapers; Granny always took something to eat and drink. This time the jar of water leaked onto Ricky's cloth diapers. We each held a diaper out the window trying to dry them. ((Wonder what people in passing cars thought.)) At the fair, some youngster came up and asked to hold Ricky, Granny was glad to hand him over, the kid took Ricky out of sight. When asked where Ricky was, she said she gave him to

some boy.   Fortunately, Ricky was returned a little later—probably because his diaper was wet.   On one return trip from Columbus, when we topped the hill at the old Murray house, we saw a "shooting star"—was quite pretty. Seems like Jerry Henson went with us once to the fair. Once Billy and Laverne Powell took Barbara and Annelle to the fair but first met at Joyce and Gene's house. Wonder how may people Joyce and Gene took to the fair thru the years. I loved it—well not the rides— but everything else.

3.   Joyce and Gene took Brenda and me with them to Panama City. Don't remember how old Connie was but think she was about 7. First time I ever saw the ocean. We stayed in a rental house across from the beach. I had a single bed in a modified closet—most privacy I had in long time . Managed to lose my billfold on the swings on the beach—good Lord was watching so was able to find the billfold later—it contained all my money for the trip. Going down there, Gene used his watch to check speedometer by setting car on 60 miles per hour and seeing if it went one mile a minute. Don't know if we helped pay for the rent or the groceries or the gas— probably not, but we had a great time and lifelong fond memories.

4.   Joyce and Gene took Brenda Jane and me with them to Columbus shopping. We always met at the back of Kirvens*. We had to wait our turn to get to sit on the bench there—but we always worked our way to the front of the line and got the bench. Spent many hours waiting there at the back of Kirvens. But always loved going to Columbus.   On one trip, saw Bim Wiggins (cousin)

219

driving a delivery truck (company was Georgia something) and hollered at him. He parked and came over and we talked for a while. Seems like I remember seeing a Columbus Christmas parade or two. Once Gene was logging, I think on Fort Benning, and Joyce drove there and we picked him up. He cleaned up and changed his clothes and we were off to shop or to the fair.

5. Joyce and Gene sometimes dressed up and went to Columbus (I think, dancing). Granny would keep Connie and Peggy for them. Remember Gene looked so handsome when he dressed up in his nice suit.

6. Once in the car, Joyce lit a cigarette for Gene by puffing on it to get it started. I looked at Brenda and wondered if we should tell on Joyce to Dad/Papa. ((Cartons of cigarettes were often given as Christmas presents.))

7. Gene had a chain saw repair shop in back yard of their home (the one that Miss Brady later bought). He would repair them and rev them up—guess chain saws do better when revved up a lot. He had lots of parts, oil, equipment, etc., in the shop—it was a neat place to meddle around in—until he shooed me out. Don't know long he had that shop or what happened to it—guess he sold it. ((Wonder if neighbors complained about the noise).

8. Gene built or bought a large sand box in the back yard (near the chain saw shop). It had a tall slide that ended in the sand box—sand to cushion the landing. Think the box was painted dark green. It was there for years—

enjoyed playing in it too. ((That house is on quite a large lot.))

9.   Gene had arthritis pretty badly in his hands—and possibly other places. He said when he applied for a job once, they asked him about his hand and he said "you know what it is"—think he got the job. When arthritis flare up, he hurt badly.

10.   Seems I remember Gene coming to the house (maybe before marriage?) and he drank a lot of ice water. I pronounced "Billy" as "Biwwy" and "Sally" as "Sawwy", and so on, and it always cracked Gene up. Helped me slow down and pronounce it as two words—Bill—Lee.

11.   Gene played baseball with the Buena Vista city baseball team. Remember going to several games in BV and away to Elleaville, Lumpkin, or Richland (possibly others).   At Ellaville, Gene was playing outfield (Centerfield?) and made a long, long running catch—great play. Joyce honked and honked the car horn cheering for him. At Lumpkin (or Richland) one BV player (I think Baywood McManus) hit a long home run over the left fielder. I was near the left fielder when Baywood came up again—the fielder backed up a lot and said "let's see him hit it over my head now". He shouldn't have said that because that is exactly what Baywood did—probably the longest ball ever hit in Lumpkin/Richland (maybe in Georgia).   At one BV home game, a batter broke a bat which I eagerly claimed. It had a sharp point so Gene used his pocket knife to cut off the sharp point. When I got the bat home, used glue, hammer and nails and tape to try to

repair the bat—was the best bat I had for long time—but it did have that empty space where Gene had cut off the sharp point. At one game, Coach McGlaun was the umpire but stood behind the pitcher to call balls and strikes. One hit him in the back and he called the batter out—not sure that was the right call but I sure wasn't going to question it. In one game in BV, Bump was on third base when the ball was hit and he came charging home: the catcher tripped him ((probably accidentally)) and it sort of knocked the breath out of him and by then the catcher had the ball and tagged Bump out. Bump ragged the catcher for a few innings until he came over and apologized to Bump. (Oh, Plains had a team too; remember their third baseman wore shorts but stopped everything hit to him, so we quite ragging him about his shorts.)

12. Joyce and Gene lived in a house behind Dillard's grocery store. Think Joyce said they rented some rooms there. ((Not sure if this was the boarding house?)) Also lived in a garage apartment across from back of Baptist church and across from what is now Subway Sandwich. Then I think they moved to the house across from the Garrett's (house later bought by Miss Kati Lou Brady).

13. I used to cut the grass at Joyce and Gene's (later Miss Brady's house). It was a big yard, I loved the money but, being basically lazy, did not like the work. Cutting the slopes in front was particularly challenging---hard to push/pull the mower up the slope--if mowed back and forth, gas would leak out on the mower—but mower never caught on fire or blew up. In the back yard there was a metal anchor for a power pole—it ruined a

few mowers—would just throw itself under the mower, somehow. Seems like Bill Brady used to cur grass around town too.

14. Joyce and Gene had nice white (?) big Plymouth Fury with big fins (cars had fins back then). Loaned it to me for Junior-Senior ball (don't know if it was as Junior or Senior). Liked driving it—was automatic. Here are a few cars they had that I think I remember: dark Green dodge?; two-tone blue and white Pontiac (with rounded fins), and the white or tan big finned Plymouth Fury.

15. Don't remember the jobs Gene had but think there were several. He worked with different people in sawmilling/logging. Seems I rode with Dad/Papa on the gas truck up to Fort Benning (?) where Gene was working. Another job, maybe part time, was the chain saw repair shop. Was he a city policeman?

16. Don't remember how Joyce and Gene met and started going together. Maybe we can get Joyce to tell us. Don't remember their wedding—where was it—did I go—am sure Granny went but not sure about Papa. What job did he have when they got married? Was Joyce working in Columbus when they got married? Seems Joyce worked at the Firestone (?) store next to Wight Motor Company. ((Later I guess Wight bought that store because they cut a hole/door between the to stores and oil was stored in back of the Firestone place.)) When they got married were we still living in the "shacks"?

17. Think they went to Panama City on their honeymoon—and maybe stayed at the Barney Gray motel???

18. Remember Joyce, Gene, Connie and Peggy came to Delores and Donnie's wedding (1966) down past Valdosta at little town named Clyattville. The night before the wedding, Delores and I came to motel and visited everyone. Gene said tomorrow night you will have learned about all these false thing women use. Joyce rescued the moment by saying, like false eyelashes, false hair pieces and so on. Wedding was an adventure for all of us—per Mom/Granny, Dad/Papa tried to pass every car on the road—she tried to eat to calm her nerves—by the time they got home, she had eaten everything in the car (and maybe even chewed on the upholstery).

19. When Clements was in the Army, he would ride the bus from South Carolina to Macon (one time bus to Geneva) and good old Jim Wiggins would (?pick him up) take him back to Macon to meet the bus. Jim always drove very, very fast. He was a WWII vet with 3 bronze stars and purple heart(?s); limped and had a plate in his head from the war—so he wasn't afraid of anything—but I was. Weone would go—she and Clements sat close together--she liked to have me go to keep her company on the way home. One time Gene went with us (may have been more than once). On the way home Gene told Jim don't you drive real fast. Well Gene dropped off to sleep and Jim drove as usual. When Gene woke up, he asked Jim if he had been driving fast and I wanted to yell YES!—but didn't.

224

Didn't have air conditioned cars in those days so once I thought I could slow the car down by leaving the windows rolled all the way down—didn't work. Don't know if Gene went more than one time or if Jim's wild driving scared him away. ((Some of this repeated in "When I was a Boy in Georgia"*))

20 Joyce and Gene went to Macon and for some reason I went along (probably Brenda too)—if someone offered me a ride, I would go. They gave their maid, a Black lady, a ride to Macon and picked her up and brought her home. (Think it was the green car?) Don't know why we went to Macon—probably Dad/Papa and Mom/Granny urged them to go so I would be out from under foot.

21. There was a big storm in Columbus—may have been the same one that hit Warner Robins in about 1953. Joyce and Gene, and Brenda (?) and I went to Columbus to see the destruction—which was a lot—many trees blown down, men out with chain saws. (Back then, people got busy cleaning up things, did not sit around saying "where is the Federal Government, poor us"— they pitched in and started doing something.) While we were riding around, the radio announced that people should not be sightseeing, they should stay away—and there we were. After a while, I said something brilliant like, I'm tired of just riding around, let's do something else. ((Google says storm hit Columbus Saturday, Apr 18, 1953. Tornado hit Warner Robins Apr 30, 1953.))

22. Joyce and Gene took us to Calloway Gardens for a picnic and swimming (maybe more than once.) Think Mom/Granny went too. Was crowded. Had a good time.

(Did they ever take up to Idly Hour Park—seems I remember a big boat.)

23. Bim Wiggins ((his mom and my Mom were sisters)) told of a fishing trip to Florida that Gene went on too. Don't remember any details of the trip but at least the boat didn't sink (like other cousins boat did on another trip*). Seems like Gene might have hunted some too—I bought used Ithaca pump 16 gauge shotgun that he once owned (I think). He had traded it in at the old Western Auto in BV and I bought it on time there. Think he may have had something to do with the bird dogs that Clements and Stout boarded and looked after in some dog pens up on the hill. So Gene was into hunting and fishing some—don't know how much.

24. Was Gene in the Army? I don't remember. If so, where was he stationed, when was he in, was he in WWII, etc. ((Update 2018—yes he was in the Army but for a short time—think after he got in they discovered he had arthritis and he was released on disability.))

* Story told in "When I Was a Boy in Georgia" by Donnie Powell.

+++++++++++++++++++

YH. PAPA IN HEAVEN (1998) By Donnie Powell

((Note Dad/Papa died in late 1997 at age of 93—here is a fictional story I wrote to honor him and the other Powell's in heaven.))

The first angel said: "He hasn't stopped running since he got here. He always loved to run when he was young and now he just keeps on running. He also has been cruising the timber and the woods that he loves so."

The second angel replied, "Yes, and all the Powell's are having a great re-union laughing, telling stories, plowing mules, sawmilling, eating and just having a great time. Bo and Tom are showing each other their healed arm and finger and they are good as new. They all have been down at Bo's pond fishing and planning a fish fry too. Tom still jerks them out of the water and flings them half way up the bank."

First angel: "Would you listen to them. There is Clara sitting on the wood pile again and Pete saying she better come in before a booger gets her. Those Powell's are something. There is Bill adding another heater to his pickup, that is four so far, but that is all right, as long as he is busy adding heaters maybe he won't pitch a Powell fit. Eula helps control those fits some."

Second angel: "All of them are trying to round up some mules so they can do some logging, sawmilling and plowing. Call Brenda Jane and Danny and see if they can persuade Tom to wait on the mules."

First angel: "Are you kidding? Brenda Jane told Danny how much fun it was to ride fast on a ground sled and now they are looking all over for the fastest mules so they can have a sled race. Powell's, what are we going to do with them?"

Second angel: "Shim is practicing his dancing and John (or is it Johnny?) is drinking coffee and sitting in his truck and talking to Tom (when Tom will slow down enough to sit in the truck."

First angel: "Why does Tom want to build a house? He has a nice home already built from all the materials sent up here by all his good deeds? He and Mina really send a lot of building materials with all the good things they did. For example, they helped take care of Ethel and her children and Cornelia and her children. And you know what Jesus said about taking care of widows and orphans as well as those in prison and their families. Without their generosity and love, they might not have had a place to live. Mina and Tom aren't like some of those talking Christians who talk but don't help people—whose home in heaven might be a pup tent with walls made of hot air. Anyway, Tom wants to build a house and all the other Powell's are pitching in to help."

Second angel: "Tom said something about a hen house and a hog pen and I think his dad, Mr. Buddy, wants an outhouse put in. What next?"

Frist angel: "I just remembered, Tom is the Powell show said "The only lie I knowingly ever told was when we told the preacher that Mina was old enough to get married. And I have been paying for it ever since." We've laughed about that a number of times. But you know, he was telling the truth, he never told lies. A truly honest man and a truly good person."

Second angel: "But he is also very determined. He is cutting more trees. He truly loves working in the woods."

First angel: "Did he say something about squirrel hunting? He is also wanting to trade pickups and Ford tractors again. He does like trucks, dogs, mules and Ford tractors."

Second angel: "Oh, don't forget. He has been helping his Dad in the blacksmith shop. They have made horse shoes—that is mule shoes—Tom does not like horses at all. They have also made ax handles and wedges and all sorts of things."

First angel: "Maybe that is why he said something about building a workshop or shelter. He needs a place to store his tools, truck, tractors and all those things."

Second angel: "Did you hear him asking about the newspaper? He really enjoys reading them. He also said he wished he could tell everyone, especially the love of his life, Mina, that all is well and he is healthy and doing great and not to worry about him. He made peace with his Lord in his own way and is in heaven and very, very happy and perfectly healthy, and that he wants everyone to be happy for him."

First angel: "I'll say he is healthy. Guess what he is planning to do now."

Second angel: "I'm afraid to ask. But these Powell's are wonderful, and yes, unpredictable. Come on, let's see what they are up to now. Oh, would you look at what they are doing now.

((Not the end, just the beginning.))

+++++++++

YI. BROTHER RICKY'S MEMORIES   May 2009
Written by Ricky Powell, typed by Donnie Powell

Mom and Dad got married May 22, 1926. Dad was 21 at the time. Mom turned 14 on May 19, 1926. She was 14 only three (3) days when she married Dad.

Dad said the only lie he ever told was that Mom was 18 when he got their marriage license. Back then you had to post your marriage license for 3 days on the public bulletin board in the Court House. Dad posted it but under some other papers so no one would see it and tell her parents or if her father saw it, he could tear it down and rip it up thus preventing their marriage.

On Saturday, May 22, 1926, Mom and Dad got married in Richland, Ga by the preacher of her church. They were in a Ford car (?Model T?) that Daddy owned on halves with Uncle Bo Powell. They saw the preacher walking down the street and pulled up to him and he stood outside the car and married them while they sat in the car.

They went back and told her parents of their marriage. Her father who was pretty religious, said to them "Mina, I think you have played hell."

Dad wound up giving his half of the car to Uncle Bo partly I think because Bo was mad with him when he got back for having the car so long that day. Daddy said that that car was the last think he ever owned on halves. He said that if he couldn't buy it, he would just do without it or wait till he could afford to buy it. He also said he was still paying for that one lie 71 years later.

Mom's Mother saw their preacher later on and asked him, "Did you know you married my baby girl the other day?" He replied, "Yes". She asked him "Why?"

He replied that he thought it was time she got married. (Donnie comment: Think I remember Mom saying he did it because he knew they were determined to get married and if he didn't do it someone else would.)

In 1965, 66, or 67, in the summer time I think, Mom and I (Ricky) once went to Florida to see Brenda and her first husband Byron Mixon. They lived in a small white house in Graceville which is just across the Florida state line. We left early on Saturday morning. We went down US 27 thru Cuthbert. We stopped at the Kolomoki Indian Mounds near there. We had to wait awhile for the park to open at 900 A.M. We looked it over then got back on the road. I think we stayed on the less traveled roads instead of going thru Dothan, Alabama to get there. I could only navigate for Mom because I was not old enough to legally drive. Brenda and Byron took us to Panama City to the "strip" as it was called. We played Putt-Putt golf at the one with the jungle animals. I had my camera along and took pictures of Mom, Brenda and Byron and me in front of some of the animals. We did a couple of other things but really can't remember what. We even went to his parents' house.

In 1975, 76 or early 77, the Country Western look was in so I asked Mom to fix up 2 western style long sleeve shirts I had. She did a lot of embroidery work on them, back and front. On the medium rusty brown shirt, she stitched on my initials about 8 or 9 inches tall and all around the initials. She also made me four shirts from scratch—to me they looked better than any store bought shirt anybody had. She made one black with white stitching and with white and green embroidery on it. I installed white snaps on it. She made a white one with red stitching and embroidery. I installed red snaps on it, two each on both front patches, three on each cuff and six down the front. She also made me a medium dark green and a grayish brown one each with white stitching and with green, white, and yellow embroidery on them. I also had a blue denim long sleeve western shirt that she also embroideried my initials on the back of it and all the way around the initials which were 8 or 9 inches tall. (Donnie comment: Ricky told me people asked who made the shirts and were told my Mom. They often didn't believe that. Ricky bought some labels "Made by Mother" and then people believed him.) (Donnie comment: He was buried in one of those shirts.)

When I was about 10 years old, I asked (old) Mr. Burton Wight for a job. He hired me for Saturdays— that was when the Ford place and Wight Oil Co. stayed open all day. Anyway, one winter in 1964-65-66, it snowed late on Friday and early Saturday morning, but being loyal employees Daddy and I went to work. That Saturday morning, Mom went outside in housecoat and gloves and made a snowman on the hood of our 1962 blue and white Ford Galaxie car. I took pictures of Mom making the snowman and of the snowman itself which took several hours to melt. Dad drove slow and the snowman stayed on the hood till midafternoon before melting and sliding off the hood to the ground.

I also have pictures of Mom shooting hoops one afternoon at the basketball goal Dad and I put up from one of the old Sinclair gas signs and pipe frame.

I remember when I first got married, Debbie scrambled me a couple of eggs and they tasted like the iron frying pan. I asked Mom how long it took before a frying pan got where you did not taste it. She said I needed to season them—in other words you had to put a large bit of lard or grease in them and cook them on high for a while, let it cool down and then do it again. It usually helped to put an Irish potato or two sliced in half the second time you heated it up.

I never heard my Mother say anything bad about any of her sons- or daughters-in-law even when there were problems between her children and their spouses. My spouse Debbie, in 1983, had problems with her legs having blood clots in them and had to be hospitalized in Buena Vista that was when we still had the hospital here. Debbie's blood clots were not responding to what they were doing for them in BV, so they transferred her to St. Francis hospital in Columbus. I was Parts Manager at the Ford place in Americus (about 27 miles Southeast of BV) so when I closed up at 5:30 PM, I came home, changed clothes and went to see Debbie in Columbus (about 35 miles West of BV). Well Mom and Dad insisted on going with me each night for that week she was in St. Francis Hospital. That let me know how much they cared for me and my wife.

((Donnie comment: Wish Ricky had written more.))

++++++++++++++

YI-A-- Powell-ancestor-Barbara-Jan2010 .wps ----
Barbara Fincher <bpdf@pstel.net>

Date: Tuesday, January 26, 2010 7:55 AM

To: dd66rsb@cox.net

Subject: Re: Any oral stories of the "old country"?

Donnie, So good to hear from you -- especially since we don't seem to have a lot of relatives willing to write down, run down, etc., these wonderful family stories!

I never heard about anyone further back than the Powell who served in the Confederacy. I don't know that anyone even knew.

I have hit a brick wall with the "first" Reubin Powell who was in NC in 1750, with a record that says recently of Norfolk Co, VA. I'm trying to find a written record that can link me to the right Powell line in V. Some time back, I bought the book that Rev. Lucas wrote on the Powells in the 1960's & 70's, but most of the lineage groups will accept it due to errors.

Hoping to tie something down, I bought one of DNA kits, took it down to Buena Vista, swabbed Billy's cheek and sent it off. I've had a direct match but not to any line/person that I know. And this line doesn't go back as far as I can prove. I go back to Va in March or April and plan to spend some time in the VA Archives and try to find some record. It is possible our line is in the VA Colony as early as the mid 1600's, but I certainly can't prove it. I'm almost sure our line comes from the village of Howyll (I can't remember exactly how it's spelled) in Wales and if I can tie down the line, then I hope with

234

British records, I can identify, possibly, the ship that brought our ancestor over ----

I hope you have talked at length with Clements as he seems to have heard and retained more of the family stories than my brother. Billy was always too busy with his work to sit around after meals or at night to listen to any of the stories. I think I know more than he does, from what Mother told me about the Powells. Daddy didn't talk that much about the family -- except that he hated moving every year from one shack to another! Also, your mom told me a good bit some years ago.

I missed Bill Tom's funeral -- his death was a real shock as I didn't know he had cancer. I was at one of my conventions and couldn't go. He was buried at Pineville where some of my Upton ancestors are. I didn't know about Buster nor Mrs. McCorkle.

Would love to get with you sometime to compare notes. Barbara

----- Original Message ----- From: <dd66rsb@cox.net> To: "Barbara Fincher" <bpdf@pstel.net>

Sent: Monday, January 25, 2010 10:53 PM Subject: Any oral stories of the "old country"?

Barbara, Hello and how are you? Got to wondering if you ever heard any stories passed down about our ancestors coming to US from the old country, which country, what ship, where they landed, how long a sea voyage, where they lived in the old country, etc, etc.

Mom and Dad never told us any old stories like that--too busy trying to keep food on the table I guess. Probably their parents/grandparents never passed any on.

Have you or Annelle ever written any memories of growing up in good old Marion County?

Don't guess I knew that Clem and Stout were born in the house yall lived in. Found out a couple years ago when Clem's grandson Mitch got married in the house--now called (is it) High Pines.   Guess you have heard about Frank Powell's death--also recently Bill Tom Wooldrige, Buster Burgin, Mrs. Nellie McCorkle (my 5th grade teacher) and in Dec 08 Clem's wife Weone. Have lost a lot of good people in the last few years.

Better hush.   Donnie Powell

+++++++++++++++

YI-B –POWELL ANCESTORS

Donnie Powell (Born 1944), my father, R. A. "Tom" Powell (1904).   His father William Thomas Powell (1873) and his mother Mattie Foster (1876). His father William Theophilus Powell (1846—CSA Vet—married in 1866 which is 100 years before I Donnie got married) to Missouri Osteen (born 1846). Mattie's parents Elijah Eugene Foster (1840) (CSA vet) married 1860 to Zilpha D. Watson (born 1841). ::: Missouri's mother was Frances Osteen. Zilpha Watson's parents were Nathan M. Watson (born 1801) and Susan Watson (1808)

+++++++++++++++++++

236

YJ. WoodenLtrs-ShadieDavisPaper[1]-Dec08

(REPORT BY MRS. ANNE CHANCE IN NOV/DEC 2008)

In 2004, Donnie Powell of Warner Robbins, Georgia contacted Dr. John Burrison, a professor of Folklore and Folk Material Traditions at Georgia State University. Mr. Powell inquired about the possibility of having a student document wood block letters, numbers and words (referred to henceforth as "the letters") which had been carved by Mr. Powell's grandfather, Shadrack "Shadie" Addison Davis, and used to inscribe concrete gravestones in Buena Vista, Marion County, Georgia. In November of 2008, I contacted Mr. Powell and arranged to meet him, his sister Joyce Henson, and his mother Mrs. Mina Davis Powell, at Mrs. Henson's home in Buena Vista, Georgia on November 7, 2008. During this visit I interviewed Mrs. Powell regarding her father, who he was, his occupation, and what she knew about the making and use of the letters. As they were present, Mr. Powell and Mrs. Henson contributed what they knew, as well. A transcription of the interview is in Appendix A - Interview November 7, 2008.

What is known about Shadrack Addison Davis (Shadie) and his work at the cemetery is relegated to the memory of Mrs. Mina Davis Powell and the family lore she has passed to her children. Shadie was born in Marion County, Georgia, October 15, 1871. He married Malissa Cosby and had five children. He was a farmer and grew many different things, but grew cotton for his main commercial crop . Mr. Davis and many other people of Marion County suffered the economic vagaries associated with rural farming. Many people of the town were particularly affected economically when the town bank went under in 1925. Mrs. Powell recalls that her father was very good with his hands, and had a workshop shelter outside the house where he made items for family use. The family believes that Shadie carved and used the letters for the marking of concrete gravestones in the late 1920s until his death in 1930. Evidence (in the form of grave markers in the Shiloh Baptist and Smyrna Presbyterian Cemeteries) suggests a period of use from 1925 to 1946 for the letters. Only one grave marker pre-dates 1925, the marker for Lizzie Horn who died in 1910. However given that no grave markers using the letters were in evidence between 1910 and 1925, it is likely that the marker was made in 1929 when her husband, R. L. Horne was interred. This suggests that letters were carved in 1925.

Shadie carved letters, numbers and words into wood blocks to be used for inscription on concrete grave markers. It is assumed that he had created an entire alphabet, however, of the original 26 letters, 21 are extant [A,B,C, D, E, F, H, I, J, L, M, N, O, P, S, T, U, V, W, X, Y]. Similarly, of the possible 10 numerical digits, 7 remain [1, 2, 3, 4, 5, 7, 8]. In addition Shadie had created some words for epitaphs. Those that remain are BORN, DIED, GONE and NOT. GONE and NOT were used as part of the epitaph, "Gone but not forgotten." The family believes that the words "GONE BUT NOT" were once all of a piece, but have since been cut to form separate words. They believe this piece may have been burned in a barn fire (mentioned in Mrs. Powell's interview) and that the remnant words were cut apart from the damaged ones. A burn mark on the word "GONE" supports this assumption.

The letters are made of wood. Per Mrs. Powell, Shadie once worked at a sawmill and also crafted other wood items for family use. It has been suggested that the wood is either pecan or poplar, but this has not been confirmed . In Mrs. Powell's recollection of how they were made, Shadie carved the letters, possibly with a pocket knife. She recalls that he used a hot bore to burn out portions of the wood. Mr. Powell recalled that his mother (Mrs. Mina Powell) had told him that Shadie would turn the letters upside down to see if they were right. Looking at the letters, one can see marks of the strokes for hewing out the wood. Evidence is also clear for the use of a bore, as perfectly round circles can be seen on those letters with rounded shapes. The depth of each letter is a consistent 1/2 inch. The width and height of each block (letter) is a fairly consistent 1 1/2 inch and 1 7/8 inch respectively. (see Appendix B). The letter generally spans the height of the block. Mrs. Powell recalls that he marked off the blocks and cut them. Pen or pencil marks can be seen at the back of some of the letters. On the extant words, lines can be seen cut into the wood to separate spaces for letters. About a 1/4 inch space has been left on each side of each of the individual letters. Looking at the letters in profile, one can see that the letters have been carved narrower at the top and wider toward the block, with a cut-in indented furrow along the lines of the letter. The edges of the letters are beveled and triangular, in the same manner one would see on (old style) typewriter letters.

The letters, numbers and words were used to inscribe concrete grave markers. No record is available as to how, specifically, the letters were used, however some educated guesses can be made. Because the block letters are of consistent size and each letter has a consistent space to either side of it, it could be surmised that the letters were meant to be used side by side, abutting each other to create a spacing between letters of 1/2 inch. This is consistent with some of the grave markers found in the two cemeteries. Because the inscriptions on some of the markers are level, this suggests that a method of keeping the letters straight, either with string or boards, might have been employed. There are grave markers where the depth of the inscriptions are regular. In addition, cracks and breakages among the letters are fairly consistent at a 1/2 inch mark. This may suggest that a board was used to depress the letters equally. The single tablet marker found (Effie Davis - died 1925) suggests this method in that it has board-shaped regular depressions creating an undulating surface on the marker. Another possibility is that each letter was placed and pushed in to the surface of the wet cement to the depth of the letter. However, this is not consistent across all the grave markers, as some are deeper than others, though we do know from Mrs. Powell's account that the letters had a variety of users. The variation in depth could also be a result of the point in the drying process the letters were used.

The letters have been worn by use. Chips, gouges and breakages are noted on many of the letters (See Appendix B). Repairs have been made to cracks by epoxy and in one case, with the letter "E" a wire has been wrapped around the letter to hold it together. Evidence exists that the letters were used even after significant breakages. In one case, the "NOT" which can be seen now to have a portion of the N broken away was used and the same portion is missing on the inscription. (See infant Lawhorn, Appendix C).

Shadie Davis not only carved the letters, but with two friends, a Mr. Simmons and a Mr. French, dug the graves and made the markers. The use of cement grave markers is not singular to Marion County or to Georgia. M. Ruth Little and Tim Buchma in their book, Sticks and Stones, observed the use of concrete markers in rural North Carolina cemeteries. Little and Buchma note socioeconomic reasons for the use of non-commercial grave markers and comment that "white artisans" would generally try to copy the form and design of commercial markers. The use of concrete markers they trace to the late 19th century, when commercial concrete became readily available, even in the most rural of locales. Prior to this period graves may have been marked with less permanent markers, and the authors propose that these markers would have been replaced by concrete markers. These and subsequent markers would have little ornamentation and simple inscriptions. Little and Buchma do not comment on the manner of inscription.

Margaret M. Coffin, in her book, Death in Early America, does comment on the twentieth century inscriptions found in cement markers,

"There are homemade twentieth-century burial markers too...These exist in whatever shape took the maker's fancy...On the ones that I have seen the lettering is crude, the spelling primitive...Some inscriptions are 'Gone but not forgotten' and 'Standen at the cross'.

Terry G. Jordan, in his book, Texas Graveyards, similarly cites the use of concrete grave markers in Texas. (Mr. Jordan refers to them as cement, which I have discovered is not the correct word, concrete being preferred.) Jordan notes usage as beginning in the early 1900s and describes the process he perceived for the making of the markers.

"Poured into a mould of the desired shape, the cement is allowed to begin hardening before an inscription is written with a stylus, stick or some other pointed instrument."

Gregory Jeanes, in his article "Rural Southern Gravestones: Sacred Artifacts in the Upland South Folk Cemetery," also describes the use of concrete grave markers. He establishes this as a twentieth century phenomena with a period of predominant use in the 1920s and 1930s. He describes the construction and inscription as follows:

"Generally crude in design, these stones are either slab or block in form and of modest size. Inscriptions are most often made while the concrete is still wet and carved with a tool such as a screwdriver or stick."

Jeanes goes on to define concrete markers as "true folk markers". He bases his conclusion on what he calls the art of "making do." Certainly Shadie and company were "making do." However they were also following a tradition of marking graves already established in the cemeteries. A concrete marker dated _____ exists in the Smyrna Presbyterian Cemetery (illustration). In Shadie's lifetime, someone had created a concrete marker in the cemetery.

In addition, uninscribed concrete ledger markers as well as inscribed marble ledger markers abound. These are among traditional marble headstones, cairns and even graves surrounded by wrought iron fences. What is key to the use of concrete markers during Shadie's tenure is that it was an inexpensive way to mark a grave for a rural population during a time of economic duress. By creating the letters, Shadie ensured that the markers he and others made did not have the anonymity of a pile of rocks or a blank stone nor the "crudity" of a hand inscribed marker as described by the various sources cited here and which did exist in the Marion cemeteries.

Conversation by email with Keith Hebert, Historian, Georgia Department of Natural Resources Historic Preservation Division, reveals the ubiquitous use of concrete markers in Georgia . Mr. Hebert's comments indicate that other people may have crafted print letters to be used to imprint concrete markers. However, many of these had not been fashioned in mirror image fashion, resulting in the letters imprinting backwards on the marker. As noted previously, Shadie took great pains to ensure that the letters would be inscribed properly and could be read face forward. Close inspection of the letters reveal the irregularities inherent in handcrafted products. There are variations in the thickness from top to bottom, or in separate parts of the letters. Letters where angles join, as with the "X," are not exactly aligned. The "8" is formed by two bored circles which have a small space between them. The "7", has an arcing diagonal side which makes it very distinctive. It was these distinctive irregularities that allowed for a more easy identification of those markers that had been made using the letters.

Two cemeteries were surveyed to ascertain use of the letters on grave markers. These were Shiloh Baptist Cemetery and Smyrna Presbyterian Cemetery. The following notes graves determined to be inscribed using Shadie's letters (photos in Appendix C - Gravestone Photos).

Shiloh Baptist Church Cemetery

NAME	BORN	DIED	EPITAPH
P. P. Harry	n/a	n/a	Son of Mr. and Mrs. W.W. Harry
L.E. Harry			
n/a	n/a	n/a	Wife of W.W. Harry Gone but not fogoten*
R. L. Horn	Aug 12 1863	Nov 13 1929	Gone but not forgotten

244

Lizzie Horn   May 6 1874   Sep 6 1910   Gone   but not forgotten

William Hurst   (This   stone   is   an abbreviated ledger stone, about 1 foot square. The grave is also marked with a marble CSA tablet).

Smyrna Presbyterian Church Cemetery

B.B. Horne   6 - 1861   3 - 1927   none

Mrs. B. B. Horne   10 - 1855   1   -   1929
        none

J. D. Davis   Dec 9 1876   June 22 1929 Gone   but not forgotten

Mary J. Davis Mar 5 1848   Oct 25 1927   Gone   but not forgotten (this grave has a marble tablet marker with the born and died dates, the ledger bears the epitaph

Miss Ella Lawhorn   Aug 30 1895   Aug 25 1928   At Rest

Infant Son of Mr. Mrs. S.G. LawhornJuly 7, 1933   July 7, 1933   Gone But Not Forgotten

Effie Davis   Jan 8 1897   June 10 1925   Wife   of Clark Davis (this is the only tablet marker identified)

John W. Pierce   Nov 26 1847   May   5   1935
        Faithful unto the end

Nellie Saville   Aug 25 1847   March 3 1928 n/a

Nettie Gill   Nov 30 1844   Dec 12 1927   n/a

Shadrack Addison Davis   Oct 15 1872   Jan   17 1930   Husband and Father

He Hath Done What He Could

Gone but not forgotten

*Transcribed as seen

Unlike the North, particularly the Northeast, where epitaphs are ubiquitous, lengthy and often poetic, Terry Jordan notes that in the southern rural cemetery, epitaphs show an economy of words. Jordan attributes that to southern illiteracy and that "bereaved southerners have never been under moral or social obligation to place writing on the grave marker". He also suggests that what he refers to as the backwoodsman may not have had any attachment to place. That does not seem to be the case with Shadie and those who used his letters. True the epitaphs show an economy of words, but the words denote a wealth of sentiment. In addition, most were not relatives but were still neighbors. This certainly speaks to a sense of place.

Greg Jeanes negates Jordan's assumptions regarding southern epitaphs. He correlates southern gravestone inscriptions with those found in parts of the U.S. Jeanes divides types of epitaphs into four main groups, with a fifth catchall group for those that don't fit neatly into other categories. These four groups are biblical inscriptions, religious memoria, biographical and poetic. Biblical inscriptions are direct quotations from Scripture. Religious memoria invokes a Christian finality while inferring life after death. One example from Jeanes is "God's finger touched him, and he slept." The biographical epitaph gives information about the kind of person the deceased was in life. Shadie's own marker is concise in this biography, "He Hath Done What He Could." The poetic epitaph is as one might expect, verse. Shadie's constant epithet, "Gone But Not Forgotten," s well as the succinct, "At Rest," fall squarely in Jeanes fifth category, almost existential in their simplicity.

As to why Shadie made the letters and concrete markers, we can only speculate. The family believes that he was not paid to do this, and that he and the others who used his letters, made the markers out of a sense of duty. In some cases they had been made for kin. For others, we do not know the connection. In the Smyrna Presbyterian Cemetery at Church Hill, located 12 miles from town, there are several unmarked, ledger-style grave markers. Perhaps Shadie felt a sense of pity for those who would pass and be forgotten with no inscription to bear witness to the future. Or perhaps, as Howard Williams suggests in his, "Archaeologies of Remembrance", the act or practice of producing the marker was a conscious effort to connect and evoke memories, of the deceased, and of others who had passed before. Williams reminds us in producing a material culture, we materialize remembrance.

Shadrack Addison Davis died January 17, 1930. The family recounts that he had been digging someone's grave in the rain, and contracted pneumonia. As a tribute to Shadie, a ledger stone was inscribed using his letters. Probably the lengthiest of all the epitaphs using his letters, it reads:

HUSBAND AND FATHER

BORN OCT 15 1872

DIED JAN 17 1930

HE HATH DONE WHAT HE COULD

GONE BUT NOT

FORGOTTEN

+++

YK. LETTERS PUBLISHED   Mrs. Chance published the letters in the "AGS Quarterly" the Bulletin of the Association for Gravestone Studies, Volume 34, Number 1, Winter 2010. Page 12.

(this page may be blank)

YL. STORIES—GASOLINE 2006

Story #1 was from the radio.   Heard on radio that teenagers needed some gas and were going to siphon it out of the parents car but no one wanted to suck the hose and maybe get gas in their mouth. One "genius" in the group got his mom's vacuum cleaner--it sucked the gas out---then when the gas/fumes hit the motor, the whole thing exploded. Good news fortunately, no one hurt.

Story #2 from Clements. He told me some woman there in Buena Vista soaked her husband's greasy work clothes to get the grease loosened up. Then put them in the washing machine. When she turned it on a little later the fumes exploded and blew up the washer--again no one hurt.

Story #3, from Clements. He said when he was younger and sawmilling , a couple of the men (One was Gene Henson, Connie and Peggy's Dad) found an old well about 15 feet deep with lots of snakes in it. They poured 5 gallons of gas in the well but the gas wasn't killing them fast enough. So struck a match and dropped down the well--the resulting explosion was like a Georgia volcano--singed hair, eyebrows, etc. Don't know if pieces of snake landed in the next county or just disintegrated.

Should IQ's be checked before allowing people to buy or use gasoline?

++++++++++++++++++++++++++++++++

YM.   AUTOBIOGRAPHY--   Grisamore-
Assignment#1—June2013

Writing Your Autobiography for Loved Ones
Assignment # 1 Childhood and Teens

NAME: DONNIE C. POWELL BORN IN DECEMBER 1944.

1-1. Describe your house and neighborhood growing up. Landmarks? Grew up in small town Buena Vista, GA. The old home place was located on 104 acres partially within the city limits. [[Dad paid for it by doing a tough logging job. In those days, used mules, crosscut saws, "hands" or workers (today very automated), axes, a skidder, and log trucks. Dad had about 10 people working for him. Some years later he gave up logging and became a small-truck operator delivering Sinclair gasoline within Marion County. In the good deal, the owner said Dad could have any trees over a certain number of board feet and, after "cruising" the timber, he agreed and it was a great deal for him.]] The home place included a barn, shelter, smoke house, other building, and chicken house. The yard had no grass and we had to rake pine straw from the dirt yard even when no straw was there. The screened front porch was a place of greeting, socializing, talking, and visiting—and you could smell the things Mom was cooking. One step up led to the living room, later a wall was removed making it a dining/living room. This area was a gathering place for opening Christmas presents, birthdays, and so on, with some family spilling onto the porch and even outside and the den/bedroom. Past the dining room, was the kitchen where Mom cooked thousands of great meals—biscuits, hamburgers, steak, ham, fried chicken, chicken and dumplings, peach puffs, cakes, pies, butter-roll pie, fried streak-o-lean, eggs, bacon, flap jacks, and on and on. Mom was a great cook and enjoyed cooking for her loved ones—think she is still cooking in heaven. There was a small back porch that held the overworked washing machine, later a freezer and dryer. Stepping down from the living room was a small bedroom later a television room/den. From this room was a small hallway that opened to a single bathroom (very overworked room with 6 children)—yes indoor plumbing is great, had a few experiences with outdoor plumbing and indoor is much better. The hall opened to a bedroom. Back to the living room, a door opened to my parents bedroom which opened to the hallway and to another bedroom—Granddaddy Powell's room with private entrance, then my brother Stout's room, later my room, and finally my younger brother Ricky's room. Our home did NOT have air conditioning—though I grew up without it, I would be hard pressed to do without it now—though the good old days were indeed good, every single thing was not better. Our home place was a wonderful place in which to grow up, mostly because it was filled with love.

1-2. Who were your friends and why were they your friends? My friends were my relatives about the same age. Mom would make Dad take her visiting and insisted her and Dad's brothers and sisters visit us. Nearly everyone had lots of kids so we had someone to play with. Other friends were nearby neighbors— Miller, Hanner, Wade—near my age. Do not remember getting into any fights or arguments. When company came, we played outside (Did Mom lock us out?) 1-3. What kind of games did you like to play? My sister Brenda was a year and half older so whatever she played I played—and I liked it or—being the runt of the litter-- she would beat me up. Loved hopscotch, jump rope, chase, hide and seek, tag you are it, and when leaving "I got your last tag", flies and skinners (baseball), gator pit (a hole about 15 feet wide and a foot deep had a "gator" who would try to tag (or did they tackle us little kids who ran through the pit). Another favorite was "Ain't no boogers out tonight, grandpa killed them all last night" (the "booger" hid in the dark and would pounce on us as we sang and ran or skipped in the dark yard). Remember putting sand in discarded hose or sock, swinging around, throwing into the air and trying to catch it before it hit the ground.

Our favorite board game was Monopoly—we would play for hours and even days—going past "Go" so often we broke the bank and printed our own money (sort of like the Federal Government today?)—we also made special rules like getting $500 if we landed on Free Parking. We enjoyed checkers and ping pong on dining room table.

In our front yard, there were ground bees. We would place Mason jars over the hole when the bee went in and use the flat lid to slide under the jar and thus capture the bee. We would also capture bees on Mom's flowers (Crepe Myrtle, 4 Oclocks, candle lilies, daisies, etc. fertilized with "organic fertilizer" from the barn).

We made up games and enjoyed playing—was better than doing chores.

1-4. What kind of clothes did you wear? Hairstyle? Why? Wore jeans and tee shirts (?). Remember Mom sewing 25 pound patterned or white flour sacks into shirts, dresses, sheets etc. Wore shoes that had to be tied (no Velcro) and later penny loafers. Riding on back of friend's bike, my shoe got caught in the spokes which ground up the side of the shoe, the sock and a layer or two of my heel skin—so got to go without one shoe but with bandages for a few days. Back then, had hair—let it grow long and combed it over. Was blessed with wonderful cowlick so complained about it for years. God has a sense of humor—cowlick no longer a problem. Later crew cut, flat top, duck tales, became popular with the guys—but never long hair, at least not until the mid 1960s. Had my hair cut short in high school—flat top (or as a student once said, I was level headed.)

1-5. Did your family eat meals together at the table? What did you talk about? We ate meals together. Often my older brothers (Clements and Stout—one named for local merchant and one for local doctor who delivered my younger brother Ricky at home.) would work with Dad in the logging business and would gobble down 8 or 10 hamburgers on Saturday night standing up before they rushed off to dates—I could barely eat two. We got our first television (could see 3 snowy channels) in about 1954 so we did not watch tv during meals. Believe we did listen to news on battery powered radio. We did not have blessings before meals but do remember Mom quoting young Clements' blessing "O Lord for the batter cakes". Did start blessing in later years, probably after we got married in 1966. Mom did all the cooking and cleaning up the dishes and kitchen. Even at large gatherings, the women were expected to clean up the dishes. After getting married, I soon got some "training" and learned how to do dishes and even some cooking.

1-6. What kinds of things did your parents always say that stuck with you? Get a good education—their education levels were 8th (Dad) and 6th . Be honest—if Dad was going to sell something like a truck, he would fix it up at his expense. When you give your word, stand by it. If you get a whipping at school, you will get one at home. Stay out of trouble. If you can't say something nice, do not say anything at all.

1-7. Did you get an allowance? What did you spend it on? Did not get an allowance but my parents were generous and tried to provide whatever we wanted. Am amazed they did so well on such limited income. Never got food stamps or welfare. They worked hard for a living. When I got a job earning $5 a DAY in local grocery store, I was able to save a lot of it. I spent money on Saturday all-day movies, cap pistols, bb guns and bbs, pocket knives, etc. As a teen, spent money on dates to local movie theatre, bowling, basketball games, etc.

1-8. What is the best gift/present you ever received and why? Had many wonderful presents, especially at Christmas. Perhaps the best present, was a 20 inch red bicycle with training wheels that my Dad just lifted out of the back of the pick up truck and put in front of me—don't think he said a thing—he didn't need too—hope I thanked him. I jumped on the bike and rode it around the yard for a long time—even sat on it taking a break. Rode that bike for years.

1-9. Describe your school. Brand new brick school in 1950—we were first class. Lower grades were on the left, high school and library on far right with middle grades in between. Had an auditorium for assembly, plays, programs, graduation, etc. Our first lunch room was part of the old gym which was built by the Workers Progress Association (WPA—one teacher said when he was younger they said the WPA stood for We Piddle Along.) Later a new lunchroom was built with the old lunch room becoming a band room (later got a new band room). Three of my aunts worked in the lunchroom, so I probably got extra large helpings—and extra supervision who would report any misbehavior to my parents. A community school. Gym was used for Halloween Carnivals, sock hops, Junior-Senior Prom, donkey basketball, wrestling, etc., but most of all for wonderful, exciting basketball games which were supported by the community—gym always packed—back then smoking was allowed. (School too small for football.)

Playground was behind the school where we had swings, see-saws, one flying jenny, merry-go-round. Played games such as crack the whip, chase, baseball, touch football, etc. One day boys were playing war on a construction pile of dirt using dirt clods as hand grenades. Someone threw a half brick which hit Hugh in the head. He was bleeding and squalling when he went flying by me—he was hurt but it didn't slow him down. Fortunately he was ok and wore his bandage proudly. Next day, the Principal's announcement said dirt pile was off limits and not to throw bricks. He made quite a few such announcements.

Our parents emphasized a good education and good behavior. Our teachers were dedicated, professionals and very good who we would meet at the grocery store, church, etc. The students were held accountable to do their part of learning. Parents, teachers and students all did their part (unlike today where only the teachers are held accountable.) Our school was strongly supported by the community. No drugs, no gangs, little to no disciplinary problems. We went to school in a "Mayberry" type town and a "Mayberry" type time. We were very fortunate.

1-10. Who was your favorite teacher and why? All were great—difficult to pick one favorite. One was Mrs. Garrett, our English/Literature teacher—demanding but fair—helped us love literature, poetry, etc. She had us write our autobiography in the 11th and 12th grades but I cannot find it. Mrs. Lowe lectured a lot and sometimes was not exciting but I seem to remember things she said—one of my favorites was "I was 16 before I realized damn-Yankees was two words." Several of the teachers also helped with extra curricula activities such as the yearbook, cheerleader sponsor, club sponsor and even drove us to various club meetings at other schools or locations, including a week at FFA-FHA Camp (near Covington) which I truly loved, Co-Ed-Y training at Rock Eagle, Library Club convention, Beta Club convention in Atlanta, etc.

I loved school and learned many things from each of my teachers and they were all great. I hope I thanked each of them. To honor as many as I could, I recently placed a small US Flag on each of their graves.

1-11. What is the funniest thing you ever did as a child? When very little, I told my Mom to get me some water. She said my name is Mom or Mrs. Powell and you should say please. My response was "Please get me a glass of water, Mrs. Powell".

As a teenager, I happened to go to the same movie to which my older sister went on a date. I got home much earlier. So when she finally came in, Mom asked where she had been. She was quiet so I chimed in that she had been parked at the "loop". I gladly told Mom all I had heard about the loop. My sister had left the room. A little later when Mom was gone, my sister came back, balled up her fist, stuck it under my nose and said "You keep your mouth shut about me and where I go!"   (I shut up.)

This is more dumb than funny. In 11th or 12th grade, our Literature teacher had told us about the novel "A Tale of Two Cities" --how the bad woman –Madame Defarge-- hated the Aristocrats and when their heads were chopped off she would stand under them and get their blood all over her hands while laughing. A test question asked for her name. Didn't have a clue but was determined not to leave a blank so I guessed "Bloody Mary". (Hope the teacher got a chuckle out of that dumb answer.)

1-12. What is the most dangerous or daring thing you did as a child? I attended the "Barney Fife" school of bravery or not. I was just too practical and scared to try much of anything that was dangerous. I was sort of trapped into one dumb/dangerous thing. After dropping off both our dates, my friend decided to see how fast his car would go down a nearby hill—think we hit 100+. I did not scream—probably couldn't—but I wanted to.

1-13. Tell us about your first sweetheart/crush. First kiss. Prom date. I was also scared of girls (still am). Guess Karen K was my first love. Wrote her letters and she wrote to me. First date to movie at local theater. Junior prom date was Joyce and senior was Diana.

1-14. What were your chores as a youngster and teenager? Got to help hang clothes on the line sometimes. Got to rake the yards to remove pine straw. When we had a cook stove heated by burning wood, I sometimes got to bring wood inside. Once I picked up a board and found a snake, flew screaming to the house. Mom and brother came to take care of the snake. Asked which board and when he stepped on the right board, I said the one you are standing on—he moved quickly. I had asthma and could not do some chores—and I used that to my advantage whenever I could.

1-15. What was your favorite book? Song? Movie? How did it shape your life? I loved reading in school and in the summer time—books from the Bookmobile and library. I liked animal stories, biographies, boy stories, etc. A couple of songs I liked were, "Get 'Rhythm" by Johnny Cash; "Davy—Davy Crocket, king of the wild frontier" and "The Ballard of New Orleans". At sock hops, I did not like the fast dance songs but preferred the slow dance ones. Liked songs at church, such as "Amazing Grace", "Up From the Grave He Arose".

I loved movies. I was allowed to spend Saturday afternoons at the theater—one admission price and I could watch it over and over. Movies took me many places and on many adventures—westerns, war movies, movies in Africa (wild animals so impressive), Biblical, etc. Also liked the serials, shorts (Three Stooges), and cartoons—even liked the previews.

Think books and movies thrilled me and took me to faraway places and helped me form ideas of right and wrong, other points of view, other traditions, etc.

1-16. Did you collect anything growing up? Why? Yes, I had a small collection of arrowheads—it was a good "boy" collection and was fun searching for them. Also collected stamps which were so varied and had pretty art work. Letters required 3 cents. They were on letters and packages that came to the house so the hobby was cheap. (Some years ago, checked a stamp book to see how valuable my stamps were—each was worth about 14 cents, so will need to hold them another 50 years.

1-17. Did you go to church as a youngster? Did you come from a religious background? Yes, I went to the Methodist church with my older brother until my other brother went to the Baptist church so my sister and I also went there. Loved going to church—Sunday School, Vacation Bible School, Baptist Training Union, boys group called Royal Ambassadors (RA), parties, sermons, singing, etc. My Mom would attend church once in a while-- though my Mom loved going to rural churches when there was All Day Singing with dinner on the grounds.

1-18. What were holidays like at your house? We had Easter egg hunts at church or Sunday School teacher's home. Mom boiled and dyed eggs. We would crack boiled egg on friends' head. We exchanged Valentines at school. Each class would decorate a hat box and the prettiest one would get a prize in assembly. Mom said I addressed some Valentines to myself to be sure I got some. Christmas was our favorite. We exchanged gifts in Sunday School and at school. A classmate remembered his 7th grade teacher giving all the boys a pocket knife. Firecrackers were legal and we loved popping as many as we could—and Roman candles, etc. Mom bought a plaster of Paris nativity scene which I now have (must be 60 years old—an angel's head broke off and we glued it back using red fingernail polish—only angel with red ring around her neck.) We exchanged gifts on Christmas Eve for years. Santa did not wrap our presents. (After marriage, found out Santa wrapped my wife's childhood gifts—so Santa wrapped our children's gifts.) We would wake up after Santa came and we would stay up all night playing with our gifts. My gifts included a cap gun and holster set, BB gun, games, a train set, etc. Apples, oranges, tangerines, grapes, English walnuts, Brazil nuts, candy, etc were Christmas treats we loved. We kids loved singing Christmas songs with "Rudolph" and "Frosty" being favorites. Do not know how our parents afforded to buy the things they did—they were very frugal and unselfish. Christmas was just a wonderful time of the year.

1-19.What historic events do you remember as a child? Where were you? What were you doing? Don't remember any historic events as a child. I do remember listening to war reports (Korean War?) which caused me to have a stomach ache. Being near Columbus, we heard the news from that area—such as the murder of Albert Patterson, Attorney General for Phenix City Alabama in about 1954. It was on television and in the Columbus newspaper and caused the National Guard to be called out. When Kennedy was killed, I was at Georgia Southwestern College and we were all stunned.

1-20. Name the three people (other than parents or family members) that most shaped your life during your childhood and teen years? Cannot narrow it down to three but I was greatly influenced by all my teachers and Sunday School teachers. They taught love of God, respect for others, Pledge of Allegiance to the Flag, love of country ("Breathes there the man with soul so dead, who never to himself has said, this is my own my native land", or "America for Me"), love of family, how to think for myself, and so many more things.

((NOTE: I would like for there to be a special "Monument to kindness/good deeds" where people could place a small rock to honor/remember someone special—parents, family, teachers, nurses, soldiers, etc. As the pile grew, it would make a statement that while there might be a lot wrong with the United States, there is a lot right with her too.)) ((Idea came I think from memory of Rock Eagle and "Shindler's List" where survivors honored him by placing stones on his grave.))

+++++++++++++++++++++

WRITING YOUR AUTOBIOGRAPHY FOR LOVED ONES

Week Two Questions

2-.1. Was the transition from childhood to teenage years easy or difficult? My wife often says I am still in my childhood. Do not remember the transition except perhaps as I became aware of girls and did not have a clue of how to talk to them. They may have thought I was "stuck up" but I was just very shy—tongue and brain would not work very well in trying to talk to them.

2-2. Were there any circumstances that made you have to "grow up" in a hurry? I was very fortunate and blessed with a good immediate and extended family. My parents were married 71 years. My father was never unemployed and when I was in high school Mom started working in a shirt factory—primarily to help pay for college for my sister and me and possibly my younger brother.

2-3. Describe your high school. How much different were things then? Our high school was co-located with the elementary school and the transition was fairly easy. The population of our school was small, for example my graduating class had 40 members. Graduating in 1962, the schools were segregated. The local banker gave me a ride to Atlanta to have some allergy tests run. He asked what I thought of the schools closing in other states to prevent integration. I told him I was not big and strong and needed my education—I did not want the school to close and I wanted to go to college. He said if I ever needed any financial help to come see him.

Changing classes was confusing but we adjusted to it and I actually liked having different teachers. We did not have lockers but "pigeon hole" bookshelves made by our shop class.

2-4. What kind of clothes did you wear? What were the fashions of the day? The boys wore jeans or slacks and tee shirts and white socks and Keds tennis shoes. The girls wore dresses with crenlins but no slacks or shorts in class.

2-5. What kind of music did you listen to? Did you play an instrument like the guitar or piano? Loved country and western songs—especially those with stories such as "Big John", "The Battle of New Orleans". In 5th grade took music and played a training flute, but that was the high water mark of my musical career. In college I visited a friend whose family played the "William Tell Overture"—that is when I learned it was not the Lone Ranger Theme Song.

2-6. What kind of dancer were you? Self taught and terrible especially fast dancing the "jitterbug"—probably looked worse than I thought I did. Preferred slow dances—how girls can follow is still a mystery—do they all know what is on our mind and know what we are going to do before we do it? That is scary, but explains a lot.

2-7. What were required social skills of the day? We said "yes sir" and "no Mam" and were respectful at all times. Our high school English teacher told us how to introduce people and how the girls should stand with feet heels touching at about 90 degree angle. Remember in first grade, I was holding a spoon in my fist. My first grade teacher did not say a word, just opened my fist and put the spoon in the proper position. In typing, if our elbows stuck out too far, she would whack them with a ruler. (I spent more time erasing than typing. Really loved computer screen where correcting mistakes was easily done with back spaces.) When picking up a girl for a date we did NOT blow the horn and wait for her in the car. Never did enjoy talking to her parents while waiting for her to come into the room. She had to be home at a certain time and we dared not be late.

2-8. Did you play sports or involved in other extracurricular activities? I was not good enough for our varsity basketball or baseball teams. (Too small to have football, tennis, etc.) But enjoyed playing "pick up" games of touch football, baseball, and especially tennis and basketball. Also enjoyed ping pong at the First Baptist Church. Was in as many clubs as possible, such as Future Farmers of America (FFA—would have starved, just joined to go to summer camp with FHA), Beta, Library, Future Teachers, Co-Ed-Hi-Y, Future Business Leaders of America, "Vistan" yearbook staff, Manager of the boys basketball team in 11th grade, and Baptist Royal Ambassadors (RA). Liked the conventions and socials.

2-9. Did your high school yearbook have a quote about you or predict what kind of career you would have or person you would become? Don't think so but think my friends knew I was going to college and believe my teachers did also.

2-10. Who were your closest friends and why? My earliest close friend was Ernest Hart—got to spend nights at his house and he at mine. Our sisters were in the same grade and were close friends who were roommates at Georgia Baptist College in Atlanta. In about 1959, we got a new preacher and his son Billy Moore became a close friend—he is now a retired doctor. We were about equally matched in basketball, tennis, ping pong, etc. We talked about girls and even double dated some. We could talk about anything and we both studied because we knew college was in our future. We also went to Camp Pinnacle Baptist camp for a week with his father driving us there and back. We worked in the same grocery store on Saturdays for $5 a day—working with someone helps you understand them.

2-11. Did you go to the prom? What do you remember about the experience? Yes I went to the Junior prom—date was Joyce McCorkle, daughter of my fifth grade teacher. (Years later her niece married my nephew.) In my senior year, I failed to get a date and was planning to go "stag". Then Diana Brannon broke up with her boyfriend and she agreed to go with me—hey I would rather be second choice than no choice.

2-12. What do you remember about your high school graduation? It was very respectful and full of "pomp and circumstance". No air conditioning so it was very hot. As honor graduate, I had to give a speech that my teacher totally re-wrote—very nervous and this pesky fly kept buzzing me and I was afraid he would fly in my mouth. We also had a light-themed Senior night, a baccalaureate sermon, and then graduation. At the time I knew high school was over, but did not realize the significance or import of that event. I would never see some of my classmates again. At our 50th reunion, 6 of the 40 had died, and some were unable to attend. Those of us who moved away, were no longer close to any of our classmates—those who lived locally remained somewhat close. ((Note: Since we graduated in 1962, we could all have invested in Apple and Microsoft and become millionaires—if we had only known. I would probably have invested in "Eastern, the wings of man".))

Graduation was a wonderful sense of accomplishment but for me, college was somewhat more of the same.

2-13. Did you know what you wanted to do with your life? Some wonderful teacher(s) or someone, told me about a State of Georgia scholarship to recruit teachers. The state would pay for room, board, tuition, books, -- just about everything. Requirements included a "B" average and teaching in the state of Georgia for three years. Some teacher told me about it, probably helped me apply and even recommended me. Without the scholarship I probably would not have been able to go to college and my life would have been very different. The scholarship provided a path to a good career which was what I wanted to do at that time. Have no idea of what might have happened had there been no college— perhaps a job locally or in nearby towns with no future, marrying a local girl,---just unknowns. Would not have met and married my wife, and would not have had our wonderful children and grand-darlings.

2-14. Were the plans you made after high school (college, military) decisions you made or were they made for you? The plans for after high school were mine and were supported by my family. My family always treated me with dignity and respect and as if I were a mature person (sometimes I was).

2-15. What was your first experience being away from home? I was able to go to summer camp for a week each several times. My first experience "living" away from home was living in the dorm at Ga. Southwestern College. Had to study to keep my B average, had to watch my budget, worked in the library, learned there are many different personalities out there—one "scrounger" borrowed anything and everything and returned nothing. Met people from other counties, states and a few from other countries. A very broadening experience.

2-16. Did you make good decisions? Did you "sow some wild oats"? Basically made good decisions. Back then, girls were "good"—several dates to hold hands, and even more to get a good night kiss. The girls in college had an early curfew—if the college controlled the girls then the boys pretty much had to behave. It takes two to sew wild oats. In college, some had a hard time adjusting to having no parental supervision— partied the first quarter, on probation the second, and gone the third. We would ask, where is old "Partying Joe", oh, he flunked out. Have advised college bound family members to get high grades the first year—build up a cushion of "A's"—and tell them about old Joe.

2-17. If you could do anything differently, what would it be? Perhaps, apologize to a few people (one who is dead) for not being kind. Perhaps going back and personally thanking each teacher and even writing them a thank you letter. (Since all are either dead or cannot contact, it is too late. However, last year, I placed a small U. S. Flag on the graves of my teachers as a way of saying "Thank You". The flag seemed appropriate since teachers are very patriotic, taught us love of country, and the Pledge of Allegiance to the Flag. Thank you.

2-18. When did you experience the death of a family member or close friend for the first time? My grandfather Powell died when I was about 9. The death that hit me the hardest up to that time was when my sister Brenda died of cancer in 1981. Had a hard time believing and accepting her illness and eventual death.

2-19. When did you own your first car? What kind was it? Color, make, and model? My last year of college at Georgia Southern in 1964, my Dad traded in a pickup truck and co-signed a loan so I could get a little light blue 1960 Ford Falcon, standard shift. Improved dating possibilities in college—could go to drive-in theaters— also called "Passion Pit". When I got married in 1966, it had become not only my dating car but became our honeymoon car. My wife could not drive and I had difficulty teaching her, especially since it had standard shift. It was doomed. Traded it in on 1966 dark green Fairlane Ford (also without air conditioning) automatic transmission. Some of the best money we ever spent was to pay for my wife to get professional driving lessons—in the automatic car. Getting her driver's license made her even more independent and self confident—and I didn't have to go everywhere she went.

2-20. When was the first time you realized you were really in love? Knowing high school and then college was temporary or short term, I never got serious until getting a job teaching math in Dougherty Junior High School in Albany, Ga. There were lots of new teachers and I dated several. Then at a county wide teachers meeting, I saw this young lady—hardly noticed her— who was wearing a dark blue A-line skirt, white blouse, bright red lipstick, hair in a bun, thin and cute—but hardly noticed her---"It was an enchanted evening, I met a stranger, across a crowded room, and somehow I knew I would see her again and again...." But first, I dated her roommate Karen and she dated Grady—some time later we sort of swapped—Karen and Grady got married and Delores and I got married. Guess I realized I was really in love when we were dating and became engaged.

2-21. Was there someone you almost married but didn't? Not really, though I did date Karen and others. At Karen and Delores' 50th high school reunion, Karen confessed she did not remember dating me. I was lucky to find someone like Delores—would rather be lucky than good.

2-22. What were you looking for in a husband/wife? The most obvious are the tangibles—pretty, cute figure, a job, smart, sexy, etc. But it is the intangibles that are the most important—trustworthy, honest, religious, supportive, sense of humor (required to live with me), good mother, tough, determined, loving, flexible, willing to tolerate me, etc.—basically a good, good person.

+++++++++

WRITING YOUR AUTOBIOGRAPHY FOR LOVED ONES

Assignment #3 Middle Years and Beyond

3-1. What kind of childhood did your children have? We were middle class living in small town (Warner Robins) in Georgia. Took them to church and supported them in getting a good education and in everything they undertook. We talked at meals with tv off. As a Christmas gift in 2010, I asked them to write some memories of their childhood, and according to them, they had a wonderful childhood. When they were little, we read to them each night and tried to spend time with them. We tried to be open to them and encouraged them in all areas. We said prayers with them at night and went with them to church.

3-2. What were some of the memorable things they said growing up? Daughter—there was enough gas in the car to coast into the yard.

3-3. What kinds of things did your parents say to you that you found yourself repeating to your children? Tell the truth and be honest. Get a good education. If you cannot say something nice don't say anything at all.

3-4. Did you move around to other cities? States? Houses? Why did you move? How did you pick the neighborhood where you live? Due to being asked to participate in civil service Reduction In Force (RIF) at the Marine Base, moved from Albany, GA to Warner Robins in 1971 and to a slightly bigger house eight years later. Neighborhood was one in our price range.

3-5. What were some of the vacations and trips you took as a family? Was there a special place you always went? Each summer we went to my wife's family reunion for several days. We also enjoyed vacations to such places as Panama City, Gatlinburg, Disney World (our favorite), once to Jekyll, once to Fort Mountain State Park. We were blessed to be able to have these vacations.

3-6. Who were your friends and neighbors? How did you meet them? Our closest friends were people in our age group attending the same Sunday School class ("Becomers") at Trinity United Methodist Church. Our next door neighbors were also close. It helped that we had children about the same age.

3-7. What were some of the rules of your household? Let us know where you are going to be—this was before cell phones. Our daughter gave us some challenges in this area. Do your school work.

3-8. What part of parenting are you most proud of? How could you have done better? That our children are good, good people.   Spent more time with the children. Been more aware of problems.

3-9. What kind of activities did you involve your children in? Little League? Scouts? Theater? Ballet? Tee ball (best game ever), Little League, Boy Scouts, karate (2 black belts), band (2), church youth choir and activities (Sharon), ballet and piano (Sharon), etc.

3-10. What kind of career and jobs did you have? What were the ups and downs? Taught Junior High math for three years then to civil service career in Civilian Personnel. (Wife is retired elementary school teacher.) I was very blessed and in retrospect, progressed further than I probably deserved.

3-11. If you could have had any other career, what would it have been? Would have enjoyed teaching till retirement. Could have liked being an engineer. (Who wouldn't like to be a professional baseball player but no chance of that.)

3-12. How did your values and tastes change as you got older? Guess I became more tolerant in some areas. I learned to never say "no child of mine will…"

3-13. What kind of charity or volunteer work did you involve yourself in? Involved in church activity. Also did some Scout work.

3-14. What was your proudest moment during those years? Our children's graduations, marriages, employment and birth of two grand-darlings.

3-15. What was your most embarrassing moment during those years? Losing my temper.

3-16. What kind of modern conveniences came along in your life that made things easier and better? Color TV, air conditioning, indoor plumbing, cell phone, www, computer, VCR/DVD, . Sadly, divorces became easier and more prevalent.

3-17. What kind of books did you read? What kinds of shows did you watch? What newspapers and magazines did you subscribe to? Liked to read the Bible, religious books, westerns, mysteries. Like old movies, westerns, action, comedy, nature and History Channel. Liked reading Readers Digest.

3-18. Did you have a particular hobby? How did it get started? Have enjoyed golf, tennis, jogging, briefly fishing, reading and dabbling in writing, going to yard sales. Passing out wooden nickels thanking "Veterans". Recently putting small flags on graves of my teachers and veteran relatives (idea came when I saw article about a veteran placing flags on graves of 50 veterans plus seeing large flags in front of Westside Baptist honoring 9-11. Made pedestals to hold small flags and placed in front of church on Veterans, Memorial, and Independence Days, plus for funerals at Trinity (have turned that over to Scouts.) Last year (in 2012), started buying, cleaning and giving away stuffed animals (idea just sort of came). With help of church and others, have passed out about 1500 (as of June 2013)—to lots of thank you's, smiles and some hugs.

3-19. What was your favorite place to shop during those years? Sadly, Wal-mart, so convenient and good prices.

3-20. How much has the church been a part of your family's life? Always has been a major part of our life and always will be. Our daughter married in our

273

church—Trinity United Methodist. Was very, very difficult to "give her to Tommy", but he is such a good, fine person she could not have done better.

3-21. What kind of political views did you develop and did they influence others in your family? Common sense. Balance the budget.

3-22. Did you ever have jury duty? What was the experience like? Almost, for a murder trial—glad I was not selected but would have done what was necessary (he was found guilty).

3-23. Did you develop a sense of patriotism and why? Yes—have realized where we would be without our military/veterans. Love our country—probably 70+% of world's population want to live here. Am very fortunate. Believe in Constitution, laws, education, freedoms, etc.

3-24. What were your views on race growing up and how have they changed? What changed them? Grew up in segregated South. Once the law changed and working with minority helped change my thoughts. Some policies have made things worse for example, now 73% black babies born to single moms—and with no dad to help raise them, almost guaranteed poverty and problems.

3-25. (DEEP THOUGHT) The values I learned as a child that stuck with me through all those years were.

Work for a living. Respectful. Punctual. Honesty. Hard work. Love others. Give benefit of the doubt.

3-26. (ADDED BY DONNIE). TELL SOME FUNNY THINGS YOUR CHILDREN/GRANDCHIDREND DID OR SAID. TELL SOME STORIES ABOUT YOURSELF/WIFE. ANY PET STORIES?. Our daughter Sharon said she used to sneak into her older brother Richard's room and make his Star Wars figures kiss her Barbie dolls. He would set traps for her. He once set strings/etc trap and caught his Mom and said, ah, ha, I caught you.

Richard tried to do a chin up on the towel rack in the bathroom—it broke away from the wall and he called for Dad—he was just standing there holding the broken towel rack.

Ben snuck into Sharon's room and got one of her razors. Mom had told her to keep them put up or she couldn't shave her legs any more. He tried shaving his lip and cut it—cried out and we came running. I asked what happened and he said I don't know. But it was bleeding quite a bit.

Richard was standing at the head of his bed when his feet slipped down between the mattress and headboard hurting him. His alarmed cry brought us running and we were able to free him with just some bruised leg.

Ben and his friends Scott and Stuart liked to climb the hall walls—literally. One foot one each side of the wall and they could climb up to the ceiling. We didn't mind, just let them play. When Scott's dad came to pick him up and saw him up at the ceiling, he almost had a something.

When we got puppy Scooter, Richard and Sharon ran and ran with him in the back yard—I cautioned they would run his legs off. Scooter was Pekinese with long hair which we had cut in the summer time, making him look like a bulldog.

Sharon was not afraid of frogs but Richard did not like them. She picked up on and said "yahhh" as she stuck it in Richard's face.

Sharon had some small frogs and decided they needed a bath, with soap. It killed them (yes they "croaked").

We cut the last orange into slices so Richard and Sharon could share. Richard exclaimed, "She licked all the orange slices so I wouldn't get any."

Sharon had interesting way of saying things. Learning to read, she sounded out the letters for "up". U sounds like U and P so the word is UUPP ("you-p"). I corrected her but realized it should be pronounced that way. Instead of saying lets dig that up, she said lets un-plant it.

When Sharon asked why I quit playing church softball, I said, Oh I'm too old and ugly to play. She said, you are not too old.

+++
++++++++++++

Grisamore—Assignment#4—June2013

WRITING YOUR AUTOBIOGRAPHY FOR LOVED ONES

Part IV: Now and Beyond

4-1. What is different now about your home than the home your raised your family in? In the not-to-distant future, we may have to move into assisted living but for now, this is the same house in which we raised our family. But now it is more empty and quiet—and less alive-- with the children gone. Our children visit for a few hours and occasionally our two grand-darlings (Rylee and Haven) stay overnight. But the house misses our children's vibrancy and aliveness--and them. ((Younger son and friend used to literally climb the hallway walls. Of course the house misses that.))

4-2. HOW HAS YOUR COMMUNICATION WITH OTHERS CHANGED OVER THE YEARS (EMAIL, PHONE, ETC.)? We used to write and receive hand written letters from each of our Mothers. Now about the only letter we get is from Delores' oldest sister Laurie who does not have a computer. Cell phones/smart phones make it easy to call and send short messages instantly no matter where the person is, which can be nice. (Some nuts text while driving—guess they do not mind the possibility of killing or being killed.) Smart phone was helpful to get and send emails and calls when Delores was in the hospital overnight. (It also has weather and map features which are nice.)

4-3. REFLECT BACK ON SOME OF THE PLACES YOU HAVE TRAVELED OVER THE YEARS. HAVE YOU EVER TRAVELED TO A FOREIGN COUNTRY AND WISH YOU HAD LIVED THERE? Never been to a foreign country (does Washington DC count? Joke). Have travelled to a number of other states—each state is beautiful in its own way. Rocky Mountains, Niagara Falls (why doesn't it run out of water—being replaced at the same rate), the Alamo, River Walk (someone said friend fell into that river panicked, yelled I can't swim—friends yelled "stand up" only 2 feet deep), Garden of the Gods, etc. Always glad to get back to Georgia. Born and raised in Georgia and do not want to live anywhere else.

4-4. HOW HAS TIME CHANGED YOU PHYSICALLY AND EMOTIONALLY? In so many ways. In my mind I can still do the things of my youth. Now that I am 68, my body often tells me when I shouldn't do something—or should not have. Now mostly bald (like by "hair brush for bald men", brush with no bristles.), waist line up to 36 inches, weight 165 (when married 28 in waist, 125 pounds), still about 5' 6". In Dec. 2004, had back and leg injury—putting my tiny grand-darling in low to floor play pen and bone broke off spine hitting nerve sending lightning bolt pain down my left leg. Had surgery but left leg atrophied some, weakness, numbness, but am blessed, can still walk, climb stairs, etc. Cannot jog or run—used to jog in 10K (6.2 mile) races. Cannot play tennis. Might could golf but not sure good for back or leg. Used to play softball for Trinity United Methodist but age suggested I give that up some years before my back injury. Still enjoy going to yard sales. Could cut grass but have decided to hire someone to do it. We also have someone help clean the house once a month. My wife has had three back, three shoulder and several other surgeries. She is not home-bound but is more restricted in the last several years. I now do most of the cooking, laundry, etc. Being her (part-time) care giver has changed what I do and her condition changed what we attempt. Traveling is not much fun any more—do not plan to go to Disney, the beach, the mountains, etc. any more.

EMOTIONALLY—Retirement helped ease many stresses and pressures. In some areas, am more tolerant, try to laugh instead of getting upset. ((Charles Kurault, "On the Road", told of visiting Indian tribe who said "the little people" made them drop things, or hid things and laughed instead of getting angry. I am trying to laugh with the little people.)) Sadly, my temper is still volatile when I sometimes do not get my way. Try more and more to see the lighter side of life. A quote from high school "laugh and the world laughs with you, weep and you weep alone" is so true. I enjoy jokes and funny stories perhaps more than ever. My wife also is humorous. My stories in "When I was a Boy in Georgia" were nearly all "non-serious" or a light look at life. Try not to take myself too seriously. Recently, on second floor in Atlanta hospital, lady was "whisper-shouting" at a friend going down the escalator but friend could not hear her. I asked the lady what was her friend's name, she said Sharon. I leaned over and shouted very loud "SHARON"—friend looked up. Guess we are afraid of what strangers will think of us. Older I get, less I care about what strangers think. Family and friends already know I'm a little "unusual or eccentric" in some ways. At my sister-in-law's funeral, it was windy and cold, I was very cold. After that, I decided, "I'm old enough, cold-natured enough and bald headed enough that I will wear a hat anytime and anywhere I want to, regardless of social conventions." I might look a little strange sitting in church with a knit hat on, but at least I am warm. I keep a sweater in our Sunday School room. I take a jacket with me to all doctor offices because they are often cold. Yep, carrying a sweat shirt in the summer might look strange but I prefer to be warm.

4-5. IF YOU HAVE BEEN SLOWED BY AGE, WHAT ARE SOME OF THE SIMPLE ACTIVITIES THAT YOU MISS DOING THE MOST? When married, the limitations of one affect the other. I miss the physical closeness that is now more difficult. Have found that gravity is very quick. That the ground/floor is further away than it used to be. Now when something falls to the floor, we get the "helper, extender, picker-upper" with which to pick it up. Think I must be getting taller, because I cannot reach my feet to clip my toenails. Memory wise, seems I have trouble remembering simple words sometimes—later it will come to me and I wonder why I couldn't remember it. ((Recent thought: Only two people can make our marriage better or worse.)) Eyes have some floaters (or dent on retina) which reduces my desire and ability to read, and I have always enjoyed reading.

4-6. WHAT TYPE OF ACTIVITIES DO YOU NOW ENJOY? ARE YOU SURPRISED AT SOME OF THEM? Have become more of a watcher than doer—enjoy watching television (too much) such as westerns, sports, classic stories, history, nature, etc. Enjoy yard sales, last year started buying stuffed animals, washing, drying, tagging and giving to others or groups with note saying "do a good deed and pass me on, or keep me". This has been well received, with lots of thank yous, smiles and a few hugs. Still enjoy reading but somewhat less. Recently took trip by myself to Camp Pinnacle, Clayton GA to give the camp 350 stuffed animals to give to the girls and staff there. Sort of a "thank you" to the people who made my trip there in 1959 and 1960(?) so memorable (first time I saw mountains) and special. Enjoy riding down back roads (when able to take a trip). Enjoy "piddling" projects around the house and sometimes at children's houses.

4-7. DO YOU ENJOY OUTDOOR ACTIVITIES SUCH AS GARDENING? WAS THIS SOMETHING YOU DEVELOPED OR HAVE ALWAYS ENJOYED? Never liked gardening or yard work, it was work. Enjoy watching grand-darlings swim next door but water is too cold for me. Walk around block or at mall sometimes but leg/ankle/knee pain limits. Tend more and more to be inside person.

4-8. WHAT ARE SOME OF THE "JOBS" YOU CONTINUED TO DO, EVEN AFTER YOU OFFICIALLY RETIRED? When I retired in 2003, I retired. Took off my watch because for years very controlled by it. My wife and I each wanted little to no commitments. There is a Garfield cartoon that shows him lying flat on his back, his thoughts "I like to start my day slowly", next panel he is still lying there with no caption, and final panel he is still lying there with caption "Then build up to this". That is my retirement goal. As I grew up, noticed how hound dogs just lazied around—again something to which I aspire.

4-9. ARE YOU SENTIMENTAL? HOW OFTEN DO YOU PULL OUT OLD PHOTO ALBUMS AND SCRAPBOOKS? Yes I am sentimental. Enjoy old childhood photo albums as well as newer ones of our children and grand-children. Enjoy reviewing my high school yearbook, and remembering the good old days.

4-10. HAVE YOU EVER HAD A BRUSH WITH FAME AND FORTUNE? No to both—we are great strangers. Ed Grisamore wrote an article about my giving wooden nickels to veterans and included it in one of his books ("Never Put a Ten-Dollar Tree in a Ten-Cent Hole", page 173).

4-11. WHAT HAS BEEN THE ONE NATIONAL NEWS EVENT DURING YOUR LIFETIME THAT HAS FACINATED YOU THE MOST? DID THAT EVENT (OR OTHERS) CHANGE YOUR UNDERSTANDING OF THE WORLD? Greatly shocked by Kennedy's assassination. Also greatly shocked by 9-11—many changes resulted from this and will continue for a long time—such as increased security, Iraqi War, increased national debt, etc.

4-12. HOW HAVE YOUR TASTES CHANGED IN FOOD, BOOKS, MUSIC, ETC? I still want to eat some things that my body dislikes such as onions, spicy food, greasy food, etc. More and more leaning toward bland and blander diet. Don't read as many westerns but prefer mysteries more. Like short stories more—perhaps indicating a declining attention span? Have always and still like country and western music, and religious songs. Favorite singers are "The Statler Brothers", especially "the Class of '57". Really like "Hymn of Promise" and its comforting thoughts about heaven.

4-13. DO YOU READ YOUR BIBLE DAILY OR MEDITATE? Not daily but am religious and love Jesus. Have been blessed to receive religious Christmas stories—usually one a year. Sometimes when I re-read them I say "did I write that?" (think I got "Help").

4-14. IF YOU ARE A GRANDPARENT, HOW DOES IT DIFFER FROM BEING A PARENT? Love being a grandparent—our two grand-darlings are just wonderful. Their parents have the responsibility and we get the enjoyment. Their love and innocence rekindled loving impulses, laughs, love of life, joy of new discoveries, etc.

4-15. DO YOU HAVE ANY RECURRING DREAMS AT NIGHT? WHAT DO YOU THINK THEY MEAN? One dream is a bear is chasing me, getting closer and closer—I wake up and and and…it is my wife snoring. (My grand-darlings love it when I tell about that dream.) Another is tornadoes—have always been afraid of tornadoes. Recently, tornado came and got me and I kept saying, "I love you Jesus, I love you Jesus…" That was encouraging. One is I am looking for a bathroom and cannot find one—wake up and realize I need to go to the bathroom. In another, am on a trip and get lost—may indicate doubt about what I am doing.

4-16. OF ALL YOUR PERSONALITY TRAITS, WHICH IS THE ONE YOU HOPE FAMILY MEMBERS WILL REMEMBER MOST ABOUT YOU WHEN YOU'RE GONE? WHAT IS THE ONE

TRAIT THAT HAS NEVER CHANGED ABOUT YOU? Tough questions. Perhaps, love of Jesus, love of family, my sense of humor, sometimes generous in small ways, hopefully honesty, etc. One unchanging trait is my most basic belief "GOD IS"; another is love of children and grandchildren, honesty.

4-17. HAVE YOU BECOME MORE TOLERANT OR LIBERAL ABOUT THE IDEAS AND LIFESTYLES OF OTHERS AS YOU HAVE GOTTEN OLDER? With influence from my wife, have become a little more tolerant of gay lifestyles. Am more conservative politically--$17 trillion national debt is scary. Am less tolerant of those who do not want to work and have several generations on welfare, food stamps, etc.

4-18. WE ALL HAVE "BURNED BRIDGES." DO YOU HAVE ANY REGRETS? Nothing comes to mind about burned bridges. Regret not recognizing our children's medical issues earlier.

4-19. WHO ARE SOME OF YOUR FRIENDS OR FAMILY MEMBERS FROM EARLIER YEARS THAT YOU REGRET HAVING LOST CONTACT WITH? We keep planning to get back together with our friends the Walters. I looked for Charles Peterson from college but could not find him—need to try again.

4-20. THINK BACK TO SOME OF THE GOALS YOU SET EARLIER IN LIFE. DID YOU ACHIEVE THEM? WHY OR WHY NOT? Wanted a college degree and teaching job which I achieved. Wanted to get married and have children, which I did. Wanted to be a published author—can now publish my autobiography—but also would like to publish "Some Christmas Stories". Wanted to be financially rich and have not accomplished that—except by comparison—people in third world countries would consider our small home a castle and us rich. So I am blessed.

4-21. WHAT IS NOW YOUR DEFINITION OF A FULFILLED LIFE? We are blessed—had a good Civil Service career, have three good, good children, two good, good grandchildren. Married in 1966—never thought anyone would put up with me that long—after all, my parents "kicked me out" at 17 to go to college. Most important is love of God and Jesus as my savior.

4-22. A HUNDRED YEARS FROM NOW, WHAT DO YOU THINK YOUR GENERATION WILL BE REMEMBERED FOR? For the National debt. For allowing illegal immigrants to flood the country and turn the US into another bankrupt Latin American country. For our being so naïve about people taking advantage of well-intended laws. For our generosity. For our military protection of the world. For the decline of the family and church. Sometimes God gives us what we want, not what we need, and our free will makes a mess of things.

4-23. AS YOU HAVE GOTTEN OLDER, WHAT HAS BEEN YOUR ATTITUDE ABOUT DEATH? As more of my family and friends—sometimes younger—have died, I have realized death is coming closer. It is inevitable. Sometimes when great suffering exists, death may be welcome. I used to not go to visitations or funerals—scared me—now I go to many to at least pay my respect to the person and family. Am confident

Jesus will save me and take me to heaven. At funeral, celebration, have thought it would be good to sing "O Happy Day when Jesus took me to heaven to stay..." Also, "Hymn of Promise" is comforting.

4-24. "IF YOU HAD TO WRITE A NOTE—ONE NOTE—AND LEAVE IT PROPPED AGAINST THE SUGAR BOWL ON YOUR KITCHEN TABLE FOR FUTURE GENERATIONS TO READ, WHAT WOULD YOU SAY IN THAT NOTE?" (Question from the book "Notes from the Kitchen Table.")   Love God and Jesus—remember "GOD IS", love your family, try to love others as yourself, as Jesus said. Anyone can be a jerk, be a special good, good person. Upon seeing first born, thought "This is what life is all about." Cherish every minute of life.

4-25. OTHER. Like the poem "Keep A Goin'" and its meaning. Like "The moving finger writes and having writ, moves on...."   Like "O wad some power the gift to give us, the power to see ourselves as others see us." One of my sayings, "The GREAT I CHOOSE, is real and there are consequences to our choices".

++++++

YO. --

Grisamore-All-4-Assignments—June2013 (JUST THE QUESTIONS TO AID YOU IN WRITING YOUR OWN AUTOBIOGRAPHY)

((There was more—but I stopped here.))

++++++++++++++

7. VETERANS--WE THANK YOU. The following article was published in the Macon (GA) "Telegraph" in November 2005. It is my attempt to honor current military personnel and veterans.

United States Military Service By Donnie Powell

U. S. Military Service is a noble calling. The frozen, barefoot military of Valley Forge were the midwives at the birth of this country. Through the years the military has provided the shield to allow freedom to nourish and grow.

The military allows us to have a Republic, liberty, freedom of religion, freedom to assemble, freedom to bear arms, schools, courts, society, and on and on. Each military person takes an oath to protect and defend the United States against all enemies and to protect the Constitution. Liberty and freedom are not just words but are worth dying for to them.

Military service is a life changing event. It broadens the perspective of the individual member. It challenges the member to become a part of something special, something important. If in combat they are asked a lot at so young an age—to put themselves in harms way for others. Most who are in the military realize they are part of something bigger than themselves and are willing and able to rise to unbelievable heights of service and devotion. It makes them better people and better citizens.

The military has become a strong arm of democracy but willingly controlled by the civilian sector, ensuring a peaceful continuance of the government of the people, by the people and for the people. The United States, with all its faults, continues to be the country most sought after by the peoples of many, many countries, who continue to try to come to this country for a better way of life and to breathe freedom—to let their soul taste the sweetness of freedom for the first time. The U. S. military protects many countries of the world, just by being in existence. The U. S. military also is able to reach out a helping hand to many countries especially in times of disaster.

General Patton supposedly said "war—all other forms of human endeavor pale in comparison to it". A paraphrase might be "military service—all other forms of human endeavor pale in comparison to it". The military accept a sacred trust to preserve the United States.

Most military personnel look back and know they did something truly worthwhile—that on their watch the country was safe—freedom continues to breathe. For their entire lives, most know their military service "was my finest hour." The end.

THANK YOU FOR YOUR SERVICE!

+++++++++++++++++++++++++++++++

A BABY IS JUST AN ANGEL   By Donnie Powell (Written about 1970 and modified ever since)   (Baby is Angel-Feb07)

A baby is just an angel, without any wings.

A baby is just an angel, crawling on the floor.

with baby food on his face.

that wets you now and then.

without any hair.

you rock to sleep every night.

keeps you awake all night.

A baby is just an angel, who needs all your love.

that gets sick sometimes.

learning to turn over for the first time.

taking his first steps with hands in the air.

who makes you smile quite a lot.

that makes you sing nearly all the time.

who is entrusted to your care.

A baby is just an angel, with her daddy wrapped around her little finger.

who is born prematurely and scares you a lot.

that makes you thank God more.

who is nearly perfect in almost every way.

that strews toys faster than two adults can pick them up.

loving life to the fullest.

crying during the family photo session.

A baby is just an angel, who is what life is all about.

playing in the bath tub surrounded by 1,000 toys

and when the bath is over, has dry soap and washcloth.

learning to run, swing, swim, play ball.

hugging and kissing you goodnight.

that has more energy than two parents.

A baby is just an angel, who makes your heart skip a beat with love.

that grows up all too fast.

skipping out to climb into her bus to go to kindergarten, with her lunch in one hand

and her dad's heart in the other, and there I stand with a lump in my throat and tears in my eyes.

wanting   a   puppy,   kitten, hamster, parakeet, etc.

who cries almost as much as you do when he goes to first grade.

going to her first dance and is more beautiful than a heavenly angel.

who for no reason says he loves you.

who has a broken heart and all you can do is suffer with him.

A baby is just an angel, that is suddenly a teenager, but, it seems, was born just yesterday.

graduating from high school.

going out into the world with all your prayers and hopes.

A baby is just an angel, that you love all your life.

A baby is just an angel, who will be with us in heaven for eternity.

Yes, a baby is all of these and more; Thank you God, for loaning us three of your angels.

Added after grandchildren born; A baby is just an angel who says yes I want to marry, I love him with all my heart; who says "Are you ready to be grandparents?"; who has two little grand-darlings you love as if they were your own children; who says "I love your O-MA and O+PA". Who make your heart smile with warmth whenever you think of them. (Dedicated to our three angels, Richard, Sharon, and Ben—add lines for your angels.) (Copyright 1996)

++++++++++++++++++++++++

PRAISE GOD! IT'S A WONDERFUL LIFE!

++
+++++++

EXCERPTS FROM

POWELL'S MISCELLANEOUS THOUGHTS AND STORIES   (Published 2018)

#17 TRIBUTE TO TRAVIS   (1978)

He's been dead since 1965. I don't know why I still think about him but I do. Usually, it is when someone mentions competitiveness. He and I were high school classmates and he was the most athletically competitive person I have ever known. He was not blessed with great size or ability, but was slightly above average in both. We had no football or track team but he could have made our basketball team most years. However, our class and the ones ahead and behind us were laden with talented players so he did not make the team. But that did not stop him from competing in "sand lot" baseball, basketball, touch football and his best—tennis.

As the luck of the draw or choosing would have it, I was usually—if not always—on the other team. I never was the best on my team so I didn't have the responsibility of "head to head" or "face to face" confrontation with him. But I could easily observe his competitiveness. To Travis, if it was a game, it was worth winning. If hustle, determination, and aggressiveness could give the edge or the victory, then he had them. Bear Bryant's philosophy of "winning is the only thing", described Travis perfectly.

He was not great but he was always one of the best in sand lot games or on the tennis court. Have you ever seen people play tennis who have had no coaching? That was us. But since we played so much, we began to develop quite a bit of skill. Travis was not a great tennis player when serving or playing the baseline, but on the net he was devastating. His form was wrong (mine too) and he played too close to the net. Had a well-coached player seen him, he would have said, "He doesn't know how to play the game", or "He's out of position". But I have never seen anyone play the net any better. He had an instinct for playing the net. Many a time I made what I thought was a good or great shot, only to see Travis make a tremendous effort and with that quick, strong wrist action, bounce the ball not only over my head but over the screen!

He was particularly good in doubles, especially with his usual partner Billy who was an exceptionally good baseline player. They did not play up and back together as well-coached players do. Billy played base line whenever possible, and Travis owned the net, not just his side but all of it. Or at least you'd think he did the way he played it. Probably any good team that had been coached and had practiced together could have beaten them. But they were the best in that small town of Buena Vista GA. Maybe everyone didn't know it, but I sure did. And they were the best because they worked around their weaknesses, and worked well together as a team, and because of Travis' competitiveness.

Because I was usually on the other team—and therefore usually the loser—I didn't like Travis very much. But in looking back, I can see that he had many good qualities. He was from a family that was poor— perhaps poorer than mine. That alone should have made me feel a close kinship to him but it didn't. I regret that I never invited him to my church. As far as I know, he died in an auto accident without knowing Jesus. This I deeply regret. But if there is any way that he and I can get together after I die, and if such trivials as tennis are allowed, I'm sure he and I will play one more game. And when he slams that shot of mine over him head, over the screen and maybe even clean out of heaven, I'm sure I won't mind as much as I used to.

God bless you Travis.   (End)

UPDATE: His sister Carolyn messaged me through facebook that Travis went to Union church regularly and she was sure he was a Christian.

++++++++++++++++++++++++++

66.   LIFE-CHANGING EVENT BY ONE OR MORE TEACHERS   By Donnie Powell   June 2012 (File name is Powell-life-changing-June2012)

Marion County High School, Buena Vista GA, Class of 1962 just had its 50th reunion which prompted a lot of reminiscing, thoughts, stories, etc. After the reunion, it dawned on me that one or more teachers had a hand in a life-changing event for me.

My academic grades were good and I had dreams of college but my parents were not financially able to pay for my college education.

In the mid 1960's, to help alleviate a teacher shortage, the State of Georgia provided scholarships which paid for room, board, books, etc., as long as the student maintained a B average and paid back the loan by teaching in Georgia for three years. Do not remember how I learned of this scholarship but I am sure some teacher took the time to get an application form, encouraged me to apply, and probably gave me a good recommendation. I happily received the scholarship, completed 2 years at Georgia Southwestern (then) Junior College and graduated from Georgia Southern in 1965 with a teaching degree in math. I taught math for 3 years in Albany, Georgia and then obtained a civil service position in civilian personnel.

In looking back, I realized without that teacher's scholarship, I would not have gone to college,

not become a teacher, not met my wife, not qualified for the civil service position in civilian personnel which resulted in a good career, not have been the father of my wonderful children, and so on. What job(s) I would have landed without college is only speculation but would not have been as rewarding, and whom I might have married (if any) I cannot guess.

The light bulb came on. Some wonderful teacher(s) went out of his/her way to help me go to college—a life-changing event that I only just recently recognized. Wish I could remember who and I hope I thanked them.

++++++

NOTE: I want to thank Dennis Parker whose tribute to one of his teacher's got me to thinking about the impact on my life of un-remembered teacher(s) who steered me toward a teacher's scholarship and how different my life would have been had this not happened. Though my experience is far less dramatic than Dennis', it was still a life-changing event. I suspect many classmates have been shaped and helped by our teachers, often in un-remembered ways.

+++++++++++

(2018) Had another life-changing event or thought while waiting for interview for summer job. My brother Stout worked at trailer plant in Americus, GA and had arranged for me to have an interview. While waiting, the thought occurred that if I went to summer school for three summers I could graduate a year early and land one of those "high paying" teacher jobs. So I thanked the receptionist and cancelled the interview (think Stout was disappointed), rushed back to class, went on to summer schools and graduated college in 1965 instead of 1966. Having started first grade at 5 and a half, plus going to summer schools meant the ladies I dated while teaching in Albany were probably 2 or more years older than I. It also meant, had I graduated in 1966, I might never have met my wife-to-be Delores—been married 51 years.

(2018) How did we meet? It was "Some Enchanted Evening", and I saw her "across a crowded room---and somehow I knew I'd see her again and again"……..

+++++++++++

MR. MOSS AND STOUT

Mr. L. K. Moss was the Vocational Agriculture teacher for many years. One of his favorite sayings was "I said all that to say this". When my older brother Stout got married in the middle of his senior year, he dropped out and started to work. Mr. Moss went the extra mile--he pulled Stout's records, came to Mom and explained that Stout had enough credits to graduate and get his diploma—all he had to do was complete a test (or something). Stout did and got his diploma which may well have helped him in future jobs—certainly it helped his confidence and feelings about himself. Mr. Moss did not have to do what he did, but he, like all our teachers, was not just a good teacher but a good person who cared for his students and helped people. I say all that to say this, "Thank you Mr. Moss for being a good, caring teacher and a Christian who put his faith to work in helping Stout."

+++++

70. FLAGS   (2018)

I made cement and wood pedestals to hold small U. S. Flags which were placed in front of our church Trinity United Methodist in Warner Robins GA on special holidays such as Memorial Day, 4th of July and Veterans' Day. Upon request also put them out for funerals of veterans at Trinity. After a few years, turned the flags over to the Scouts in Trinity. Also gave about 6 of the pedestals and flags to Parkway Funeral Home which they display on holidays. During one service at Trinity, gave a small flag for auto windows to each veteran—at the time over 50. Preacher allowed me to give this salute to our veterans in church—"(with two middle fingers curled signifying "Love") "From our heart, we the people thank you for your sacrifice, courage, devotion and service—May God bless and keep you. " (Then led them in Pledge of Allegiance to the Flag.) Several have expressed appreciation of the flags in front of the church. On occasion, have given a flag to veterans I have met.

Several years ago, placed a flag on the graves (the ones I could find) of my former teachers and high school classmates—tried to honor them in some small way. Have some relatives who were veterans of WWII, Korea, or Vietnam—placed a flag on their graves. Also placed a US Flag on known graves of my ancestors in Marion County, Georgia—some were veterans of the War Between the States. (Interesting that after I placed a US Flag on a Confederate veteran graves, someone (a cousin I guess) placed a Confederate flag on the graves. My thinking was they were born and died under the US Flag and answered the call to arms for the Confederacy so they are deserving of both flags.)

Placed flag on great-uncle Stephen Davis' grave—he was Ocilla policeman killed in the line of duty. (He is buried at Smyrna Presbyterian cemetery in Marion County, GA area called Church Hill). I heard about the Public Safety Memorial in Forsyth, contacted them, got supporting documentation to have his name (and two others J. P. McInnis and T. W. Sheffield) added to the memorial. Mother (Mina Davis Powell), her sister Sarah D. French and daughter Cornelia and I went to the ceremony on May 26, 1998 where Stephen's name was added—very solemn and impressive.

Placed flags on my ancestors including Shadrack Addison Davis, who carved wooden letters backwards and used them to write on the cement slabs of deceased friends and neighbors. (He was digging a grave in bad weather, caught pneumonia and died in 1930. The letters were used to write on his own grave.) A graduate student Anne Chance (student of Dr. John Burrison, professor of Folklore and Folk Material Traditions at Georgia State University). , documented the letters and published her findings in "AGS Quarterly", Vol. 34, No.1, Winter 2010. Donated the letters to Museum (acceptance of the letters was approved by Dr. Burrison), in Atlanta so they would not be lost.

WITNESS TO WAR. In 2011, heard about this non-profit effort to video veterans (mainly of WWII) as they told of their experience. Wanted them to interview WWII veterans in our church—contacted them ((witnesstowar.org)) and they asked me to set up the meetings—arranged two meetings at Robins AFB Museum of Aviation. Names of some interviewed:

Sam O'Quinn (radio operator on three planes that crash landed—See Macon Telegraph, Nov 9, 2013, page 1D), Carswell Wynne, Winton Cain, Larry Westbrook, J. B. Fauscett, Clyde Mathe, Sr (think he was in WWII, Korea and Vietnam—not many did that), Ralph Pannell, John Manning, Gene Sullivan (see Macon Telegraph, 29 May 2011, page 1A he put Flags on Graves of Vets), Buford Cummings (See Perry Home Journal, 1 June 2011, Page 1A), Jim Lane (Emily Carley interviewed him at home.)

NOTE: I encourage any veterans to record your story— witnesstowar.org is one organization to consider. In 2023 helped 4 Vietnam veterans video record their story—one has since passed. Some are unable to talk about their experience. Thank you all veterans.

++++++++++++++++++++++++++++++++

73. BROTHER RICKY'S MEMORIES   May 2009
Written by Ricky Powell, typed by Donnie Powell

Mom and Dad got married May 22, 1926. Dad was 21 at the time. Mom turned 14 on May 19, 1926. She was 14 only three (3) days when she married Dad.

Dad said the only lie he ever told was that Mom was 18 when he got their marriage license. Back then you had to post your marriage license for 3 days on the public bulletin board in the Court House. Dad posted it but under some other papers so no one would see it and tell her parents or if her father saw it, he could tear it down and rip it up thus preventing their marriage.

On Saturday, May 22, 1926, Mom and Dad got married in Richland, Ga by the preacher of her church. They were in a Ford car (?Model T?) that Daddy owned on halves with Uncle Bo Powell. They saw the preacher walking down the street and pulled up to him and he stood outside the car and married them while they sat in the car.

They went back and told her parents of their marriage. Her father who was pretty religious, said to them "Mina, I think you have played hell."

Dad wound up giving his half of the car to Uncle Bo partly I think because Bo was mad with him when he got back for having the car so long that day. Daddy said that that car was the last think he ever owned on halves. He said that if he couldn't buy it, he would just do without it or wait till he could afford to buy it. He also said he was still paying for that one lie 71 years later.

Mom's Mother saw their preacher later on and asked him, "Did you know you married my baby girl the other day?" He replied, "Yes". She asked him "Why?" He replied that he thought it was time she got married. (Donnie comment: Think I remember Mom saying he did it because he knew they were determined to get married and if he didn't do it someone else would.)

In 1965, 66, or 67, in the summer time I think, Mom and I (Ricky) once went to Florida to see Brenda and her first husband Byron Mixon. They lived in a small white house in Graceville which is just across the Florida state line. We left early on Saturday morning. We went down US 27 thru Cuthbert. We stopped at the

Kolomoki Indian Mounds near there. We had to wait awhile for the park to open at 900 A.M. We looked it over then got back on the road. I think we stayed on the less traveled roads instead of going thru Dothan, Alabama to get there. I could only navigate for Mom because I was not old enough to legally drive. Brenda and Byron took us to Panama City to the "strip" as it was called. We played Putt-Putt golf at the one with the jungle animals. I had my camera along and took pictures of Mom, Brenda and Byron and me in front of some of the animals. We did a couple of other things but really can't remember what. We even went to his parents' house.

In 1975, 76 or early 77, the Country Western look was in so I asked Mom to fix up 2 western style long sleeve shirts I had. She did a lot of embroidery work on them, back and front. On the medium rusty brown shirt, she stitched on my initials about 8 or 9 inches tall and all around the initials. She also made me four shirts from scratch—to me they looked better than any store bought shirt anybody had. She made one black with white stitching and with white and green embroidery on it. I installed white snaps on it. She made a white one with red stitching and embroidery. I installed red snaps on it, two each on both front patches, three on each cuff and six down the front. She also made me a medium dark green and a grayish brown one each with white stitching and with green, white, and yellow embroidery on them. I also had a blue denim long sleeve western shirt that she also embroideried my initials on the back of it and all the way around the initials which were 8 or 9 inches tall. (Donnie comment:

302

Ricky told me people asked who made the shirts and were told my Mom. They often didn't believe that. Ricky bought some labels "Made by Mother" and then people believed him.) (Donnie comment: He was buried in one of those shirts.)

When I was about 10 years old, I asked (old) Mr. Burton Wight for a job. He hired me for Saturdays—that was when the Ford place and Wight Oil Co. stayed open all day. Anyway, one winter in 1964-65-66, it snowed late on Friday and early Saturday morning, but being loyal employees Daddy and I went to work. That Saturday morning, Mom went outside in housecoat and gloves and made a snowman on the hood of our 1962 blue and white Ford Galaxie car. I took pictures of Mom making the snowman and of the snowman itself which took several hours to melt. Dad drove slow and the snowman stayed on the hood till midafternoon before melting and sliding off the hood to the ground.

I also have pictures of Mom shooting hoops one afternoon at the basketball goal Dad and I put up from one of the old Sinclair gas signs and pipe frame.

I remember when I first got married, Debbie scrambled me a couple of eggs and they tasted like the iron frying pan. I asked Mom how long it took before a frying pan got where you did not taste it. She said I needed to season them—in other words you had to put a large bit of lard or grease in them and cook them on high for a while, let it cool down and then do it again. It usually helped to put an Irish potato or two sliced in half the second time you heated it up.

303

I never heard my Mother say anything bad about any of her sons- or daughters-in-law even when there were problems between her children and their spouses. My spouse Debbie, in 1983, had problems with her legs having blood clots in them and had to be hospitalized in Buena Vista that was when we still had the hospital here. Debbie's blood clots were not responding to what they were doing for them in BV, so they transferred her to St. Francis hospital in Columbus. I was Parts Manager at the Ford place in Americus (about 27 miles Southeast of BV) so when I closed up at 5:30 PM, I came home, changed clothes and went to see Debbie in Columbus (about 35 miles West of BV). Well Mom and Dad insisted on going with me each night for that week she was in St. Francis Hospital. That let me know how much they cared for me and my wife.

((Donnie comment: Wish Ricky had written more.))

+++++++++++++++++++

85. AN AUTO ACCIDENT IN 1956/7 NEAR TAZEWELL (Note: True story. This article in "The Journal" –Buena Vista GA, on Nov 16, 2016, Page 4 & 9)

BACKGROUND: Henry Harbuck, a minister, led the ceremony celebrating the life of his brother Paul. A number of family and friends (including five of Paul's high school classmates) were in attendance there at the Tazewell Baptist Church on 5 Nov. 2016. The following was told by Henry Harbuck to Donnie Powell (a classmate of Paul's) and several others. Paul's other

304

classmates in attendance were Dennis Parker, Bobby Woolridge, Robert Matthews, and Jack Christopher.

+++++++++++++++++++++++++++++

When asked if he was in "the wreck", Henry said "Yes" and shared his memories of it.

Four of them were returning from Marion County High School band practice in Buena Vista, GA. Benny Pike was driving with Harbuck siblings Paul, Henry and (?) Ellen as passengers. Benny wanted to impress--or maybe scare--sister with his driving skills. Henry and Paul told him to slow down but he did not-- even as they approached the bad (worse back then) curve near Gin Creek just outside Tazewell. They went off the road with auto turning over several times—no seat belts back then. Henry got out and wondered if he was in a dream. He heard his sister screaming (the Owens who lived about a quarter of mile away, also heard her). Later learned she had a broken back which took several years to completely heal. Benny had broken leg and Paul was injured too.

Henry realized he needed to get some help. Saw a car coming from Tazewell and ran into the road to flag it down. Briars and the wreck had scratched him and tore his shirt and he was bleeding some but he managed to stop the car—which came to a screeching stop. Henry told the driver, "We have had a bad wreck and people are hurt. We need to get them to a doctor or they might die." The driver said, "I'm Doctor Robinson (from Buena Vista), and I'll take care of them." And he did. One of God's angels at the right place at the right time.

Henry later learned a miraculous fact about the doctor being there. Doctor Robinson, had received a phone call from the daughter of a patient in Butler (Tazewell is on the road between Butler and Buena Vista). He drove the 25 miles to the patient's house, but the daughter said she had NOT called him. Confused and puzzled the doctor started his return trip home. And just outside Tazewell he saw someone in the road waving him down.

Henry said that event had a profound effect on Doctor Robinson the rest of his life. Henry shared too that was when he began to think about the ministry. Benny went on to become a medical doctor. Paul and Ellen remembered the event for the rest of their lives and were shaped by it.

+++++++++++++

NOTE: Dennis Parker, a classmate of Paul's has read a book "God Winks" and recommended it. The author gives examples of when such unusual circumstances occur that it can only be the work of God's action— when He winks at us. Think the wreck and Dr. Robinson being there was truly a God Wink. The word "circumstances" can often be spelled-- "G-O-D".

+++++++++

Cemetery. Headstone or obelisk (about 2 feet tall) fell over. (It was for my great uncle Steve Davis who was killed in line of duty in 1910—provided info and had his (and two others) name added to the memorial at the Georgia Safety Training Center in Forsythe. He is buried at New Smyrna Presbyterian cemetery about 12 miles south of Buena Vista GA.) Obelisk too heavy for me to pick up—so got a bunch of short 2 by 4 boards, tipped it up onto one board, rocked it over so could place 2 boards under other side and so on. Had to raise it about a foot to get level with the foundation stone. Going good until almost to the top and for some reason the boards would tilt and not let me raise it any more—lowered obelisk some, tried again, same thing. So just went for it and it worked. Put some putty around it and last time I checked—still standing. My sister Joyce was with me (we had been to a Powell reunion at Union Methodist)—when I finished she said—you are your father's son.

In same cemetery, grandfather Shadie Davis (and others) buried there. Noticed Chinaberry debris had covered his concrete slab covering his name etc. on it. (He had carved (backwards) wooden letters to write on cement slab graves. Mom said they used those letters to write on his grave—in a way he wrote on his own grave.) So decided to clean litter off the grave but also came prepared to cut down the tree—about 30 feet tall. No chain saw (I'm afraid of them), used hand saw, rope, etc., Did not want to damage the graves and was able to use rope to pull it right into an open space—almost—broke one of the cement blocks surrounding the graves. Don't tell EPA, but then used gasoline to pour over the tree stump and bushes to keep them from growing back. Need to make another trip over to visit my ancestors—

and be sure China Berry tree hasn't come back. (2018) (excerpt from about page 389 in book).

++

106. Stout, My Brother   by Donnie Powell 2018

Hello Stout,

Don't know that I have ever told you how much of a positive impact you had on me and my life. Wish I could remember more but here are some ways both you helped shape me, both directly and indirectly. Thank you more than I can say. Donnie

.1. You went to the Baptist church in Buena Vista and took Brenda Jane and me with you. That church had such a big and lasting impact on me. Even got to go to Camp Pinnacle, in Clayton GA twice—got to see the mountains for the first time and they left a lasting impression on me. Had you not attended First Baptist, I might not have turned out as well as I did—could have been much worse—who knows. Our family and the church helped me have an inner direction that served me all my life.

2. You were one of my role models—and still are. You were honest and always hard working—around the home place, in the logging business (doing a man's job at a young age), at Wight Motor company, New Moon, farming, Sumter County, etc. Always working and doing things.

3. You know/knew so many people. No matter what was wrong or broken, you seemed to know someone to call. For example, when Danny's leg was broken and he

308

was in the Americus hospital, I drove up (I think from Albany where I lived single from Aug 65 to Aug 66 then marriage) in the blue Falcon. When I left his room to return home, the car battery was dead—it was Sunday. You called someone who went to his service station/store and brought and installed a new battery and you paid him (hope I said thanks—if not, here is a very belated thank you very much.)

4. You arranged a job interview in the summer of 1963 at New Moon. As I sat waiting to talk to Loomis, it dawned on me that instead of a job, it I went to summer schools I could get a "high paying" teaching job a whole year earlier. Waiting for the interview, probably scared me with the realization that I might get this real job, a physically demanding job, and not being very mechanically inclined or coordinated, I would probably fail miserably. That realization motivated me to finish a year early and enabled me to meet Delores—had I got the summer job at New Moon, I would probably have tried to get one the other summers and have graduated in 66, Delores would probably have been swooped up—who knows who I might have married (if any) and I would not have had three wonderful children, two great children in law, and two super grand-darlings—you indirectly contributed to those wonderful blessings. So thanks for the sobering chance at an interview.

5. When you were working at Wight Motor Company, you could do just about everything—drove cars to Columbus, cemented base for gasoline pump, pump gas out front, find parts in the parts department, and many other things I don't remember. Back then, the Firestone

store was next door, and one day I followed you there and you tossed me a white football and said, "You can have it" (or maybe happy birthday). (Hope I said thank you—if not, here is another late one.) So, early on you helped me begin to learn the joy of giving. When Dad had to be out with his back surgery, he had me try to work in his place a few weeks one summer (maybe 1962). Believe Mr. Wight thought I could do everything you could but he was sadly disappointed—just little to no aptitude. But that experience did serve to motivate me to study harder.

6. Think maybe on my first day(s) of elementary school, Brenda Jane rode on bike behind Clements and I rode behind you—thanks for the ride (never did like to walk to or from town/school/church). Maybe I rode with you on your motor bike (or regular bike with a motor installed).

7. We hiked in the woods behind the house some—if you hadn't been with me I would have gotten lost—might still be lost to this day.

8. You gave us Scooter, the special dog that the kids loved until he died. Had a big impact on them and helped them love that dog unconditionally—which in turn helped shape them in a positive way.

9. You finished high school when it would have been easy not to (you were in the "Class of '57", a favorite Statler Brothers song). You always did well in later classes such as at Forsyth in a Georgia Public Safety class. You are/were very smart and capable and could have done well in the academic world but chose to work

with your hands building and creating things--while I just pushed paper to which I was more suited and you had an impact on me being able to do that.

10. You let me ride on your pet calf. I probably begged you to let me ride and you put me onto its back—which served as a launching pad when calf bucked me off. Again a good learning experience—be careful what you ask for you may get it and you might not like it.

11. At Uncle E. R. Jernigan's July 4th celebration, you warned me to "watch out, there is a deep hole there". But being an early smart alec, I said I won't step into it—glub, glub—can still remember seeing the bubbles as I sank like a rock. Your warning had alerted Clements who got to me first—I screamed and stayed away from the deep hole. But later I did learn to swim. So thanks for helping save me and motivating me to learn to swim.

12. You enjoyed dancing and you could dance. I just sort of took up space on the floor but I enjoyed trying. Once when fast dancing, I glanced at the girl and she was smiling—dawned on me later that she probably was not smiling at enjoying dancing but at my efforts to dance—thankfully she was kind and silent. Had you not been out there dancing, showing the way, I might never have tried it and missed out on a lot of fun.

13. You were the first of us to go to FFA/FHA camp and hearing you talk about it encouraged me to want to go. (Have no idea how Mom and Dad could afford to send us to camp.) Camp was a lot of fun and got to meet new people and learn new things—like square dancing

(mostly confused stomping around), shuffleboard, badminton, crafts like making a lanyard, etc. Camp created many life long memories. Had you not gone, I might have missed out on that.

14. When Ricky was no longer able to drive, you also took turns driving him to Albany for his doctor's appointment, to Plains for medicine and Americus for shopping—usually several stops plus helping him unload groceries at his home. When Ricky died, you took the lead in going through his things, organizing them, disposing of many, and again knowing someone, this time someone who had yard sales inside where we were able to sell some of his things. It was a sad and challenging time and it would have been impossible without you and your efforts.

15. You were a comforting big brother to me when I had a medical panic—well maybe I was just a bit skittish (no I was scared)—you and Barbara advised to just wait for the medical exam and hope for the best. Good and accurate advice—as usual.

16. You are and were a role model as a husband and father—for example, camping and boating—say didn't you (or someone in your boat) try to jump from your boat to a runaway boat to keep if from crashing or running over someone—even if I had thought about that I would not have attempted it—way to go.

17. You stood up with me when I got married and supported me in that major life event.

18. In the Bible story of the Prodigal Son, the younger son asks for his inheritance early and leaves. I have

always known that had I done that, my brothers would have come looking for me until they found me and brought me home.

These are just a few of the ways you helped shape me in a positive way—there are many others that neither of us remember. You have always been a good good person and someone I could count on and look up to. You have had a positive impact on many lives—especially mine. Thank you for being my big brother.   Donnie

((Added later: Stout said in passing a car, don't pull over until you see their headlights/front of car in your rear view mirror—still use that tip.))

+++++++++++

109. PARKER, DENNIS: A HIGH SCHOOL MEMORY 2012 By Dennis Parker

(Included with his permission)

Out of all my high school years, there was one teacher that I did not particularly care for at all. She gave me no reason for this and was never unkind to me in any way, in fact the opposite, but I just didn't like her!

In the tenth grade, Miss Evie White taught a class called "Typing I" and I enjoyed it because it was something different. In the eleventh grade it was "typing II" and again I enjoyed the class but not the teacher. I actually became quite good at typing and Miss White sent me to the boys district and state typing contest where I won 1st place in district and 4th place in state. Although the yearbook shows only "4th in district", I still have the old award certificates and pins for both.

In the senior year, I had one credit more than the number required for graduation and was assigned two "study hall" hours in the library. I was excited about this arrangement because a class friend and I enjoyed playing games with the librarian trying to keep her guessing who was talking when she turned her back.

Somehow Miss White learned about my free hour and insisted I take "Typing II" again that year with no credit and "just for the experience", thus eliminating my plans for an extra hour of fun in the library. When I tried to argue she put her hands on my shoulders and said, "You are going to do it and some day you will thank me!" Perhaps someday, but certainly not that day, as I now disliked her more than ever!

Five years later, I arrived in the Republic of South Vietnam with a MOS of "Heavy Equipment Operator". At a processing center in Cam Rahn Bay I was assigned to the 45th Engineer Group and put on a C-123 plane to their Headquarters at Qui Nhon. There I was placed in a hot transient tent while orders were being cut for me to move on to one of their five batallions in the field as a bull dozer operator clearing jungles to build roads.

A young clerk came in the tent asking if anyone there knew how to type. I half-way threw up my hand and he asked me to go with him, explaining on the way

314

that the Group commander's clerk was about ready to rotate home and they needed to replace him. After meeting the Colonel and a brief "typing test" my orders were changed from Heavy Equipment Operator to "S1 (administrative) Clerk" and I was assigned to the Group Headquarters for my year in sunny southeast Asia.

The Group soon moved north to Da Nang where the construction battalions were to build a road called "Hai Van Pass" over a mountain which was in hostile territory. Headquarters units were always located in the safest places possible and we were in a Marine compound built on the side of a small mountain. I felt perfectly safe there. My duties as S1 clerk switched from general office work to full time processing casualty reports from the five field battalions. Casualties did not happen in "shifts" so I worked 24 hours seven days a week and slept when I could .

The procedure included taking the details of the casualty from the field units by radiophone, typing them up in military reports, which were very detailed, and getting the "killed in action" ones on the next plane to Graves Registration in Saigon. I also worked closely with the Red Cross getting emergency messages to the field troops, including family deaths at home and some happy ones such as "you have a fine baby girl at home".

At first these reports bothered me, but eventually I learned that I could not dwell on the details and sadly, they became routine as more and more began to come in with deaths and all types of injuries.

One morning about 2:00 am I began to notice the statistics from our field unit casualties: "Dozer operator hit by sniper fire", "Bull Dozer hits land mine", "road construction crew ambushed", etc. The number of heavy equipment operator deaths was startling! Later that morning when I finally got to bed I couldn't sleep. I lay in my bunk thinking that I was processing the casualty reports of the people that were doing the job that I was originally assigned to do. I prayed, and I thanked God that I had been pulled out of the transient tent back in Qui Nhon and assigned to office work at the safe Group Headquarters, and right in the middle of that prayer, I thought of the name "Evie White" for the first time since high school.

Evie White! The high school teacher that I disliked so much! The high school teacher that saw something in me that I didn't see in myself! The high school teacher that placed her hands on my shoulders and said, "You are going to do it and someday you will thank me"!

History shows that the February 1968 Tet Offensive was the worst part of the Vietnam conflict and I was right in the middle of it. In a wart that took more than 58,000 lives and maimed more than 153,000 others, I came home with no close calls and no entertaining war stories, yet to this very day I live with two regrets: First, I never got the chance to apologize to Miss White for my unfounded dislike of her, and second, I never got to thank her for making me take typing three years and learn to do it well, which I truly believe, saved my life in Vietnam.

Thank you Miss White, wherever you are!

The End

By Dennis Parker, Class of 1962, Marion County High School, Buena Vista, Georgia.

(9532) MISS EVIE WHITE The 1959 Yearbook was dedicated to her and Mr. Mathews, the Principal. Thanks Dennis for your moving tribute to Miss White.

+++++++++++++++++

110. SALUTE TO JIM WIGGINS—WW II DIASBLED VET (2018)

Jim was my cousin (his mom and mine were sisters). He was badly injured in WWII, had a metal plate put in his head and walked with a limp and had trouble with his arm (right I think). He received three bronze stars which (I think) means he was in three major campaigns. When I knew him growing up, he was always happy and fearless--he drove his car at "warp" speed (scaring me when I rode with him—but I was easily frightened). Later it dawned on me, "after what he (and other vets) had seen and been through in battle, nothing could scare him—ever. Looking back, wish I had asked him about his military service--wish I had told him "thank you for your service—which very nearly cost you your life and did cost you the full use of your arm and leg. You, Jim, have earned the respect of us all and rightly deserve the title Hero."

Note: Though Jim was not killed in battle, he was only a few inches from making that ultimate sacrifice. Belatedly, I did place a US flag on his grave as a small tribute to him. He had a brother Curt in WWII and another Clinton "Bim" who was in the peacetime Army (and another brother whose name I have forgotten). His widowed mom struggled but raised four fine sons who served their country well.

+++++

On one June 6, Mr. L. G. Scott told my brother Ricky that at this time of the day back in 1944, "I was scared nearly to death. I was on Normandy Beach."

+++++++++

Comment: Here is a salute I have given to a few veterans and it applies to all veterans—"From our hearts, we the people, thank you and salute you for your dedication, service, devotion, courage, and sacrifice. May God bless you and yours." ((Published in Marion County, GA, "Journal", May 30, 2018, Page 4))

++++++

Again thank you all veterans.

++

++++++++++++++++++++++++

EXCERPTS FROM

POWELL'S #2 MISCELLANEOUS THOUGHTS AND STORIES 2020

++++++++++

.1. MONSTER IN MARION COUNTY? (Based on foggy memory of true events.) Rumors circulated about sightings of some kind of creature—around Walker Williams Lakes, out in the country near Brantley, and so on. One man found an unusual footprint—someone heard a noise in the bushes and shot the bush—some were not scared but as usual I was the scaredest—tried to hide it but stayed close to others. The monster or creature even got the notice of the Columbus tv or newspaper. Was a favorite topic of conversation. Finally, some actual facts were disclosed. The footprint was a regular print modified with a nail—others admitted what they saw was imagination in overdrive— and so on. Some were disappointed that Marion County did not have a monster—I just breathed a huge sigh of relief—one less thing to be afraid of. ((English teachers especially Mrs. Garrett would have me say "one less thing of which to be afraid."))

+++++++++++++++++

4. AGE OF FAMILY MEMBERS (true)

In high school had to fill out some forms listing various information including the birthdays of my parents and brothers and sisters. Of course I did not know so sort of guessed. When done, noticed that when the eldest was born Mom would have been about 10 years old. That night got info from Mom so would be prepared next time. Have found it easier to remember birth years than ages. By the way, Mom got married at age 14 and Joyce was born when Mom was 18, not 10.

319

++++++++++++++

... #5... L-12—(True) In 1960 when in tenth grade, for some reason, school had a "Powder Puff" (girls) touch football game. At first practice, some of us guys were there and played defense for a few plays. On first snap, I slipped thru the line, had a clear shot at touching the girl quarterback—but I had a problem— where could I touch the girl without getting into trouble—so missed her and she ran for yardage. Next play, their coach told the line to raise their elbows thus preventing me from getting through. Not sure which team won the game but think all had a good time—glad I was helpful in helping the "line-women" block for their quarterback.

M-13—(True) In elementary school (about 1956?) in an assembly program, a man used clay to sculpt heads/busts of famous people, one being Mark Twain. (Memory came as I watched PBS production about Mark Twain.) A classmate Lonnie Pike (?), had read story about him and we asked if the sculptor looked like Twain—he nodded confirming that it did. Wonder who the other busts were—guess I'll never know. Learned a lot at assemblies—in one we sang a dumb song "Pine Tree"—those were the only words. We would sing various songs (one "Up on the housetop click click click--and a classmate asked what is click click click), clubs would present programs, sometimes there would be a play, etc. –sadly often a wasted effort when trying to bestow art upon me.

N-14—Dad (born in 1904) said the school had a water bucket with a dipper shared by all the students.

He said students with runny noses would take a sip from the dipper and drop the un-drank water—cold germs and all—back into the bucket. I would have had a hard time dealing with that—ugh.

O-15—When a kid, someone would place forefinger and middle finger (spread open) on top of the same fingers of their other hand—with thumb hidden below. Then they would tell gullible person to stick their finger in there and "feed the crow"—when they did the thumb or "crow" would pinch/hurt the finger of the feeder.

When we would find a discarded pack of camel cigarettes we would remove the blue stamp and sometimes there would be a letter underneath—don't remember all of them but a "C" meant the person finding it would get or give a "crack" on the arm (ouch)—and an "H" meant a hit on the arm. If done just right, blow would raise a bump on the arm.

++++++++++

33. Memories from Joyce—Nov 2018

From Donnie--a suggestion--interview Joyce 16 Jan 2017

Lauren   Landrum   lauren.m.landrum@gmail.com 1/18/2017 3:16 PM

To   dd66rsb   dd66rsb   Quick   replyReply allForwardDelete

Hi Uncle Donnie,   Thank you for talking to Grandmother about this and sending this information!

It's really cool to hear about all of these things. Great stories.

It's a great idea to do interviews and capture all of this oral history. I'd like to set up some time with her to do that.

I wish there had been a way to do that going back generations, it sure would be interesting to have more information like this about the distant past.

Hope you are well!   Love, Lauren

On Mon, Jan 16, 2017 at 9:50 AM, dd66rsb dd66rsb <dd66rsb@cox.net> wrote:

Hello Lauren,

A couple of months ago, had opportunity to ride around with Joyce. Realized she is one of the oldest ladies in Marion Co. Thought it would be great for someone who knows how, to interview her and I thought of you. A few things/thoughts:

1. She remembers rationing during WW II. for just about everything including shoes--she saw a pair she wanted in one store.

2. She and maybe Grannie told of Grannie helping Papa work in the fields while Joyce was left in the house with her dress anchored to the bed.

3. She said when she and Gene got married they lived in a boarding house--one bath--five other men lived there.

4. Think she worked in Columbus for awhile.

5.   Society changes---when I was little almost no divorce. Also no Hispanics. Segregated schools. (Per news reports--back then 70+% of black households had father--now 70+% births are to unmarried girls. etc etc) Most women stayed home ---fathers worked.

6.   Technology changes--wow--she remembers Granny using outside washpot to boil water and wash clothes. I remember our first tv--3 stations--had to go outside and manually rotate the antennae.   No computers, no cell phones, etc etc.   She will remember party line phones. All cars made in USA--no seat belts--gasoline was cheap--maybe 33 cents a gallon.   No air conditioning. No clothes dryer --in winter clothes would freeze on the line.   She might remember non-electric irons to iron clothes. Cooking on a wood fueled stove. etc etc.

7.   High school ended in 11th grade--she was Valedictorian.

8.   Think we were living in the "shacks" (where Brenda Jane and I were born) when she got married. --think she got married at the Baptist church--though a member of the Methodist church--wow she has probably been a member of that church for 75-80 years?   (We called them shacks because I think there were a couple of old trailer/shacks made into a house--also might have added a room or two.)

9.   Think she walked to school--so did Clem and Stout-- later they rode bikes and let Brenda and me ride on the back.   Remember Brenda walking home from school.(School with no air conditioning).   Teachers were big part of the community--would see them at church,

grocery store, etc. Teachers were great--helped us learn--cared about us--taught us to be good citizens and good people, --so did our parents.

10. Granny and Papa raised 6 of us--just one bathroom. He was logger/sawmiller--self-employed and later became gas truck driver--dawned on me that it was probably difficult to go from being your own boss to working for someone else. His dad lived with us a few years--had a black smith shop just outside the house. Joyce would remember more than I about him. Grandpa Davis died the year she was born in 1930.

11. Might be good to have Stout there to add his memories --they might spark memories from each other. I asked him at Christmas to tell again his memories of Papa's shotgun (which I have) misfiring and blowing Papa's right forefinger off. Could have easily injured Stout and Clements.

I do go on and on--will hush.   Have a great week. Donnie

+++++++++++++++++++++++++++

39. BASKETBALL MEMORY BY ROCKY   JAN 2019

((This one was posted in "Boy In Georgia" but just added the last sentence.)) 37. Coach (as state champ?) named Brownie to the South All Star game in 1962. When asked, Brownie suggested player (Peek??) from Edison also be named. Later Brownie said Lee Martin from Perry was very good, especially at passing; said after a couple of practice games between first and second team, some changes were made because the second team won both games. Do not know if he got to play much in the all star game but it was quite an honor for him.   Bobby said the championship players got to keep their uniforms—and Sonny Duncan treated the team to steak dinner.

38. (Added 2019) Rocky Wade shared this story. In one game, other team was roughing up our players and the refs were not calling any fouls. Coach called time out, he was fed up. Wayne Thompson ("Cheyenne") was on second string and he was big and strong—if basketball had a linebacker position, Wayne would be the linebacker. Coach told Wayne, "hear me now—I'm turning you lose—yes I'm turning you lose" (Modern movie "Clash of the Titans", used the term, "Release the Kraken"—that's what Coach did.) So when Wayne got the ball he headed straight to the basket—there were 3-5 opposing players in the way—he plowed through them with elbows flailing, and opposing players being knocked left and right. Refs called him for charging. Next time he got the ball, only a couple between him and the goal, "Charge" with same results. Third time he got the ball—not one player was between him and the goal. After that, the opposing team got the message and both teams settled down to basketball instead or rough-ball—and besides, with Wayne on the bench, Coach could always "release the Kraken" again.

++++++++++++

50. MEMORIES—GRANNY-OTHER-TYPED 3-2019

(Note: Missing first 2 entries, so started with 3. Granny is Mina Davis Powell, married 71 years to Roy Alton "Tom" Powell (Papa) —my parents—typed by Donnie Powell)

.3. How did you and Papa get to know each other?

Roy Daniels and Tom were good friends. Roy dated my sister Clare Davis. That's how they got to know each other. Uncle Bo (E.E.) Powell went with my sister Jessie Sarah (we all call her "Bunch") some. (Donnie Comment: Had they married, would Billy Powell have been Cornelia or Edith???) All sis, Bo/Bunch, Roy/Clare and Grannie/Papa went in a car to see Fortune Teller on Sunday. Fortune teller looked at coffee grains left in the cup. Told Grannie she would have two husbands (Grannie said it is not true—yet)

.4. Papa and Bo bought a car together before Grannie and Papa got married. Papa helped Bo pay for it and let him have it. Papa bought brother A. A ("Shim") 1 or 2 mules and a wagon while Shim was living in house were Thomas Miller lives. Papa helped brother John when their baby died (after Elaine) at age of about 6 months. Papa bought the casket. Baby buried at Union Methodist Church cemetery.

.5. Papa and Grannie lived in "Shacks" and Uncle Bill lived in what I call our home place. Papa built a nice front porch on the shacks. Granny put baby bed there during the day because it was cooler and had more room. (Note: Shacks is where Brenda Jane and Donnie were born. Later Ricky's trailer was on the spot where the shacks were.) Papa bought Uncle Bill's place and we moved from the Shacks to that house (at night). The shacks were empty and so a number of people lived there, through the years. (Papa and Grannie were always very generous and helpful, so people stayed there, probably rent free.)

The other house is where Clements and Weone lived for a few years and where Leta, Alton and Nenia were born.(Note: Clem and Weone lived with Papa and Grannie and us, with only one bathroom when they first married.)

So with two empty houses, a number of people lived in one or both of them. Papa's brother Pete and his wife Clara lived in the Shacks for a while. (Pete drove gasoline truck before Papa did.) Papa was a mechanic with Burton Wight. Wore white coveralls. Grannie boiled the clothes in the wash pot and got them clean.) Papa's brother John and family lived in the shacks. Grannie's sister Ethel (also called Mamie Ethel) and Clinton "Bim" lived in the house that is now Ricky's storage house and later in the shacks for a while. Bim living there when he went into Army and later got married. Jerry Davis lived with them for awhile. (Grannie said Bim and Clements caught snakes and kept them in the old barn that was near the shacks. She found one in a big jar and it scared her.

Stout and Shirley lived in one of the houses. When they got married, Stout was not going to go back to school. Mr. L. K. Moss came out to the house and talked about Stout getting his diploma (he had all the credits just needed to take a test or something) and Stout did get it.

That was nice of Mr. Moss. Stout and Shirley had a trailer at the Hall's.

Cornelia (Bunch's daughter) and her 3 children lived in the house that became Ricky's storage house.

.6. Clem and Stout rode bikes to school and would give Brenda and Donnie a ride (wonder if they charged us for that taxi service?).

7. Grannie said when they were living at Uncle Bo's old house, one Sunday, Papa went down to Bo' and Pete was there and Pete and Papa got into an argument and Pete hit Papa. Papa then caught Pete in the collar and pushed him down. It upset Papa but he told Grannie about it.

.8. When little, Papa and Bo took a little wagon to the frozen creek and brought a wagon load of ice to the house. Papa told Grannie that his mom should have looked after him better.

.9. Clements working with Uncle Pete when had a wreck and hurt/cut his hand.

.10. Joyce, Madeline and June Goodroe moved to Columbus to work. After about a week, Papa got her a job with Burton Wight. (Donnie comment: Yep, Dads like to keep their girls close to home.)

.11. Stout and Ruben Britton got lost in the woods behind the house. Lots and lots of friends and neighbors came to help find them. Heard they went fishing. Chet Henson went down into water hold (with sewage) to look for them. Granny said that was so nice of him to do that. Neighbors do things like that—thank goodness.

Stout and Ruben followed creek until lit came out on road near a saw mill—night watchman heard a noise and shot his gun in the air. Stout and Ruben walking down the road (I would have been running) finally got a ride home. (?Mr. Murray?). Grannie said she hugged Stout. Don't think Papa whooped Stout.

.12. Grannie took extra milk to Brittons and one night Mrs. Britton said we'll have plenty of supper tonight. Always very appreciative.

.13. Stout had two wrecks. One time he ran into the policeman—Cap Henson. After he was married, he was coming back from fishing and turned a truck over. Someone was with him earlier but Stout had dropped him off. Stout had a concussion and couldn't remember what happened.

.14. (Donnie Comment: I remember one time Papa sold a mule and to deliver the mule, Brenda saddled the mule and rode it while I rode in the pickup with Papa. (Let's see, she rode on bouncy old mule and I had to ride inside the truck on soft seat—yep, I got shortchanged again. Ha ha.)

The end.

++++++++++++++++++++++++

51. Granny-Papa-said-Mar2007

My name is Donnie Powell, I am typing this up on 4 March 2007. These are some things that my parents Roy Alton (Tom) Powell ("Papa") and his wife Mina Myrtle Davis Powell ("Granny"), said/heard/etc., and I jotted a note down—will try to list the date of the note when known.

1. Granny and Papa (Note dated 9 June 1979): Shadie Davis used to keep bees. William Thomas Powell (Papa's father) also had about 3 bee hives. Sam Davis teased Mina and Clare a lot. Her grandfather Grandsa (Jack) Davis, had scuppernongs, currant bushes. Mina was walking on "paling" fence, slipped, foot got stuck. Clare went and told their Granny. Grandsa brought axe and Mina said, Grandsa don't cut my leg off. He laughed and used the axe to knock a board off the fence so she could get up.

Mina, Clare and Myrtice Powell set woods on fire. Mr. Lowe said they wouldn't have set woods on fire for nothing. Well, they set woods on fire after school. Different day, these three were also going to get in a boat and go fishing. Saw a big snake eating a fish. Scared them away from boat. Mina thinks that is what kept her from drowning. They went to old maid's house and while (?adults were) eating, the 3 got into lotion and spilled it on the floor. Myrtice got it up with her slip.

Powell's had a family Bible about 14 inches by 14 inches; a puff of wind blew the loose pages out and were lost. Papa had a gold watch the Gene Henson bought for him in Columbus. Pineville Cemetery has, we think, Papa's great-granddaddy buried there. W. M. Powell, Papa's granddaddy, is buried at Union Church in Marion County.

Papa helped build the Arthur Boyette home ((on Broad Street, adjacent property to ours)). He was between sawmill jobs. Even helped lay the foundation. (Donnie comment: I vaguely remember this, so must have been about 1950??)

Papa and Granny: Said Christopher "Kif" (Shadie's brother) was very mean. He poisoned dogs, pouted for two or three days.

Granny and Papa had many tomato plants and Granny was very mad about having so many plants. Said go did a hole in the hard dirt, plant them and next morning they are wilted.

Granny took train ride to Cottonton, Ala. Went to see big old gully, had bridge over it. Mina and Clare wanted to go down in it; wouldn't let them. They threw a rock in it.

Granny –Mina-- was cut on the head by her sister Clare. Mina wanted to climb up on bale of cotton to eat cane. Clare had knife peeling cane and dared Mina to climb up on bale of cotton. When Mina did, Clare whacked her on the head, and cut it. Still has scar. When they took Mina inside, Clare grabbed her leg from under the steps to keep her out.

Granny said iron fell on her finger and made nail come off. Looked bad. Grandsa (her grandfather Jack Davis) came over to their house and said let me see it. He said, well looks like the best thing is to bite it off. He pretended to bite it off. Granny said "no Grandsa, don't bite it off."

Granny said Grandsa and them "made nothing over us. Didn't hug or love them." Only had one Christmas tree in middle of the house. Shadie read Christmas story that one time.

Papa said he was sick till about age 16 or 17. Legs swelled up. Dr. Boyette said was "heart dropsy". Then he got well and really enjoyed running and doing things till late at night. When sick, they'd press on his leg with finger and the "dent" would stay there. He used it as an excuse to keep from going to school.

Papa ("Tom) and his brother Pete and three others went to Yatesville or somewhere near Atlanta and drove new model cars back to Buena Vista. Papa tried to say in sight of Pete on dirt road because Papa did not know how the way back home. Dirt roads all the way to Atlanta.

Granny (Mina) had rheumatism till they took her tonsils out; Dr Wise took them out. Mina had leg ache about every day. Papa heard about the surgery at school.

John Powell (Papa's brother) had a double barreled shot gun with pull-back hammers that belonged to William T. Powell. Bill Powell may have a picture of William T. Powell's wife , Mattie Foster Powell. Picture is big and cost $9. and William scraped up money for it, wouldn't let them take it back. (Aunt Lucille may have it).

Granny: On Grandsa and her Grannie's birthdays, kin folks would usually come. That may be when the picture of the entire family was taken in front of their home.

2. Granny and Papa (note dated 21 Mar 1982) One house they lived in was pushed off the pillars in a strong wind. After that Papa was even more afraid of bad weather. When we were in the shack, he'd get us all up and go sit in the car until it passed. I remember that I think. I also remember that after we moved into the "home place" ((203 South Broad Street, in Buena Vista, GA)), he'd get us all up and get in one bedroom. Made us put our clothes on. (?Must have been a tornado.)

I (Donnie) remember my stomach hurting when I heard on the big battery radio war stories or reports of war stories. Granny, ((my Mom)) said I'd get scared and have a stomach ache.

Clements and Stout got in a lot of wrestling fights: one time they even broke the bed in Papa and Granny's room.

Papa said his brother EE "Bo" and he (Roy "Tom") said older brother Pete would beat them up. But then the 2 of them would take up for each other and if Pete jumped on one the other would jump on Pepe and together they could handle him.

Granny said Claire and she said if they ever had boys that fought as much as Aunt Ethel's oldest two did, they'd kill them. Be careful what you say.

Tom Hollis ((business man in town)) said that before Granddad Powell grew up, you couldn't get him to say a word and now you couldn't get him to shut up.

Granddad (Papa's father) was so "curious" ((or eccentric)) he wouldn't even use a bathroom inside. He'd go to the out house.

Uncle Rag ((Granny's brother)) said Papa and Granny kept their home lit up like a road house. (I asked how he knew about a road house.)

3. On 27 March 1982, cousin Allen Davis came by and I shared what I had on our ancestors. He's really done a lot. I need to get a history of Webster County (also Stewart County). He said Shaddie A Davis fell off a mule, got tangled up in lines and was dragged. Said he broke or cracked his neck. Only one bald headed Davis. He said Uncle Christopher "Kif" used to pout a lot, and they'd tell Allen not to pout like his Uncle Kif. He said Shadie really liked to sing. That he'd get song book on front porch on Sunday morning and sing some hymns. ((Donnie comment: my singing is so bad, that when I sing they make me leave and get on the front porch.)) He led singing in church.

4. Papa: (Note dated 13 June 1986) Said he lied that Mina was 18 when they got married. Only time he knowingly told a lie and had been paying for it ever since. He hid their marriage license under some stuff on the bulletin board. Had $6, paid preacher $2.

((Donnie comment: best money he ever spent.)) Married in Richland, GA. On 22 May 1926 (I think while sitting in the Model T??).

Granny: Said her father (Shade A. Davis) said, "Mina, I believe you have done played hell." Said her mother told the preacher, "you married my baby" and he said yeah, I know, it was about time she married. (Think he also said, they were going to get married by some preacher so I did it.)

Asked Papa," If your wife died, would you marry again?" Papa, said, "I'd bring one back from the graveyard". To which, Granny said, "That's the only kind you could get (Dead). (This from Ricky.)

Papa's grandfather had a double barrel muzzle loader. Doesn't know what happened to it. "He was scared of the weather. He'd say, Granny Welthie, ain't no use to plant it, we won't live to see it."

Granny: Said she and her sister would rub poison ivy on themselves to try to get it to keep from going to school. It didn't work.

5. Granny (Note dated 20 June 2003): Granny (sometimes spelled Grannie) and her sisters used some of her mom's snuff a few times. Put it in their cheek.

Granny: As a child, she poured too much syrup and if she did not eat it all, she would have to eat it at the next meal.

Granny: She was 12th child, 3 were born dead and one died after only 9 months old.

Granny: Her dad (Shadie) smoked "bull Durham" rolled cigarettes.

Granny: Her mom (Malissa Jane ("Lis") Davis had long hair; girls would plait her hair and brush it.

Granny: Her dad Shadie worked on the grave of granddad of Myrtice Upton Powell (?), caught pneumonia and died. He had carved letters backwards to write on the cement slab over graves. Those letters were used to write on his cement slab—in a way he wrote on his own grave. ((Donnie comment: Those wooden letters are still in the family and hopefully won't be lost—perhaps it would be good to have them in a museum somewhere??) (Note 9 June 1979, I used some of the letters to print in cement and they still work.)

Granny: Granny's grandfather, Grandsa (Jonathan Davis, guard at Andersonville) had a long beard and Granny would plait the beard, with tobacco juice in it.

Granny: Granny remembered a little about the swine flu of 1918. She would have been about 6 years old.

Granny: Her dad Shadie had about 100 acres he bought from her grandfather Jonathan (Jack) Davis.

Granny: Granny said the wood bridge over the Kinchafoonee Creek was scary. Her mom scared. Rode over it in a wagon to go to church at Seminole (over Kinchafoonee and Dry Creek).

Granny: Granny's mom Malissa Jane was Baptist and her dad, Shadie was Presbyterian and his mom was Presbyterian. Granny's sister Clare joined church when traveling (I can't read next word but looks like women) preachers came by.

Granny: Granny seldom got to go to town. Her dad took bale of cotton to town, said Clare and Mina could go to Buena Vista. Shadie gave them a nickel each and they bought candy. Trip was about 12 miles on dirt roads. Her Aunt Mag Davis Maddox lived in BV and she stayed with her on trip to BV while Shadie took mules to barn.

6. Granny said "Cousin" Cleona(??) once said she wished she could stand up in church and talk but could not. As she was poking the fire with a stick she said, you know both ends of this stick are important, the one that pokes the fire and the end I hold. So whether you are in the fire (speaking in church) or just serving as the handle (doing other things), everybody in church is important. So I won't worry about not being able to speak in church.

7. Granny said when I (Donnie) was little (in the shacks—the house where Brenda and I were born, which is about 100 yards from the "home place"), I asked for a drink of water. Granny said I have two names, Mama or Mrs. Powell. Then I said "Mrs. Powell, will you give me a drink of water?"

Donnie Powell Warner Robins GA.

++++++++++++

GRANNY INTERVIEWED BY GREAT-GRANDSON TRAVIS DAVIS 1996 ((Thanks to Travis' mother Rhonda Powell Davis for mailing me a copy of the interview in 12/96))

For my English assignment, I interviewed my Great-Grandmother, Mina D. Powell, who lives in Georgia.

.1) How old are you? "Eighty-three years old." When and where were you born? "I was born on May 19, 1912 in Marion County, Georgia."

.2) What items dis you have at age of 14 that are rare today? "We didn't have very many toys at all when I was a child."

.3) Describe you home that you lived in as a kid. "It was a gray house made of pine. It had 4 rooms and was very small. We lived on a farm and had a barn out pack."

.4) Who was president when you were a teenager? "I can't remember who was president then."

.5) What grammar school did you go to? "Sandhills Grammar School in Georgia."

.6) What was your way of transportation to school? "We had a horse and a wagon and sometimes we would ride in the wagon and sometimes we would just go on horseback."

338

.7) What type of food did you have back then to eat? "Mostly vegetables, hog meat and chicken."

.8) What type of clothing did you wear back then? "Cotton dresses and sweaters. We made our clothes from cotton and flour sacks."

.9) What type of hair styles were popular? "Slicked back or straight back in ponytails."

.10) What type of school danced were popular? "We had no dances at all."

.11) Were you born in a hospital or at home? "I was born at home. They didn't have hospitals where I lived."

.12) What kind of pets did you have? "We had farm animals such as horses, cows, hogs and chickens."

.13) How many children do you have? "I have six children." How many grandchildren do you have? "We have 10 grandchildren and 8 great-grandchildren."

.14) Did you have a milkman back then that delivered milk? "No, we had to get our milk from cows. We had to milk them ourselves."

.15) Were your children born in a hospital? "No, they were all born at home, just like me."

.16) How old were you when you got married? "I was 14 years old."

17. Where did you husband propose to you? "In a car in front of my house. We then drove to Richland to find a Justice of the Peace. We stopped him as he was

driving down the road and Papa (her husband) lied to him about my age and he married us right there in our car."

18. What historical events have you lived through? "I can't remember anything except John Kennedy being shot. "

19. What were some of the jobs you had? "I worked at the shirt factory in Americus all my life. I was an inspector." ((Note: She started working at Manhattan shirt factory about when Ricky started to school, about 1959.))

.20) What are you words of advice to a happy life? "To just be yourself, always be truthful, and try to be the best you can be."

++++++++++++

SECOND INTERVIEW BY TRAVIS DAVIS

For my second interview, I am interviewing my Great-Grandmother. Her name is Mina Davis Powell. She was born May 19.1912. She is 83 years old.

The two areas that I found most interesting were about her childhood and about her children. So, my second interview will be questions about those two area.

.21) Question: How is your childhood different from childhood that children have today?

Answer: The biggest difference nowadays is that children have so many toys today. I see my grandchildren getting loads of toys on Christmas Day and I remember how we were happy to get an apple and an orange in our Christmas stocking. You didn't see toys back then like you do now. Stores are full of them now. I remember getting a doll once and thought it was the greatest thing. Schools were different back then. There were no school buses.

.22) Question; If you didn't ride a school bust, how did you get to school?

Answer:: We had a wagon that the horse pulled. Sometimes we got to just ride the horse to school. I always liked that. It was always pretty bad when it rained though. You'd get wed and be wet at school all day long.

.23). Question: What did you like about school?

Answer: Everybody was always helping each other. We got along good and were all friends.

.24) Question: What did you dislike about school?

Answer: It was just too far away. It would take us over an hour to get to school each day. If it was cold or raining, it was a mighty long hour.

.25) Question: Did you have a happy childhood?

Answer: Yes, for the most part, I would say I did. I enjoyed growing up with my brothers and sisters. Times were hard but we loved each other and helped each other out.

.26) Question: How many brothers and sisters did you have?

Answer: I had five brothers and four sisters.

.27) Question: Are they all still alive?

Answer: No, I only have one sister left. We see each other quite a lot. She comes and visits m a lot.

.28) Question: Describe a special moment that you remember from your childhood.

Answer: When I was probably about 9 years old, me and my sister were sitting on a wire fence eating berries. When we went to get down, my foot got caught on the wire and I fell on my back but my foot was still caught in the wire. My sister went to get my Grannie and she came running out of the house with an ax in her hand. She was planning on chopping the wire to get my foot out but I thought she was going to chop my foot off and I started screaming like crazy. My sister still laughs about that day. I guess it was pretty funny.

.29) Question: When did you get your first television set?

Answer: We got our first TV about 45 years ago. Of course it was black and white. I don't remember when we got our first color TV. I remember we were real excited about that first TV. The kids would watch it for hours. We all did. Before we got our TV, we would listen to the radio a lot. They had programs on and told stories and played music. I always enjoyed listening to the radio.

.30) Question: Did you learn to drive when you were sixteen?

Answer: No, I didn't learn to drive until I was 32 years old. Papa decided he would finally teach me how to drive and he did. It was scary at first. Papa probably wasn't the best one to teach me. He said my driving scared him.

.31) Question: How old were you when you got married?

Answer: I was 14 years old. My daddy was not too happy about it at first. We had to sneak off and get married in another county. Papa lied about my age so the preacher would marry us. We got married in his car on the side of the road. We didn't get married in a church.

.32) Question: How long have the two of you been married?

Answer: We've been married 69 years. Sometimes it seems like it's been that long and sometimes it doesn't. The kids always come over and we have a big dinner for our anniversary. I always look forward to it.

.33) Question: How old were you when your first child was born?

Answer: I was 18 years old. She was born at home. We didn't go to hospitals back then.

.34) Question: Tell me about your children.

Answer: Well, my first born was Joyce. She was born on November 20. 1930. My second was Clements. He was born on December 2, 1934. Then, there was Stout, your granddaddy. He was born the same day as Clements, on December 2, 1938. Then, there was Brenda Jane. She was born March 30, 1943. Next, was

Donnie. He was born December 6, 1944. And last was Ricky. He was born June 4, 1953. Ricky was a little bit of a surprise. I thought Donnie was my last one but then along came Ricky, 9 years later.

.35) Question: Were any of your kids troublemakers?

Answer: No. They were all good kids. Clements liked to play practical jokes on Donnie. Clements and Stout were always fighting, but boys will be boys you know. They always worked it out. They didn't get into any trouble. At least if they did, I didn't find out about it.

.36) Question: Tell something funny or interesting about each of your children.

Answer: Let's see. Well Joyce liked this boy when she was in school. But Papa did not like this boy at all. Papa use to be waiting for Joyce when she got off the school bus. He wanted to be sure this boy did not walk with her. It used to make Joyce so mad. Papa would walk her home down our long driveway and stop and get the mail. Joyce would come storming on in the house, mad as a wet hen.

Clements had to go to school two extra years because he was always so sick. He had to repeat the twelfth grade twice.

Stout got married before he finished school. Back then you couldn't go to school if you were married, so he had to quit.

Brenda was the smartest child. She always got all A's. She went to college and became a nurse. She lived in Atlanta a lot. She died several years ago.

Donnie got a scholarship and had to teach at school to repay the school. He's still a teacher today. (Taught 3 years then to civil service.)

Ricky went to trade school and became an electrician. Ricky also had a back operation that left him partially paralyzed. He walks with a brace on his leg.

.37) Question: What kind of chores did you give to your kids?

Answer: They had to rake the yards. They hated that. They would have to wash dished after supper and sometimes I made them do laundry.

.38) Question: Are you glad you have so many kids as you did?

Answer: Yes, I am very glad. I wouldn't trade a minute with any of them. They each were very special to me and still are.

END

++++++++++++++++++

61. ANCESTORS AND DESCENDANTS (May 2012)

They were tough, pioneer-stock hard working builders who lived in various places and times. Many are unknown, even their names, but they all helped forge me and my descendants. Some may have fought in wars and some may have fought starvation, the cold, the heat, the Great Depression, way bay they may have fought wild animals and lack of shelter. But they persevered, these our ancestors and instilled a will to survive in their descendants.

Some few I know a little about, like Grandpa Shadie Davis who died before I was born after digging a friend's grave in a cold rain. In Smyrna Cemetery in Marion County, GA (about 12 miles south of Buena Vista), on his concrete slab they used the letters he had carved to honor others, and wrote on his grave "HUSBAND AND FATHER, BORN OCT 15, 1872, DIED JAN 17, 1930. HE HATH DONE WHAT HE COULD   GONE BUT NOT FORGOTTEN." He is buried beside his pioneer-spirited wife Grandma Jane and they are surrounded by other family members who each worked so hard to make a living and a life while helping build a country. Close by is his brother who was killed in the line of duty as a policeman in 1910 and whose name is on the Georgia Public Safety Memorial, Forsyth GA. Not far away are other ancestors, some born under the US Flag, answered the call to arms for the Confederacy, and who worked at rebuilding the country and died under the US Flag—deserving of both flags.

A few miles away (at Union Methodist Church), lie my Mom and Dad, (Mina M. Davis and Roy Alton ("Tom") Powell—who lived through the Great Depression, working hard to raise 6 children. Mom found time to make quilts, one family tree quilt for each of her children. We cherish all her quilts but especially the family tree quilts. They raised us to be hard working, to love our family, country and be of faith. Their values live in us and our descendants

We salute all our ancestors and our descendants.

++++++++++++++

Note: In Pineville Cemetery, Marion County, GA there are some graves of ancestor(s). This is an abandoned or orphaned cemetery—being reclaimed by nature. Many large trees growing within a few feet of gravestones. March 2012

Shadrach Pearson Born 28 Dec 1807, Died 16 Sep 1896. (An old note of mine said Shadrach Davis (S. and E. C. Pearson lost 4 children below age 10 from 1842 to 1864, so sad.)

+++++++++++++++++++++++++

+++++++++++++++++++++

72. HOT PEPPER RUBBED ON PEANUTS from 1961 typed 2019 (true story)

In 1961, I was initiated into the Beta Club which meant for one day at school, I had to wear a cigarette sales girl outfit and provide peanuts to senior club members. (Side comment: One classmate had to dress up as Raggedy Ann, when he bent over his book, his mop wig flopped down around his face and almost cracked up our stoic coach/math teacher—it was quite funny.) Being a bit of a smart alec, I sort of resented giving them peanuts, so I rubbed some hot pepper on them while Mom watched. Next day I provided the doctored peanuts and the seniors said "these peanuts are hot". I innocently said, "There were some peppers near them on the table, I guess that's how they got hot." That night Mom asked how the hot peanuts worked out and my sister Brenda Jane—a senior Beta Club member—

overheard and got to the bottom of what happened. Thought I'd be in trouble, but she didn't tell on me (Thanks Sis) or if she did, they thought it was funny.

Today, looking back, guess I invented hot Cajun peanuts but didn't know it at the time.

+++++++++++++++++

((Note: Want to write a book about women—they are amazing, they endure so much, they persevere, etc.---title to be

WOMEN—STRONG, TOUGH, RESILIENT—AND LOVING .

WOMEN—STRONG, TOUGH, RESILIENT –AND LOVING By Donnie Powell July 2019

INTRODUCTION: From the women in my life, there is no doubt, they are strong, tough, resilient and of course loving, compassionate, determined and on and on. Decided to write a book honoring them, starting with my Mother, deceased Wife, and adding others. The fact that they put their lives on the line by becoming pregnant and having a child—that alone qualifies them to be in this book. How many of us men would risk our life to father a child? But so many women—some who are not mothers—brave unbelievable hardships and persevere and keep going. It is hard to imagine the drudgery of hard, physical labor sometimes 16-20 hours a day every day all their lives. Heroes—yes every one. Often their faith in God carried them through. A special salute to all single moms—who are both mom and dad all year long—each one qualifies for entry into this book.

You are invited to write up and submit information on some woman you know who you think is strong, tough, resilient—and loving. Here is a suggested format to get you to thinking. You may use any format. (You will note my write up on my Mom and Wife are not in this format, so use whatever you want.) (NOTE: As of April 2023—I have written only three—so my book idea may never happen—but I think it is a worthy project.)

.I. NAME   YEAR OF BIRTH, WHERE RAISED

.II. EARLY YEARS—THROUGH HIGH SCHOOL

.III. THE 10 YEARS OR SO AFTER SCHOOL (FOR EXAMPEL MARRIAGE, JOBS, ETC.)

.IV. MIDDLE YEARS

.V. LATER YEARS

.VI. SOME   SPECIAL   STRUGGLES   AND TRIUMPHS

.VII. OTHER

++

.1. POWELL, MINA MYRTLE DAVIS Born 1912, raised in Georgia

EULOGY--MINA MYRTLE DAVIS POWELL— also known as "MOMMA", "GRANNY", "GREAT GRANNY", "AUNT MINA" "MRS. POWELL"

…Preacher: Reference "Hymn of Promise"

++++++++++++++++++

Preacher: Now I'll read what her children wrote which expresses the feelings for all. This shows among other things how much Mrs. Powell loved her family.

(In some language somewhere, the name "Mina" must mean "love of family".)

Mina Davis, the youngest daughter of Malissa Jane Cosby and Shadrack (Shade) Addison Davis, was born on May 19, 1912 and was only 14 years old when she married Roy Alton ("Tom") Powell on May 22, 1926.   During their 71 years of marriage they had 6 children—Joyce, Clements, Stout, Brenda, Donnie, and Ricky. All of these children were born at home without any kind of pain medication. They now have 11 grandchildren, 10 great-grandchildren, and 3 great-great-grandchildren—the first one's middle name is "Davis" in her honor.

Before getting married, she was raised in a family of 8 siblings. This was during the horse and buggy days when you washed clothes by hand, drew water from a well or carried it from a spring. They cooked on a wood stove, went to the fields to pick cotton, stack peanuts, pull corn; they raised their own vegetables in a garden and chickens in the yard. They killed hogs on very cold days, milked cows and did many other farm jobs. She walked to school even with ice frozen on the sides of the dirt road.

Then Daddy married her and whisked her away to--well, more of the same. They were a great team—they had to be. They lived through the Great Depression or, as they called it, "Hoover Days" and World War II. They lived by the slogan "use it up, wear it out, make it do, or do without". When we children came along, we learned never to get sick, or act like we felt bad because we knew we would get a BIG, HUGE, LARGE dose of castor oil. It was so bad, each of us said we would never give our children castor oil.

All of her children and grandchildren had to have quilts to keep warm. So she spent many, many hours piecing together scraps and then quilting them. Each of us also received a unique "Family Tree" quilt where she had embroidered names of all her siblings and their families, plus Daddy's families, as well as each of our families—these are treasured heirlooms. She had a talent for making many other things including "Western" style shirts, special outfits for grandchildren, etc.

Through the years, she spent a lot of time babysitting her grandchildren and great-grandchildren, loving them and always letting them do things her own children were not allowed to do. She always welcomed new in-laws into the family and never said anything negative about them.

We were lucky to have her as a grade mother. This involved helping 3 or 4 other mothers serve goodies and drinks for parties, such as Christmas, Valentines, Easter, etc. She attended almost every school function including plays, programs, graduations, etc. She supported all of us children and strongly encouraged us to get a good education.

351

After her youngest child started to school, she got her first paying job at Manhattan Shirt Company. They carpooled to Americus, and between the 4 or 5 women riding together, we're sure they had some very interesting gossip—Momma was very friendly and loved to talk.

Her family always came first—she loved each and every member dearly. She did without many, many things for herself but was very generous in giving to her family; she was totally unselfish—and she never complained. Somehow they managed to always have bounteous Christmases whose memories we still cherish today.

We think her favorite passion was cooking. She always cooked big meals each Sunday hoping her children and their families would come. Anybody else that came was always welcome. No matter when you went to see them, she always wanted you to eat. This was her way of showing love. Some favorites were chicken pie, cakes, pies, biscuits, peach puffs, sweet potato biscuits, vegetables, fried chicken, cracklin' corn bread (crumbled into a glass of buttermilk), hoke cakes fried on top of the stove, fried side meat, home-made ice cream, ambrosia, butter-roll pie, roasted pecans, and on and on.

She endured many heartaches during her 97 years—the death of her parents, all her brothers and sisters, her beloved daughter Brenda Jane, a son-in-law, her husband, a grandchild and a daughter-in-law.

Proverbs 31:28 say, "Her children shall rise up and call her blessed".

Today, as we her children, other family members, and friends, say our final goodbye to her, we give thanks to God for this special lady, her love to us, and her blessings of 97 years. Lets us not just mourn her passing but celebrate her most remarkable life.

(Written mostly by Joyce (Powell) Henson).

((Note: Another thing Mom did was to write handwritten letters to her children away from home in college, the Army, etc. She was very faithful in keeping in touch with her family.   Handwritten letters are increasingly a thing of the past.))

++++++++++++++

HYMN OF PROMISE   BY NATALIE SLEETH, 1986

1. In the bulb there is a flower, in the seed an apple tree

In cocoons, a hidden promise, butterflies will soon be free

In the cold and snow of winter, there's a spring that waits to be.

Chorus: unrevealed until its season, something God alone can see.

2.   There's a song in every silence, seeking word and melody,

There's a dawn in every darkness, bringing hope to you and me.

From the past will come the future, what it holds, a mystery

Chorus: unrevealed until its season, something God alone can see.

3. In our end is our beginning, in our time, infinity

In our doubt there is believing, in our life, eternity.

In our death, a resurrection at the last, a victory.

Chorus: unrevealed until its season, something God alone can see.

+++++++++++++

((Note: We put some items in Mom's casket that had special meanings. For example, needles, thread, a big spoon (castor oil and cooking), a small corner cut from a quilt, pictures of family, etc.))

((Note: When Dad died, she said her last goodbye by caressing his cheek and saying "Good bye Tom." It was a holy moment that opened the floodgates. I followed her example in saying goodbye to her.))

++

++

EXCERPTS FROM

POWELL'S #3 MISCELLANEOUS THOUGHTS AND STORIES 2020

++++++++++++++++++++++

#9. POWELL—AUTOBIOGRAPHY—1962   By Donnie Powell

Autobiography my Senior Year. English 12 Mrs. Pearl S. Garrett May 16, 1962

(Note: Mrs. Garrett had us write our autography in the 11th grade and then update it in the 12th grade. So glad she required this—brought back many memories and things I had forgotten. Hope you enjoy.)

The Junior-Senior Prom Dance highlighted a wonderful Junior year for me. I escorted Joyce McCorkle to the Prom and had a wonderful time. On the way home, the police stopped us and I asked if I was going too slow.

Commencement exercises were the last of May, and since my sister Brenda Jane, was graduating, I attended all the services. The day after graduating, I received my report card, thus ending my Junior Year.

June 1961 flew rapidly past, again I spent my free time doing nothing. I even failed to read any books. I was first introduced to the great sport of tennis in June. I shortly afterward bought a tennis racket and spent many an hour of my vacation at the tennis court.

July, 1961 went much like June, with one main exception I had been awarded a week's vacation for my family and myself at Ida Cason's Callaway Gardens. We enjoyed the wonderful recreational facilities of the Gardens, mainly swimming, boat riding, and the Florida

State University circus whose summer headquarters were there. I even tried skiing for the first time, I was a big splash. The week's vacation ended with a dance on Saturday night. We had round and square dancing, and I just had a ball. (Note: Met many other students from other schools and I learned how to juggle three balls. While there, Roger Maris hit four of his 61 home runs during one double header—just happened to remember that.)

Back home, I got into the old grind of doing nothing, except taking care of Ricky, because both my parents worked.

June French, Co-Ed-Y vice president and I as Chaplain attended the YMCA leadership conference at the 4-H Center at Rock Eagle in August. I went prepared to study and learn my duties as Chaplain, but I also went to enjoy the fellowship of others my age. We had some wonderful socials, speeches, and games; and a spiritual experience which I shall never forget. June's parents were considerate and provide return transportation for us. I enjoyed the trip home even though I was slightly ill and very sleepy. (Note: One night at Rock Eagle, I was sick and took my asthma medication on an empty stomach which mace me very sick. Next morning in line for breakfast, two nice guys let me go in front of them. Later as students at Southwestern they remembered me as the "green" guy at 4-H camp.)

My senior year began on September 1, 1961. The senior sponsors were Mrs. Pearl S. Garret and Mr. Gary Simpson, the two best sponsors in school. The seniors bestowed the honor of President of the senior class upon me. It was the greatest honor I had received from my fellow students.

Besides being president of the senior class, I was Chaplain of the Co-ed-Y Club, District president of the Library Club, a member of the Future Teachers Association, and a member of the Beta Club. My subjects were as follows: first period—Typing II, Second period—English 12; third period—advanced math; fourth period—Physics; fifth period—American government; and sixth period—study hall, in which I served as a library assistant.

In October, 1961 the seniors and juniors were permitted to take the preliminary scholastic aptitude test. I took it mainly because it helps to prepare a student for the Scholastic Aptitude Tests.

October 18, 1961 was college day at Americus, which was attended by a group of seniors and juniors, myself included.

The Senior English Class of which I am a member, gave a play entitled "Punktown Court" on October 27, 1961. The play was a big success mainly because of the determination of the Seniors and because of the encouragement and guidance of Mrs. Garrett.

Senior rings arrived on October 30, 1961, making me feel that I was officially a senior.

Co-ed-Y members and officers were installed at the Baptist church on November 9.

The big day arrived. The third district west Library organization held its annual meeting in the auditorium of

Marion County High and as president, I presided. I was scared but knew all the other officers were pulling for me and somehow I made it through the meeting.

Thanksgiving holidays were November 23 and 24. I enjoyed the days by quail hunting mostly.

On December 2, 1961, I was one of a number of Seniors who took the Scholastic Aptitude Test in Americus. When the scores returned, I was delightfully surprised to find that I had a score of 590 in the math, the highest from our school, and on the verbal I received 428, about average.

December 14 saw me taking the Department of Labor Tests, which were given to Seniors to help determine their future careers.

The much awaited day of December arrived to my keen joy. The Christmas holidays began, giving me a few days rest from the burden of homework.

On January 6, Mrs. McGlaun, Librarian, and George Grier, local Library Club President, and I attended the state Library Club executive board meeting at Camp Jackson, at which meeting, plans were made for the annual state convention. I was appointed to the Careers Committee of the state educational department.

Co-ed-Y club officers were guests of the Lions club at the January 16 meeting, and everyone enjoyed a delicious meal, but afterward the officers gave a short talk on the different phases of the Y Club.

February 9 was the end of basketball season with the girls having a record of 19-4 and the boyw 21-2. I had enjoyed most of the games and also enjoyed working in the concession stand at some of the home ball games.

Admiring dancing the way I do, I naturally went to nearly every social that I could. At the FHA Valentine Social, I became a "Twist" convert and twisted at every social that I could for the rest of the year.

Beta Convention was March 9-11 in Atlanta, and along with about ten other Betas from our school, I attended. Since I was involved complications naturally resulted and things worked out so that Billy Moore and I got to see the Marion County Red Foxes win the State Class C championship by defeating at the state tournaments, respectively: Laurens, Western, Coosa, and Jackson. The Mighty Red", had previously won the sub-region, regional and many games during the season, all with only two defeats. The Marion County Red Vixens— rather Foxetts—did their best (but the fans didn't do their best because very little support was given the girls) and got second place in the sub-regional tournaments, and third in the regional tournaments.

Allergy tests were scheduled for me starting March 26 in Atlanta. The tests took only about four hours Monday and an hour each Tuesday and Wednesday. To my keenest delight the tests were completed on Wednesday and I happily arrived homed Wednesday afternoon. (Note: My Dad arranged a ride there and back with Mr. Sonny Duncan and I appreciate his giving me a ride. He asked me what I thought about some schools closing due to integration and I'm not big and strong, so I need my education. I do not want our schools closed. He said if I needed help (financially) with schooling, to come see him (the banker). During the pollens part of the allergy tests, the nurse said my back "lit up".)

Why was I happy because a trip had ended? Was I slipping? No! For on the following day, Thursday, March 29, Mr. Charles Burger, June French, Annelle Powell, Vicki Pope and I left for the convention of the Future Teachers Association at Jekyll Island. We had interesting meetings, talks, and experiences, which were highlighted by a banquet and dance Friday night. Again, I twisted and also danced and as usual regretted the time when the last dance was over.

April seemed to stimulate the teachers for they really piled the homework upon us. Perhaps they knew that we could stand anything now that the diploma were almost within reach and getting nearer.

April 27, 28, and 29 were the dates for the annual GALA convention, which this year for the first time was held at Camp Jackson. Third District West, the one in which we are in, was in charge of souvenirs and Mrs. McGlaun and the rest really did a lot of work and a good job.

At the Ga Association of Library Assistants (GALA) convention in 1961, I had met Annette Bell and she was at the 1962 convention, so we renewed our friendship and I really had a ball. There was a dance Friday night, a banquet, and a dance Saturday night and we seldom sat a dance out. But all good things must come to an end, and I left Camp Jackson realizing that I would porbably never see the camp or Annette again.

The Senior play is one of the big events of the Senior year. I was chosen to be the cruel murderer of the play. (Quite fitting wasn't it?) Many practices and much determination, plus the encouragement and guidance of Mrs. Garrett were needed to overcome the speeches, difficulties and accidents which pertained to the play. But on May 4, the Seniors turn in an excellent performance, in my opinion, the best in the history of senior plays of our school. (Note: Doug Jones broke his ankle as he burst through a stage door and had to be replaced by Barney Miller with only a few days of practice left. Barney worked hard and did a good job. After the play, Doug told Barney, "you did a better job than I would have done"—way to go Doug.)

The Senior year's big social event, the Junior-Senior Prom Dance was help May 11. I was at first unable to get a date and had determined to go "stag" But I was lucky and had the honor of escorting classmate Diana Brannon to the Prom. The decorations were superbly beautiful (in the old gym) and the band was very good— the theme was a "Roman Holiday"—so how could anyone keep from having a good time?

The biggest event of the Senior year is of course graduation, and with graduation, Class Night which will be May 25, and the Baccalaureate sermon which will be May 27.

Each previous graduating class had had four honor graduates and the fifth highest as alternate. But since I was involved, naturally things had to be complicated. (It seems I'm always messing things up.) Shep Pryor and I were tied for fourth, so on Graduation Night, May 31, there will be five speeches. The valedictory given by Fran Brooks, the salutation given by Annelle Powell, Brenda Henson third, and Shep and I fourth. We were thrilled with the honor, but realize that with all honors come responsibilities. We are working on our speeches and will present them on graduation night, May 31, 1962.

The End (Or The Commencement)

PS—The gym, classrooms, and auditorium were NOT air conditioned.

+++++++++++++++++++++++

#14. WAS AARON OLDER THAN MOSES?   (True) APR 2020

I asked in Sunday school of my teacher Bob Swint was Aaron older or younger than Moses since he was not killed when the baby boys were killed in Egypt. No one knew. But next Sunday Mr. Arthur Boyette read the Bible and found the answer. Aaron was older. Exodus 7:7. (I cheated used electronics to help me.)

Mr. Boyette, the Postmaster there in Buena Vista told us to get our parents' approval. When I was in elementary school, we could buy Savings Bond stamps—the red ones were 10 cents and the blue or green ones were 25 cents. We pasted the stamps in a folder or bond and when full it was worth $18.75 or $18 something and if we held it for 7 years till maturity it was worth $25. I tried to cash mine to get the $18 there at the post office but Mr. Boyette had other ideas. Don't think I ever got my parents' approval. Not sure I ever cashed that bond.

++++++++++++++++++++

#73. MY BAPTISM (True) Aug 2020

When I was in about the fifth grade, I gave my life to Jesus Christ and was baptized in the First Baptist Church in Buena Vista, Georgia. The baptismal pool was under the pulpit and when enough members were ready to be baptized, they would fill the pool with water (cold I think), the preacher would (I believe) put on a white robe, enter the pool and then we (I think wearing white robes) would come one by one to the pool. I guess they had put down tarps to keep the carpet dry and had told us to bring towels and extra clothing. The person in front of me (Earl Brannon) took a big gulp of air just before the preacher immersed him. (Don't remember the preacher's name.) Then it was my turn. I stepped down into the pool, the preacher turned me around, put his hands on me and said "I baptize you in the name of the Father, the Son and the Holy Ghost" (or something like that) and dunked me under, symbolizing the washing away of my sins and my devotion of my life to Jesus. I have been far from perfect but have always known that my most fundamental beliefs are these: GOD IS. JESUS IS THE LIVING SON OF THE LIVING GOD. JESUS LOVES ME. JESUS IS MY LORD AND SAVIOR WHO DIED FOR MY SINS. JESUS WILL TAKE ME TO HEAVEN WHEN I DIE. I LOVE JESUS, GOD AND THE HOLY SPIRIT WHO LOVE ME INFINITELY MORE THAN I CAN COMPREHEND. THANK YOU.

++++++++++++++++++++++++++++++

#84. MISS VERNA ALLISON - My favorite teacher
By Jack Christopher (True) Oct 2020

(Used with Jack's permission—see below)

MISS VERNA ALLISON - My favorite teacher By Jack Christopher

I never experienced Mrs. Moss' class but had the distinct pleasure of being a student of Miss Verna Allison for 3 years of grammar school. The first years included grades 4 and 5 which took place in a little 2 room Schoolhouse in Tazewell, Ga. It was actually one large room with a divider in the middle which accommodated grades 1 through 3 in one section taught by Mrs. Chloe Croxton and grades 4 through 6 in the other section being taught by Miss Verna Allison. There was also a small kitchen/dining room off to the side which served some outstanding country dinners (we referred to lunch as dinner back then). These meals were prepared by Mrs. Elizabeth McCorkle, wife of Jabez McCorkle who drove the school bus for many years from Tazewell to Buena Vista. Quite often these meals were prepared using fresh vegetables from her garden or from one of the many gardens of other generous Tazewell neighbors. Since this was a time before the advent of indoor plumbing, there was also a modest 2 – hole outhouse situated slightly behind and away from the main Schoolhouse. This Schoolhouse still stands and serves as a Community Center for the citizens of Tazewell.

This schoolhouse was heated by two large pot-bellied stoves that were located in the center of each room.

These heaters were fueled by coal that was stored outside in a pile near the side entrance. One of the duties of the male students was to periodically replenish the coal bucket whenever it became empty. No one ever complained about these duties since most of us were performing the same duties at home.

Our water supply was powered by a windmill near the coal pile that pumped water into a holding tank. We didn't use much water back then since our toilet was located in the outhouse and did not have running water. We were sometimes asked to carry a bucket or two of water into the kitchen for Mrs. McCorkle.

There was another small room off the main section called the "Cloak Room" which was used to store our coats in the wintertime. It also served as a "Time Out" detention area where we would be banished to whenever we misbehaved or committed some other offense during class. This was also the area where we would be subjected to a more severe punishment for offenses of a more serious nature. This involved a "whooping" or paddling administered to the rear end by Miss Allison with her favorite disciplinary device which was a large wooden paddle that she always referred to as the "Board of Education". I must have been one of her favorite students because I remember quite a few visits with her into the Cloak Room with the Board of Education"

While most of my visits to the Cloak Room were justified, there was one that I have to this day considered to have been a major miscarriage of justice. In the small town of Tazewell it was customary for us to go barefoot starting in the springtime and continuing throughout the summer. This was also allowed in school and most of us really looked forward to the time when we could toss the shoes and run around barefoot all day until the end of the school term and the rest of the summer.

In this particular situation, unbeknownst to me the removal of shoes was permitted only after an official date that was determined by the teacher in charge. It was early spring and since we were already going barefoot at home with the permission of my parents, I naturally assumed that it was also OK at school. I remember that day quite well. It was springtime and a little cooler that morning so I wore my shoes to school as usual. It got much warmer during the day and when recess time came around it had turned into a very warm summer day. Since I had the permission of my parents I could not resist and off went the shoes. This did not remain unnoticed by Miss Allison who promptly escorted me into the Cloak Room for a vigorous session with her and the Board of Education. I tried to explain that my parents had given me permission but that fell on deaf ears. Looking back, I guess that was my first introduction to conflicting rules of conduct that might apply differently in different situations. Back then we respected all of our teachers and never questioned anything they said or did. Our parents shared the same respect for teachers, in fact one of the common conventions back then was "If you get a whooping at school, it is not over because you will surely get another when you get home".

Miss Allison was a devout Cristian who did not hesitate to share her Christian beliefs with her students, which was perfectly acceptable at that time. We always had to recite the Pledge of Allegiance every day of school and often the Lord's Prayer as well. She taught us quite a few Hymns such as "Onward Christian Soldiers", "Swing Low, Sweet Chariot", and "Amazing Grace". I remember several occasions when she would take us on a short visit to a local elderly person who was very ill or near death and we would gather around and sing those Hymns for them. They always seemed to enjoy our serenades.

Miss Allison also had us memorize numerous religious poems and prayers. Among those were "Abou Ben Adam" and "A Tribute to Christ", not to mention some bible verses such as the 23rd Psalm.

There weren't many students in Miss Allisons' classes in Tazewell. The ones I remember are Brenda O'Hearn, Paul Harbuck, Billy McElmurray, Gloria McCorkle, Karen Welch, and Judy Halley.

Shortly after the 5th grade, the Tazewell school was closed and we had to take the bus to Buena Vista for the rest of our grammar school years. Miss Allison also moved to the Buena Vista school and taught me in the 7th grade which was in a basement room located underneath the grammar school. I distinctly remember that when it rained heavily, sometimes the lower walkway into the schoolroom would flood and we might have to walk through some standing water to get to class.

I also remember that Miss Allison had developed a new disciplinary action to take the place of the Board of

367

Education. I think at that time, paddling had been discontinued by the individual teachers and was turned over to the Principal's office for execution. I can distinctly remember on many occasions having to write "I will not talk in class" over a hundred times on the blackboard until it was completely filled up. I thought I was pretty smart and started gradually writing my sentence with larger letters to take up more space but Miss Allison caught up with that trick in no time and made me erase what I had done and start over.

On a more personal note, Miss Allison had a sister who died of cancer at an early age, leaving behind two little boys name Chap and Charles Stevens. Miss Allison told us that she had made a promise to her dying sister that she would take care of those two boys. She honored that promise, never married and looked after those boys as if they were her own. She was always talking about Chap and Charles throughout the school year and I could tell that she was completely dedicated to those 2 boys.

I am not sure what happened to Miss Allison later in life but do remember that she had to give up her teaching job because she was living in the same house as the two boys and their Father which was not proper back in those days. I am sure of one thing and that is that she would never have done anything unethical or immoral in any situation whatsoever. She was merely keeping her promise to her sister and was willing to give up her profession that she dearly loved in order to do so. To me that is one of the greatest sacrifices that a true Christian can make by placing the welfare of others above one's self in order to keep a solemn promise made years ago.

In spite of all of our misunderstandings and disciplinary situations, I still regard Miss Allison as the best and most influential teacher that I have ever had the pleasure of being taught by. She was a very stern, honest, dedicated, faithful Christian teacher of the highest degree who taught me many life lessons that I still abide by to this day and will continue to do so. She was truly a wonderful, caring teacher and a beautiful human being.

++++++++++++++++++++

Ok to send anywhere you choose. This started out as just a couple of sentences but once I got started, old memories just kept pouring in. It is just sad that teaching has seemed to have gotten corrupted just like most everything else. Who would want to become a teacher or police officer these days? Things were a lot simpler and saner back then. We didn't have much but we were much better off.   Jack

++++++++++++++

Donnie, I just got the email about Mrs Moss and prayer in school and started an email response about that which has grown into quite a lengthy essay.   Then I remembered that you asked about experiences growing up in Marion County which I had intended to respond to at some time but never got around to it.

Anyway I just completed it and am sending it to you in response to your initial request. This has morphed into a sort of tribute to my favorite teacher but does contain quite a bit of the grammar school experience in Tazewell, Ga.

I am inserting it below and also as a PDF attachment. I don't have a recent email list of classmates so please distribute to them or anyone else that you would like to. Jack

.--

EXCERPTS FROM

POWELL'S #4 MISCELLANEOUS THOUGHTS AND STORIES—2021

#1. BOTTOM OF COKE BOTTLES (True) Oct 2020

Background: When I was growing up in Marion County GA, my Dad owned a logging business which he gave up to drive a small gasoline delivery truck for Wight Motor Company, located on the square in Buena Vista. I was fortunate enough to be allowed to ride on the truck with him sometimes and between trips hang around Mr. Wight's place. (By the way, at the top of the building, were the numbers 1917 or 1918 meaning I think that the building was built in that year. Also, the cement between the bricks had reddish sand which was interesting.) There was always some type of Coca-Cola dispensing machine inside with Cokes costing 6 cents (and more later) and in GLASS bottles—yes glass bottles. The little bottles were I think about 6 or 6 and a half ounces and we old timers always said the best tasting cokes were in the small glass bottles. The glass bottles were manufactured at many locations all over the United States. My friend Kathy and I recently visited Buena

Vista, the old School and Gym where we found a couple of the small coke bottles which brought back an old memory.

Sometimes, several men would decide to buy a Coke at the same time and agree that the bottle with the location most distant (or maybe closest) would have to buy cokes for everyone. So as soon as they got their drink, before opening it, they would look at the bottom and announce the city and state where their bottle was manufactured. Helped me with geography. When Kathy and I found those two bottles, the first thing I did was look at the bottom. One was from Denver CO the other from Chattanooga, Tenn. (thicker, old time bottle). So I think I owe her a Coke.

PS: The Cokes back then did not have plastic screw on caps like the plastic bottles today but metal caps that had to be removed using a bottle cap remover usually part of the Coke dispensing machine. We kids would often collect the bottle caps and use them for a variety of things including checkers—upside and downside. Making your own checker board was fun if not exact. At least once, we also nailed the caps (cap up) to a board and placed at the front door as a door mat to catch some of the multitude of sand tracked in from our sandy yard. Doubt the plastic caps of today would be stand up to the job—the hammer would do them in.

Old memories and old cokes—still the best.

(End)

(NOTE: I submitted this to the Marion County, GA, local newspaper "The Journal" which published the article on page 8A, October 28, 2020, Volume 25, Number 41.)

++++++++++++++++

++++++++++++++++++++++++++++

+++++++++++++++++++

#4. TOMOCHICHI MEMORY (True) Oct 2020

After seeing a road named Tomochichi today, had an old memory. At Marion County Elementary School in about 1950-54 or so, an upper classman Rocky Wade was on stage in a play in about the 6th grade dressed as Tomochichi (shirtless) with Indian pants and with a feather in his hair and a tomahawk in his hand. He pointed with the tomahawk and said some Indian sounding words (which I don't remember). That's about all I remember.

Guess Mary Musgrove was on stage too but she didn't impress--Rocky stole the show.

Funny how something will trigger an old faded memory. (Now maybe you can remember some school plays.)

(End)

+++++++++++++++++++

#12. PAPA'S SHOTGUN MISFIRE—AS TOLD BY STOUT POWELL To Donnie 12/6/2020 (True)

Three of us-- me, Dad, and Clements going squirrel hunting. Stout was about 10-12. Covey of quail ran across the road in front of us. Clements had shot the double barreled shotgun with some wet shells in the yard before we went hunting and the wadding stopped up the barrel. Dad stopped the truck to shoot the quail on the ground. He laid the barrel across the truck (or stood by the truck) and when he shot it blew the side out of the barrel, and blew a hole in the hood of the truck, and Stout was sitting in the center directly behind where it hit the hood–had it come through the windshield it would have hit him in the face. Dad killed three quail. (May have shot both barrels, don't remember.) Clements could drive but did not have a license so Dad would not let him drive so Dad drove. (He was tough.)

One of us got the three quail. His finger was hanging by skin (or vein) so he wrapped it with his handkerchief (which he always kept one in his pocket).

It was Wednesday. Momma was not home. Went on the Ellaville to Dr. Stout Boyette but he was not home— Closed on Wednesday. (BV closed on Thursday).

Went on to Americus to Dr. Thomas. Dad said Doctor cut that little piece of skin off and it shot blood all over his shirt. Doctor bandaged it up. Dad drove home from Americus.

We lived in the shacks at the time. About 1948 or so. Dad went to work for Burton Wight in 1953 driving Gasoline truck.

(Donnie Comment: I think Dad said he got the shotgun from Roscoe Welch. I vaguely remember: Think someone said barrel had "caps" stuck in it. I got a roll of my cap pistol caps and asked if it was like these caps and they said no, cap or top or wadding of a shotgun shell. In the old house we called the "shacks". Guess we remember traumatic events. As of Dec 2020, I still have the shotgun with side barrel blown out.)

Note: Dad/Papa's name: Roy Alton ("Tom") Powell (Oct. 12, 1904-Nov. 21, 1997) Buried Union Methodist Church, Marion County, Ga.

++

PAPA LOGGING As told by Stout Powell to Donnie 12/6/2020

Worked half day may have paid full day on a couple holidays ??

Dad/Papa had one log truck driver and later two drivers. Hauled Hands all the way to the river if needed to De Soto, GA in half-ton pickup. Had about 7 Hands not counting Stout and Clements in Summer. He hired Jim Wiggins to haul mules in bigger truck or if close Clem or Stout would ride the mules to next place. Would have a barbed wire pen for mules—would feed on weekends. Never lost one—sometimes right by side of the road.

Had skidder—Stout ran skidder, Clements pulled the cable. Stout not big enough to pull cable.

(interrupted)

PAPA/MY DAD SAID:

After watching Clements and some of his children and grandchildren use/play with a crosscut saw (about 6 feet long with a handle on each end), Dad said: "They should write on those saws in big letters MAN KILLER. He and his workers had used crosscut saws when logging and he would know.

#13. CLEMENTS' LEATHER SUITCASE, etc.

Clements had a red/brown leather suitcase that I guess he got as a graduation present in 1953 and he used on their senior trip to Washington DC. (Our class did not have a senior trip.). I remember he was carrying it when he returned and was very excited to come inside and see out new baby brother Ricky born June 4, 1953. He and Ricky always had a special bond.

I imagine Stout used that suitcase when he went to FFA/FHA camp. I know I used it the three times I went and probably when I went to other camps and trips. Thanks Clements for having the suitcase and sharing it with me.

After graduation, Clements went to Atlanta to a TV repair school and he used or lugged that old dependable suitcase every trip. Don't know where he stayed but he hitchhiked there and back and in those days it was "safe" to do so. In "When I was a Boy in Georgia" I told about the time Clem rode bus to Butler and Dad told Mom to not go thru Ellaville to pick him up. But

Mom said he said DO go through Ellaville. By the time we got to Butler, Clem had started walking home—yes carrying/lugging the suitcase which probably got heavier by the mile. We finally found him in crossroads called Charin (about 10+ miles). He was not happy. But the suitcase endured. Might have gone on their honeymoon. May still be in their home place—Clements didn't throw things away—wonder what's inside the old suitcase.

"SKIN NEX" "KINGS X" OR TIME OUT

Clements won a yo-yo contest I think—prize was a yo-yo??

14. Powell Home place   Dec 2020

1. The "Shacks" were I think a couple of small non-insulated sheds pushed/nailed together with a bathroom and kitchen added to make a house. Also a small entrance porch and a big porch facing the road were added. There was a hallway between the bedrooms--think I remember rolling my marbles down that hallway--wasn't level.

Brenda Jane and I were born there. People who lived there were Us, later Uncle John, Stout and Shirley, Aunt Ethel, and I think others.

2. Don't think I have any pictures of the shacks.

3. Have a few pictures of the Home place where I grew up--Papa and Granny's home. Pictures somewhere.

4. We moved from the Shacks to the Home place about 1948-49--about the time Joyce got married. Papa made a great business deal. Mr. Stephens (I think) had bought timber on someone's land and had agreed to pay for say 20,000 board feet (may have been more). He told Dad/Papa he could have anything over that amount. Dad went and looked at it and said it's a deal. It was rough, swampy work but he harvested enough trees over and above the 20,000 board feet to buy the home place. Did not owe a dime on it. Great deal for him. We had a home paid for in full. Way to go Dad.

He bought 4 acres which included a house, shelter, barn, the shacks, a couple barns near the shacks, a smoke house and another storage building near the smoke house, another storage building, and maybe Granddaddy Powell's blacksmith shop (or maybe it was built later.) Plus 100 acres of woods with streams on it.

Stout and Joyce probably remember more than I do. I'll send to them.

Love Dad.

++++++++++++++++++++++++++++++++

+++++++++++++++++++

#16.   1960 BLUE FALCON CROWDED AT CHRISTMAS SHOPPING (True)

My Dad traded a truck and co-signed a loan so I could get a little 1960 blue Ford Falcon to drive back to Georgia Southern from Buena Vista, GA in 1964. When I came home on Christmas break I loaned my Falcon to my sisters and nieces to go shopping in Columbus—my Mom may have gone with them, not sure. If I had remembered how my sister Brenda Jane drove in high school I doubt I would have loaned her the car. Off they went. My older sister Joyce always shopped till all the stores closed and sure enough, they came home after dark. But they snuck into the yard by turning off the headlights which I thought strange. They were laughing—they thought I might be mad because they had overloaded my car. They started unloading and I was truly amazed at how they got all that stuff into that little car and nobody tied on the roof. Think there were packages and a small telephone table and chair—they were good at packing. When they told that story each year, in their version, my eyes got wider and the stuff they bought grew and grew—and we laughed more and more.

++++++++++++++++

20. BULLS FIGHTING (TRUE)   (Typed Mar 2021)

When I was a boy, we had a white faced Herford bull and next door neighbor, Major Miller had one too. One day Boyce Miller came over saying they had got thru the fence and were fighting. He had a whip with wire instead of leather and had been unable to separate them. He asked Clements to come help separate them. And Clem got his leather whip and went with Boyce.

(Either Clem told me to stay home or I was too scared to go but I did not go see the bull fight or how they separated the bulls. I missed the best part.)

Questions: Did we have a white faced bull big enough to fight?

Why did we have a Herford bull--we didn't have beef cows--did we?

How do you separate fighting bulls? (Or do you let them get through fighting and then drive them home?)

Did Clements talk about that later--maybe at supper that night? If so, I'm sure he exaggerated a bit--maybe a lot? ((Maybe his version would be that he grabbed them by the horns and flipped them to the ground and dragged ours home?????))

Maybe he and Boyce just went and watched the bull fight sort of like watching a rooster fight--which might be the smart thing to have done.

Guess that's enough bull for now.

++++++++++++++++++

#51. MY GRAND FATHER'S WOODEN LETTERS— DOCUMENTED (True)

Shadie Addison Davis carved the letters and some words such as "Born" and "Died" to write on wet cement grave slabs. The letters were better than writing with a stick. He would also dig the graves and when digging one, caught pneumonia and died in 1930. The letters were used to write on his grave—as my Mom said, in a way, he wrote on his own grave. He is buried in Marion Count, about 12 miles south of Buena Vista, GA on GA highway 41, in New Smyrna cemetery in area once called Church Hill because there were 4 or 5 churches in that area, now only one.

See documentation listed here.

https://archive.org/details/agsquarterlybull2334asso/page/n11/mode/2up

Association for Gravestone Studies, Volume 34, Number 1, Winter 2010, Page 12-14 ,

Note: I may have documented this elsewhere but wanted to be sure the letters were documented at least once.

++++++++++++++

#60. HONOR GRAD SPEECH   (Fiction) May 2021 ((WISH I HAD DONE THIS.))

Before I sit down, I'd like to add something that is not on the program.—There is a fly up here trying to get in my mouth. -- I may get in trouble but I hope they will let me graduate. Those of you in the audience who have already graduated, you know how this night changes everything. We will no longer be students in this our beloved high school. We go forth into the unknown—a little scary but very exciting. Changes are coming—big changes. But citizens of the United States, Georgia, and our County will meet this change and thrive. Classmates, graduation is a big change for us—I know each of you—you are ready for this next step and the world will be a better place because of you. Ours has been the best of times in the best of places surrounded by the best of people.

If I could, let me be the spokesman for the class and say thanks first of all to God who created us and the earth we live in—this marvelous Garden of Eden. And thank you to our parents who had us and raised us, our first teachers—our brothers and sisters and aunts, uncles, grands, cousins—our loving, nurturing family that helped shape us.

Thank you to our community, our churches, the workers that make our existence possible.

Thank you to our school workers, bus drivers and mechanics, lunchroom workers and everyone that keeps the school going.

Would those in the audience please raise your hand if you attended any county school, graduated from this school or attend school here. (A lot of hands go up.) You too can appreciate what I'm about to say.

And now a special thank you to our teachers and principals from first grade to 12th. You taught us so much, shaped us, and made us better. Thank you. But that's not enough. The whole community wants to say thank you. Some of our teachers may not be here tonight but here or not I'd like everyone in the audience and on stage to give them a long overdue standing ovation. Everyone stand up! (5 minutes later applause subsides.)

Ok Please return to your seats.

Classmates—dear classmates. I know and love each of you. After tonight, we go our separate ways. For some, we may never see each other again. Thank you for helping shape me and being a part of me for the rest of my life—my classmates in my cherished school memories. May God bless and keep you.

Audience, thank you for letting me say these extra words. I'll hush before I start crying.

Now our principal will get us back on schedule.

Principal: No you are not in trouble and you will graduate.

(Laughter)

+++++++++++++++++

Note: Thought about my high school graduation in May/June 1962—40 graduated—I was tied for 4th— gave a honor grad speech. Wish I had added the above but with strict teachers, Pomp and Circumstance and tradition, I was too scared to deviate even a little—just hoped I didn't mess up too much. Hope I thanked my teachers. PS. Yes there was an annoying fly.

(end)

+++++++++++++++++++++++++++++++++

++

Made in the USA
Columbia, SC
28 January 2025

52826522R00209